THE POST NEAR CHEYENNE

THE POST NEAR CHEYENNE

A HISTORY OF FORT D.A. RUSSELL, 1867-1930

BY
COL. GERALD. M. ADAMS, USAF (RET.)

PRUETT PUBLISHING COMPANY
Boulder, Colorado

© 1989 by Gerald M. Adams

All rights reserved. No part of this book may be reproduced without written permission from the publisher, with the exception of short passages for review purposes.

First Edition

1 2 3 4 5 6 7 8 9

Printed in the United States of America

Library of Congress Cataloging-in-Publication Data

Adams, Gerald M., 1920—
    The post near Cheyenne: a history of Fort D.A. Russell, 1867–1930/ by Gerald M. Adams.—1st ed.
    p. cm.
    Bibliography: p.
    Includes index.
    ISBN 0-87108-777-4
    1. Fort David A. Russell (Wyo.)—History. 2. Cheyenne Region (Wyo.)—
History, Military. I. Title.
UA26.F655A33   1989
355.7′09787′19—dc20   89-33685
                                                                           CIP

To my wife and helpmate of more than forty years, Kathleen Karnes Adams.

Contents

Introduction

PART I:
An Army Post Beyond the Frontier, 1867–1869   1

  One:
    Finding the Right Spot on Crow Creek   3

  Two:
    Building Barracks and Chasing Indians   9

  Three:
    First Spring Campaign and the Treaty of 1868   21

  Four:
    The Army and Indian Policy   31

PART II:
Indian War on the High Plains, 1870–1879   39

  Five:
    Patrolling and Escorting   41

  Six:
    The Peace Policy and Gold in the Black Hills   49

  Seven:
    Campaigns of 1876   57

  Eight:
    The Indian Wars Ended, Almost   63

PART III:
Refurbishing Fort D.A. Russell, 1880–1889   73

  Nine:
    Surviving the Cut of Posts   75

  Ten:
    Making the Post Permanent, Finally   83

  Eleven:
    Scaling Down to Size: A Single-Regiment Post   95

PART IV:
   Cheyenne Depot, Quartermaster Supply, 1867–1889   101

   Twelve:
      Also Known as Camp Carling or Carlin   103

PART V:
   Closing Out the Nineteenth Century, 1890–1899   111

   Thirteen:
      Wounded Knee, The Johnson County War
      and War With Spain   113

PART VI:
   The "New" Fort D.A. Russell, 1900–1909   127

   Fourteen:
      The Post Expands to Brigade Size   129

   Fifteen:
      Large-Scale Summer Maneuvers at Pole Mountain   137

PART VII:
   Mexican Troubles and a War in Europe, 1910–1919   149

   Sixteen:
      The Brigade Seeks Good Relations With
      Cheyenne–Most of the Time   151

   Seventeen:
      War, Demobilization and the Aviation Era   161

PART VIII:
   The Postwar Army at Fort D.A. Russell, 1920–1929   171

   Eighteen:
      The Flying Field Moves to Cheyenne   173

   Nineteen:
      A Community Relations Committee is Born   185

   Twenty:
      Senator Warren's Last Visit   197

Epilogue   203
Sources   245
Index   263

The main gate showing the entrance to this open post, first displayed the name Fort D.A. Russell. On January 1, 1930, the name changed to Fort Francis E. Warren, and in July 1949 to Francis E. Warren Air Force Base. In 1959, the construction of Interstate-25 along the east side of the base necessitated that the handsome, structure, pictured here in the early 1950s, be torn down and the main gate be moved a hundred yards west into the base. Security police were added to the new main gate that same year when missiles arrived and the citizens of Cheyenne were no longer free to come and go. An overhead arch was not included in the new main gate, but the aluminum letters can be seen on the I-25 overpass on Randall Avenue by all approaching Francis E. Warren Air Force Base from Cheyenne.—*WY State AMH Dept.*

Introduction

Few American military installations have had longer or more illustrious histories than the post near Cheyenne, yet it has been one of the least documented. Fort Laramie, ninety miles to the north, is still the most popular of the Wyoming military sites, and its history has been recorded in more than a dozen good books, yet it served as an active military post for only forty-one years, 1849-1890. In contrast, Fort D.A. Russell, now Francis E. Warren Air Force Base, has been continuously active since 1867.

When initially established as a twelve-company-size garrison, and for several years after, the post received a great deal of attention, as did the town of Cheyenne. This was partly because of their location on the travel routes and partly because of their close proximity. The military department commander in Omaha intended to have the post located fourteen miles west on Crow Creek, away from the settlement and the unsavory elements that were often associated with railroad towns. But the department commander was persuaded in late July of 1867 to site the post adjacent to the newborn settlement, where it could offer more of an economic benefit as well as military protection.

The name Fort D.A. Russell did not catch on as well as some other western names, but Cheyenne quickly became known to the reading public, and to many who did not read. Consequently, the military garrison near Crow Creek Crossing named Fort D.A. Russell could more easily be identified as the "post near Cheyenne."

There seemed no reason to expect that Fort D.A. Russell would be more than a temporary outpost on the railroad. When the closing of unneeded military outposts in the northern High Plains area started not long after the Sioux campaigns concluded in the late 1870s, Fort D.A. Russell survived because of its location on the railroad, and because of the quartermaster depot, named Cheyenne Depot, also located there.

When the Census Bureau concluded in 1890 that the western frontier no longer existed, and the government declared that the Indian wars were over, another flurry of post closings in the West followed. Again Fort D.A. Russell survived, mainly because of its location on the railroad. It had been declared a permanent garrison in 1884 by the Arthur administration, but that lofty designation did not always protect a post when the budget cutters were at work. Permanent buildings were constructed in 1884 to replace the rapidly deteriorating temporary wooden buildings put up in 1867-1868, but for a smaller garrison of eight companies.

The survival of Fort D.A. Russell owes much to its close proximity to Cheyenne. Although Cheyenne has not been known as a service town, it has loyally supported the interests of the men and women at the military base so close by. A friendly and mutually rewarding relationship has usually prevailed. When the close relationship between the garrison and Cheyenne has broken down for short periods, cooler heads have invariably worked to mend the break. For the past two decades, a Civilian Advisory Council has performed admirably in insuring that relations remain good.

Vigorous efforts of the Wyoming congressional delegation have also been instrumental on many occasions in preserving the post near Cheyenne. The military mission has changed on an average of every ten to twenty years, and the post, now the base, has evolved from a frontier outpost to a high technology missile center. However, the physical appearance of the installation remains much the same as it did early in the century when infantry, cavalry, and field artillery were assigned there.

The name changed in 1930 to Fort Francis E. Warren in honor of Wyoming's distinguished and longtime senator. After World War II the newly independent air force acquired the post from the army, and it became an air force base. Although several attempts have been made over the years to build a permanent airfield, there are no aircraft landing runways at this air force base. Visiting air force planes continue to use Cheyenne's nearby municipal airport.

Francis E. Warren Air Force Base now serves as one of the largest intercontinental ballistic missile bases in the nation, with a missile field containing 150 Minuteman III systems positioned in northeast Colorado, western Nebraska, and southeast Wyoming. A complement of fifty of the newer Peacekeeper missiles will be on alert along with the Minutemen. The base is unique for the important role it has played in the settlement of Wyoming and the West, and for its more recent key role in the national strategy of the United States.

Entered on the National Register of Historic Places in 1969, Francis E. Warren Air Force Base was designated a National Historic Landmark in 1975.

A 1938 aerial oblique photo looking southwest shows Sloan's Lake at bottom; Frontier Park, and then toward the top and crossing Interstate 25, Francis E. Warren Air Force Base. The close proximity of Cheyenne, seen at the left of photo, to the base accounts for the good relations enjoyed for most of the almost one hundred and twenty-two years of their existence.—*Photo courtesy of Mr. Bill Metz, Ninetieth Civil Engineering Squadron.*

PART I AN ARMY FRONTIER

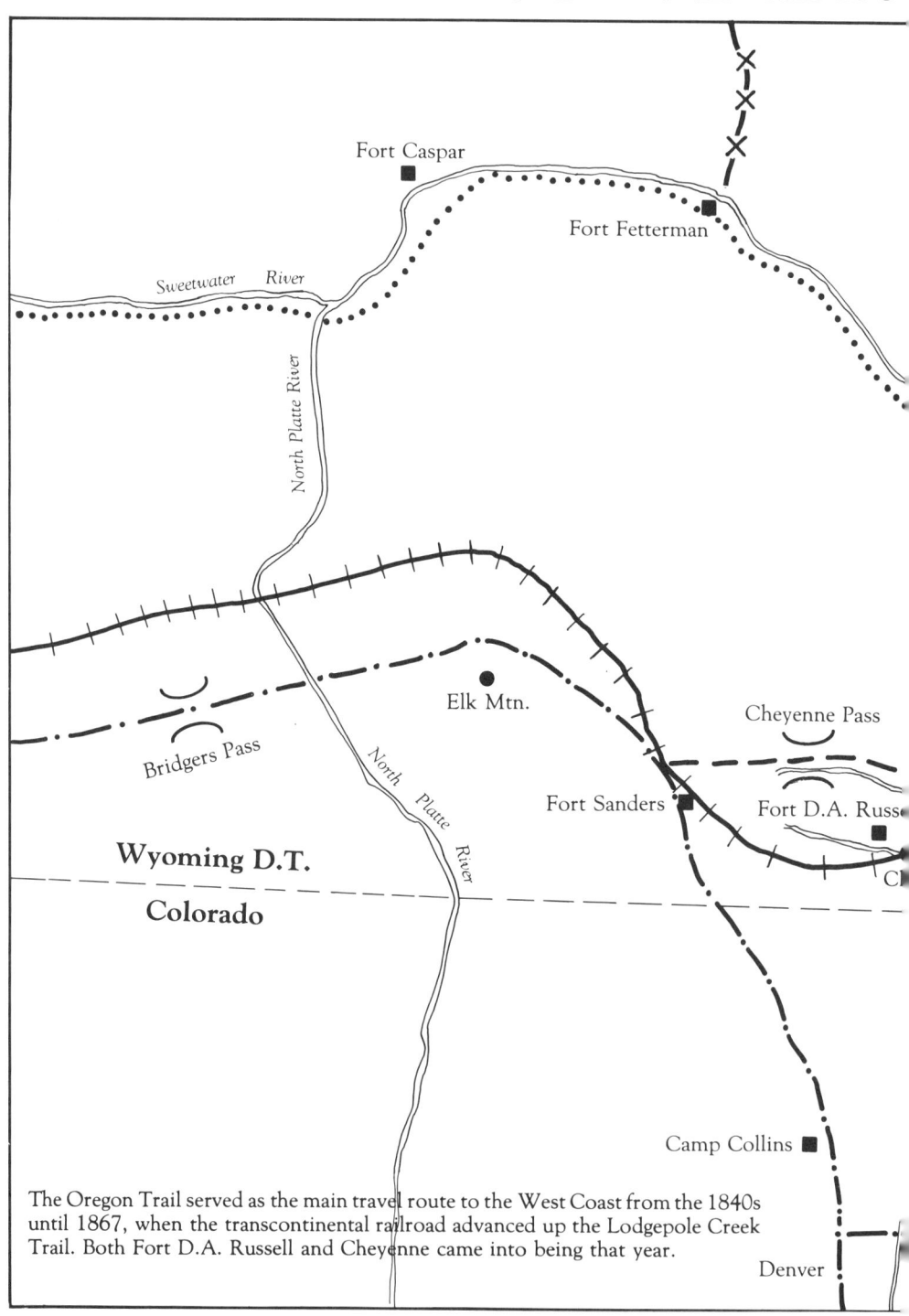

The Oregon Trail served as the main travel route to the West Coast from the 1840s until 1867, when the transcontinental railroad advanced up the Lodgepole Creek Trail. Both Fort D.A. Russell and Cheyenne came into being that year.

POST BEYOND THE
1867-1869

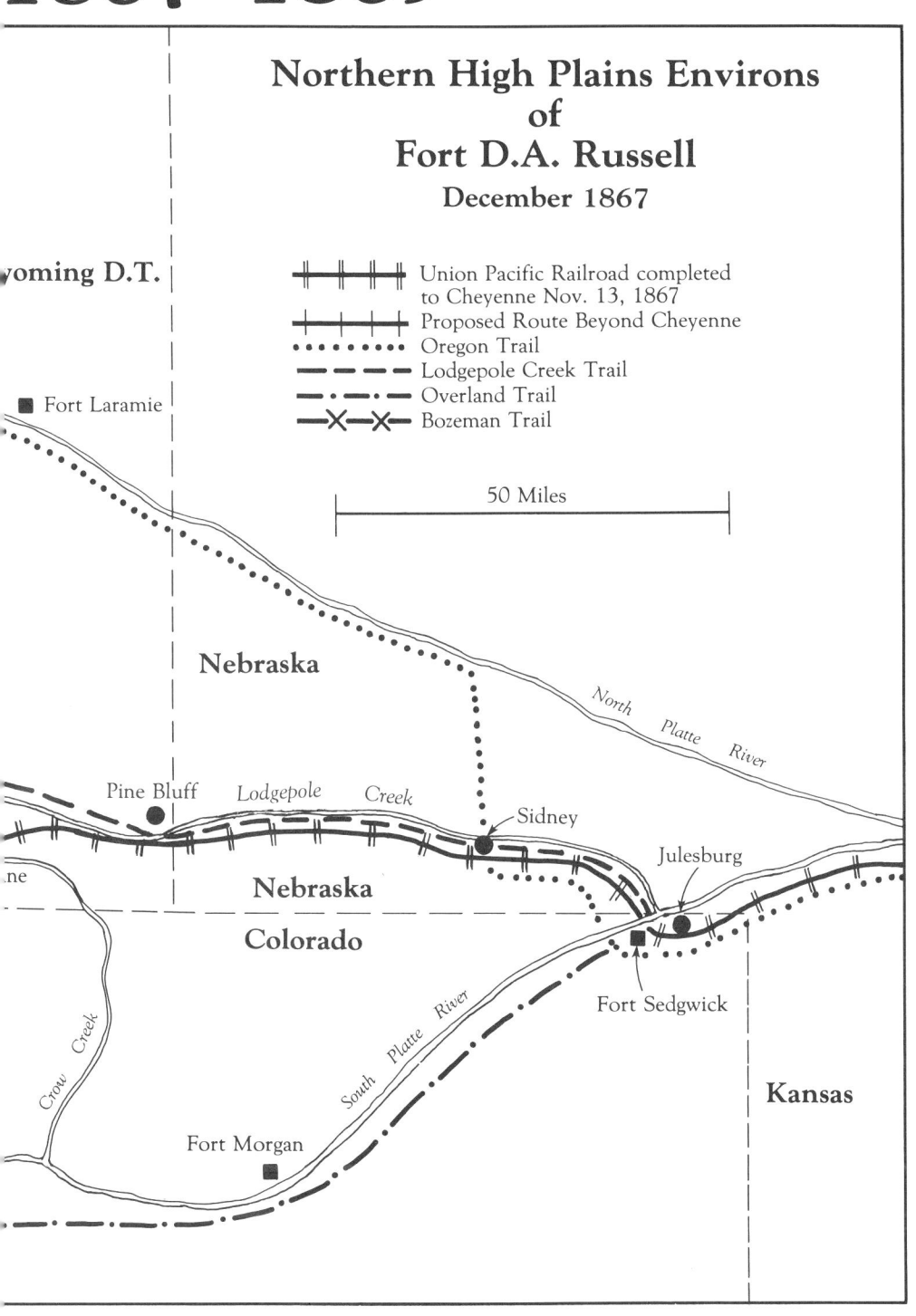

A brilliant, tough, and tenacious Civil War general, William Tecumseh Sherman served with distinction after the war as commander of the Division of the Missouri headquartered in St. Louis. He made frequent visits to Fort D.A. Russell, a new 1867 post in his Division of the Missouri which covered much of the area being settled in the West. When he succeeded Ulysses S. Grant as commander-in-chief of the army in March 1969, he continued to visit the frontier posts at every opportunity. His influence on the United States Army continued long after his death in 1891.

Chapter One
Finding The Right Spot On Crow Creek

After the Civil War ended in April 1865, the resurging westward movement dictated the need for a transcontinental railroad to link the sparsely settled West Coast with the Midwest and the western territories in between. Although President Andrew Johnson's administration focused its attention on reconstruction in the South, the northern-dominated Congress pressed for a railroad to be constructed through the central part of the West. But the Indian tribes that roamed and hunted the northern High Plains east of the Rocky Mountains where the railroad would build opposed such an invasion of their territory. Even though considerable traffic had already passed through the country over the Oregon and Lodgepole Creek trails, the "iron horse" posed a more serious and lasting intrusion.

The task of dealing with the Indian threat fell to the small reorganized regular army that had replaced the Civil War volunteers in 1866. The railroad wanted many soldiers to protect it while under construction and during its early operating stages. To provide the protection needed, the army required several new posts along the route. One key post, to be located on the eastern slope of the Laramie Range of the Rocky Mountains, then called the Black Hills, would be called Fort D.A. Russell.

The Union Pacific dealt with the majority of its own problems as they arose. But for protection from the hostile Indians, the railroad needed assistance. In order to help the Union Pacific deal with the Indian threat, Lieutenant General W.T. Sherman recommended that certain changes be made in his command, the Division of the Missouri headquartered in St. Louis:

> The construction of the Union Pacific was deemed so important that the President, at my suggestion, constituted on the 5th of March, 1866, the new Department of the Platte, General P. St. George Cook, commanding, succeeded by General C.C. Augur on January 23, 1867, Headquarters at Omaha, with orders to give ample protection to the working parties, and to afford every possible assistance in the construction of the road.[1]

Sherman's Division of the Missouri included several departments whose combined territory covered the land between the Mississippi River and the western slope of the Rockies from the Canadian to the Mexican borders. This division had the most troublesome Indian tribes, and the majority of the post-Civil War Indian disturbances occurred here.

Even though a route had been designated by Congress, the Union Pacific had some latitude in choosing the specific line for the new railroad. Instead of following the more traveled Oregon Trail in western Nebraska where the Platte River splits into a north and south branch, the Union Pacific chose a more direct route. Following the South Platte River a few miles southwest to Julesburg, the surveyors struck west along the Lodgepole Creek Trail until well beyond the Nebraska border and into Wyoming, then a part of Dakota Territory. The proposed rail route veered southwest from Lodgepole Creek as it approached the Laramie Mountains and crossed Crow Creek before entering the Laramie Mountain Range.

The Lodgepole Creek Trail, which followed the creek from Julesburg to Cheyenne Pass, was an often-used route, particularly when Oregon Trail travelers encountered hostile Indian activity or poor grazing. Moving west, this trail entered the Laramie Mountains at Cheyenne Pass and joined the Overland Trail, the Denver-to-Fort Bridger road, on the Laramie Plain where Fort Sanders stood. The Union Pacific planned to build along as much of the established trails as possible. If it had followed the Oregon Trail along the North Platte River, some additional ninety-six miles of rail would have been required on its northern loop past Forts Laramie, Fetterman, and Caspar. Had it done so, however, the building of at least three other army posts, including Fort D.A. Russell, might not have been necessary.

In late 1866, General W.T. Sherman traveled from Fort Laramie through Cheyenne Pass to Fort Sanders on a familiarization trip of the territory in his Division of the Missouri. Sherman then sent this message from his headquarters in early spring of 1867, not long after his return to St. Louis. the post and depot referred to would become Fort D.A. Russell and Cheyenne Depot:

> My opinion is that Fort Kearney may now be allowed to go to decay, only to be used as far as its present buildings are serviceable for the shelter of men and animals during the winter season. Forts McPherson, Sedgwick and Sanders should be completed but not enlarged, to be used principally for storage of troops in winter. Fort Morgan and Camp Collins should be wholly abandoned, and their stores transferred over to the Railroad about Lodge Pole Creek. At some point of the Railroad, near the Eastern Base of the Black Hills, convenient to the timber region, should be selected a good site for a depot of some magnitude, and buildings begun, which should be on a plan admitting of enlargement to the capacity of barracks for a Regiment of Infantry, and storage for, say 2,500 men. From this point for many years all the Posts north along the eastern base of the Rocky Mountains will have to be supplied.[2]

On July 4, 1867, the Union Pacific's chief engineer, Grenville M. Dodge, met with Augur where the line of the railroad would cross Crow Creek. This site on the eastern slope of the Laramie Mountains, referred to in Sherman's message as the Black Hills, met the requirements. Grenville Dodge had been a major general of volunteers in Sherman's wartime army, and he retained a close relationship with both Sherman and U.S. Grant.

Still four months from reaching Crow Creek Crossing, the Union Pacific line had been completed to Julesburg at the time of the July fourth meeting. Earlier designated a division point where the per-mile U.S. bond subsidy payment to the Union Pacific for building the railroad increased from $16,000 for plains to $48,000 for mountain terrain, Crow Creek Crossing was also designated a major railroad center. The settlement that quickly arose took its name from nearby Cheyenne Pass and the Cheyenne Indians that roamed the area.

In a telegram to General Sherman the day after his first meeting with Dodge, General Augur mentioned that he favored building the new military post and depot away from the crossing settlement and nearer wood and water. Augur had chosen a site fourteen miles west in the foothills on the middle branch of Crow Creek, near where the rail line would be laid going west.

Strong military escorts accompanied both Dodge and Augur to the early July conference at Crow Creek Crossing. Augur had arrived from an inspection tour of the western portion of his department's territory. His escort consisted of two companies of cavalry plus two companies of Pawnee Indian Scouts. The legendary Major Frank North led the Pawnee Scouts on this expedition, as he was to do many times in the following nine years. Accompanying Dodge were Major General John A. Rawlins, former chief of staff to General Grant, and a number of Union Pacific officials. The Dodge party had a military escort of two companies of infantry and two companies of cavalry. Everyone rode horseback or in wagons. Lieutenant Colonel John K. Mizner commanded Dodge's escort.

Considering the isolation and newness of the site, a goodly number of military personnel and civilians were on hand at Crow Creek Crossing on July 4, 1867, to celebrate the national Independence Day. The occasion included a rousing patriotic speech by General Rawlins. Among the civilians gathered there, in addition to the railroad surveyors and graders, were many of the first settlers of Cheyenne. Newcomers were arriving daily and setting up tent stores, saloons, and other types of establishments.

En route to the Crow Creek Crossing conference the day before, the Pawnee Scouts had clashed with a band of Arapaho near Cheyenne Pass. According to the Union Pacific surgeon who accompanied the Dodge party most of the summer, the Pawnee took eight scalps as well as the Arapaho pony herd. The Pawnee were known for their skill and success in capturing horses from their enemies, the Arapaho, Sioux, and Cheyenne. This successful engagement of the Pawnee Scouts, along with their rousing scalp dance, which continued far into the night, unnerved some of the Union Pacific party members new to the northern High Plains.

Although the Cheyenne and Arapaho were more often seen in the Crow

Two companies of riflemen from Fort Laramie moved to Cheyenne Pass in 1858 and established Camp Walbach to protect the supply trains provisioning Colonel Albert Sidney Johnston's Fifth Cavalry in Utah. Abandoned in the spring of 1859 when the situation in Utah became stabilized, General Sherman and escort camped at the site of Camp Walbach in 1866 while inspecting the territory of the Division of the Missouri. Named after the Cheyenne Indians who roamed the area, Cheyenne Pass lies some twenty miles northwest of the present-day city.—WY State AMH Dept.

Creek Crossing area, an occasional band of Sioux also came through the area. Estimated to number twenty-five or thirty bands, the Brule and Oglala were the largest, most important, and most troublesome of the Sioux. The Cheyenne and Arapaho were usually aligned with the Sioux. They often traveled and hunted together, although the Indians' favorite food supply, the buffalo, was not often seen in the Crow Creek Crossing area. The large bands of Sioux usually stayed north and east in the lower prairie where the large buffalo herds grazed.

Even though Brigadier General Augur had indicated his preference for the new post to be sited fourteen miles west, Grenville Dodge had other ideas. According to historian Gilbert A. Stelter's interpretation that appeared in the April 1967 *Annals of Wyoming*, "The Birth of A Frontier

Town: Cheyenne in 1867," Dodge considered himself Cheyenne's patron and wanted to provide protection and an economic benefit for Cheyenne, both of which could be realized by having a military post nearby. "Future merchants and saloon keepers would have a large ready made group of customers near at hand. In addition, a quartermaster depot built in conjunction with the post would provide employment for hundreds of freighters and their teams."

The unit selected to establish the new garrison on Crow Creek, the Thirtieth Infantry commanded by Colonel John D. Stevenson, had been located for some weeks on Lawrence Fork (also shown as Larrans Fork) in western Nebraska about eighty miles northwest of Julesburg. The regiment with five companies had spent several weeks there trying to contain the depredations of roving Indian war parties. Leaving Lawrence Fork on July 15, three companies (B,G, and K) arrived at Crow Creek Crossing on July 21, 1867, and set up camp about a half mile north. The site was designated the Camp at Crow Creek Crossing. The Thirtieth Infantry left one company behind on Lawrence Fork to close down that camp and one company at Pine Bluffs on Lodgepole Creek to protect the workers on the approaching rail line.

Dodge and Augur apparently reached an agreement sometime after the July fourth meeting as to where the post would be located, or else Dodge's preference prevailed. Department of the Platte General Order No. 33 dated July 31, 1867, made the name and location of the new post official: "The new military post to be established on Crow Creek, D.T., at its intersection by the Union Pacific Railroad, is named Fort D.A. Russell, after Brigadier General David A. Russell, U.S. Volunteers, Major 8th U.S. Infantry, who was killed at the battle of Winchester, September 19, 1864."

  1. General W.T. Sherman, *Personal Memoirs of Gen'l W.T. Sherman*, Vol. 2 (New York: Charles L. Webster and Co., 1891), p. 42.
  2. U.S. Army Continental Commands, Department of the Platte Records 1858-1895, Sherman's Letter to Augur, Letters Received A-Y 1867-1869, (RG 533, Roll 6) National Archives.

Colonel John D. Stevenson, commander of the Thirtieth Infantry and first post commander of Fort D.A. Russell, arrived with his regiment at the Crow Creek crossing in July 1867 and began building the post while also chasing Indians, guarding railroad workers, and escorting various visiting dignitaries.—*Ninetieth SM Wing History Office*

Chapter Two
Building Barracks And Chasing Indians

After three weeks at the Camp on Crow Creek, the Thirtieth Infantry moved on August 16, 1867, to the location chosen for Fort D.A. Russell three miles west of the center of Cheyenne. A provisional town government appointed merchant H.M. Hook mayor of Cheyenne. A survey team headed by Lieutenant R.W. Petriken plotted the boundary of the military reservation in the form of a parallelogram two miles wide and three miles long on a magnetic north axis. The parallelogram contained 3,840 acres, but additions were soon made in the southeast corner to give more space to the supply depot. One of Petriken's assistants, Lieutenant William H. Bisbee, later recalled the diverse activities of the soldiers at Fort D.A. Russell that summer: "Building involved hard work as the labor in most cases was performed by the troops whose combined duties of interior garrison work, running saw mills and chasing Indians, gave plenty of healthy recreation, amply fitting them for a fight or a frolic."[1]

The local magnetic variation of fifteen degrees, thirty minutes east skewed the north–south axis of the parallelogram to the right of true north, causing the military installation to lean on the north–south section lines. About the same time, Union Pacific suveyors laid out Cheyenne in a two-mile square town land claim and skewed the town's north–south axis to the left of true north in order to square the streets with the railroad tracks planned to run southwest through the town. Skewing Fort Russell to the right and Cheyenne to the left provided a coincidental contrast.

The garrison planned by Colonel John D. Stevenson with the help of his able surgeon, C.H. Alden, arranged the buildings around a diamond-shaped parade ground 1,040 feet long and 800 feet wide. The plan included twenty-eight double officers' family quarters on the north side of the parade plus the commanding officer's quarters set at the apex. A forty-eight-bed hospital and post trader's store were located on the northeast side. On the south side of the parade were twelve company barracks with a mess house for each company, a guardhouse, shops, and storehouses. Stevenson did not include a protective stockade as had been done in many other western posts.

The general supply or quartermaster depot, named Cheyenne Depot, stood on the eastern edge of the military reservation halfway between the post and Cheyenne. "Citizen mechanics" employed at the depot erected some buildings, with most of the rough work being done daily by details details of soldiers from the post's infantry companies. Early construction priorities centered on the barracks for the men at the post and warehouses at the depot. Tons of supplies were beginning to arrive at the depot. The Cheyenne Depot's mission was to provide supplies to all authorized users in the northern High Plains area, including Fort D.A. Russell and the army forts to the north and west, plus several Indian agencies. An ordnance depot and a commissary of subsistence depot were also established at the Cheyenne Depot, but these facilities were sub-depots and much less extensive than the main quartermaster supply depot.

The task of guarding the Cheyenne Depot and all its livestock and warehouses full of scarce commodities initially fell to the hard-pressed Thirtieth Infantry. A welcome addition to the military complement of Fort D.A. Russell arrived in mid-September 1867, when Company H, Second Cavalry, joined the garrison. A cavalry company added fexibility to this military garrison, which now totaled 243 enlisted men, twelve officers, and sixty-eight serviceable horses. More cavalry companies would soon arrive.

The Thirtieth Infantry maintained a busy schedule the first few months. Building a military post from scratch without the help of civilian contractors posed a formidable task for a fighting outfit. A large contingent (271) of recruits arrived in October from Newport Barracks, Kentucky, but they were considered a mixed blessing. Largely untrained, these recruits could still supply substantial muscle for the immediate needs of the building program underway. The urgent need for sheltering men and animals before the winter provided a strong incentive to keep the work going. Building supplies shipped by rail from Omaha to the end of the line somewhere between Julesburg and Cheyenne had to be freighted to the post by wagon train.

Local news for the new military and civilian communities first appeared in the *Cheyenne Leader*, which commenced operation on September 19, 1867, as a tri-weekly newspaper. It soon became a daily but did not carry timely national and international news until five years later. The editor and publisher of the *Leader*, N.A. Baker, included a large helping of personal opinion in every edition and served as a persuasive voice in the community. While the army in general and Fort D.A. Russell in particular were well treated, soldiers "coming to town" were sometimes subjected to undue attention if the editor thought they had misbehaved. The first edition of the newspaper reported a sergeant killed when trying to take a drunken soldier from a Cheyenne saloon. In attempting to subdue the man, the sergeant shot himself in the abdomen and died the next day. Neither the unfortunate sergeant nor the army obtained much sympathy from the editor on this occasion.

The northern High Plains Indians also received the attention of Editor Baker, who believed, along with most western editors, that Indians were being coddled by the government at the expense of frontier settlers. A local militia could deal more effectively with the Indians, he reasoned, if authorized and financed by the federal government. When a group of eastern newspaper editors visited Cheyenne, Baker reported that they were of a like mind:

> The City Hall was well filled with an attentive and appreciative class of hearers. The editors generally seemed delighted with the discussion of the Sand Creek and Indian Affairs. The civilians seemed to think that regular soldiers were not just the force to fight Indians with; and it might be confessed that right or wrong, extermination is a favorite idea with the people of the plains.[2]

The idea that a militia raised from local volunteers could control the Indians better than the regular army also seemed to prevail among local political leaders. The inability of the army to field a force on short notice large enough to put down all Indian opposition contributed to this opinion. The federal government was expected to foot the bill in any use of the militia, and it did in a few isolated instances in other areas of the West. However, those occasions did not prove fruitful, and the federal government abandoned further attempts to use militia against hostile Indians.

While engaged in protecting the railroad and the many new settlements along the line, the military at Fort D.A. Russell also responded on several occasions to the call for protection of Cheyenne against a rough element that threatened to take over the town. The provisional government formed in August 1867 did not include effective law enforcement. Army troops were the main resource available to quell disturbances that got out of hand. Other railroad settlements were faced with similar situations as the track of the Union Pacific moved west. The Department of the Platte had issued orders earlier to all its units along the railroad to help maintain civil order in the mushrooming settlements until civil authority could be installed.

An aura of hope for peace with the Indians hung over the military and civilian communities in October 1867. A peace commission had been established by President Andrew Johnson and the Congress to negotiate with certain hostile tribes in the West. Proceeding from Washington, D.C., the distinguished six-member Indian Peace Commission planned to pick up a military escort at Fort D.A. Russell for the trip to Fort Laramie, where they would meet with Indian tribal leaders. The peace commissioners expected to see the leaders of the Crow, the Brule and Oglala Sioux, the Arapaho, and the Cheyenne. Military members named to the commission included Lieutenant General W.T. Sherman, Brigadier Generals A.H. Terry and W.S. Harney with C.C. Augur added later. Civilian appointees included the Commissioner of Indian Affairs, N.G. Taylor, plus J.B. Sanford and A.S. White. The commission members were of a like mind as to what should be done with the Indians, as later reported by Sherman: "We all agreed that the nomad Indians should be removed from the vicinity of the two great railroads then in rapid construction, and be localized in one or other of the two great reservations south of Kansas and north of Nebraska."[3]

A very perceptive French engineer and writer visiting the West, Louis L. Simonin, waited in Cheyenne for the arrival of the Indian Peace Commission and recorded his impressions of Fort D.A. Russell and Cheyenne. Simonin had obtained permission to accompany the commission to Fort Laramie. An army attache to the United States Legation in Paris, Colonel Wilhelm Heine, accompanied Simonin on his tour. Simonin wrote:

> Everywhere I hear the sound of the saw and hammer; everywhere wooden houses are going up; everywhere streets are being laid out ... already there are two printing shops, two newspapers, book shops, banks, stagecoachs, then the post office and telegraph ... more than 3,000 people. It has added a thousand inhabitants each month, and the railroad has not caught up with it.[4]

The only accommodations Simonin and Heine could find on arriving in Cheyenne were in the common sleeping room of the Dodge House, the best hotel in town. The room had thirty or more beds in it, with most of the beds occupied by two sleepers. Simonin wrote that the democratic customs of the Far West permitted this "nocturnal fraternity," and the American endured it with good grace. Army friends of Colonel Heine at the post soon saved the visitors from the Dodge House:

> Fort Russell, under the tent, 1 November. The most cordial hospitality awaited us here. . . . General Stevenson, who commands the fort, the major, the quartermaster, the officers, all have received us as friends. We have sat at their mess, we have toasted one another, and drunk the sacramental glass of whiskey without which no good acquaintance is made in the United States. We have been received with all possible honors. A sentinel watches over our tent, in the evening we answer his call to return to our quarters.[5]

The post/regimental commander's commercial ventures in town also received the Frenchman's attention:

> The commandant mingles the practice of business with the profession of arms. He has bought what they call a "corner lot" in Cheyenne, one of those sites which touch on two streets at once like those so preferred by the wine merchants of Paris. . . . General Stevenson, not content with these lots, has also contrived to erect a vast storehouse in Cheyenne, a warehouse in stone, if you please, and not in wood. He hopes to store merchandise either from one or another source, when the Pacific railroad has united the two seas and has developed into the great commercial highway of the world. Every day the general in his buggy drawn by two smart horses visits his growing estate and calculates . . . how much they will bring.[6]

The colonel of the Thirtieth Infantry must have felt the investment opportunities in Cheyenne too good to pass up despite his command position. Highly visible local commercial interests could be injurious to a commander's military career. The local newspaper frequently called attention to Stevenson's downtown interests. An item on November 14, 1867: "We note an improvement in front of General Stevenson's block on seventeenth street in the shape of a substantial and broad plank sidewalk." A few days later the newspaper reported that a charitable inclination had surfaced with Stevenson's donation of four lots to the Catholics of Cheyenne to build a church.

The Peace Commission finally arrived in Cheyenne on November 5, 1867, and left the next day for Fort Laramie. Fort D.A. Russell provided them an escort of eighty soldiers plus thirty-five mule-team drivers, thirty wagons, and 130 animals. There were also various observers accompanying the commission.

Despite the great expectations for a successful peace conference, several of the principals were missing. The Sioux, Arapaho, and Cheyenne tribal leaders did not appear as expected, only the Crow. Thus, the government made little progress with the northern High Plains tribes in 1867. After waiting a respectable time at Fort Laramie for the recalcitrant Indian leaders to come in, the disappointed peace commissioners returned to Cheyenne and the East to report their lack of progress.

The peace party's military escort surely welcomed a return to Fort D.A. Russell; most of the assigned units had been in the field and on the move all summer and fall. Although quarters were still being built in anticipation of a large number of companies wintering at the new post, progress had been slow. Construction did pick up after November 13, 1867, when the railroad reached Cheyenne and building supplies became more available. Troop labor also increased as units returned to the post and winter quarters. Most of the Union Pacific track work stopped for the winter in November, and Cheyenne became an end-of-the-track winter home for construction workers, gamblers, and assorted speculators. A spur rail line was extended from Cheyenne to the post and Cheyenne Depot in December.

Although Chief Red Cloud and the Sioux had declared war on the Bozeman Trail forts more than a year before, the army started a stagecoach line in late December to the northern forts to accommodate the increased number of passengers needing transportation. A stage departed every other day to forts Laramie, Fetterman, and Phil Kearny. Set up primarily for military and postal service, civilian passengers could board by making application at Fort D.A. Russell.

Eleven companies had returned and been quartered by January 1868, seven of the Thirtieth Infantry and four of the Second Cavalry, for a total of 905 enlisted men and twenty-three officers. While wooden barracks were completed for most of the enlisted men by January, officers lived in tents until February, when their quarters were finished. The assignment of a band to the Thirtieth Infantry, one that had been destined for Fort Laramie, provided happy January news for the post. Now the military and civilian communities could have some music to enjoy, even though at Fort Laramie's expense.

An 1868 artist's rendition of Fort D.A. Russell shows the good progress made the first year. Officers' family quarters are shown to the left and enlisted mens' barracks to the right of the diamond-shaped parade ground. Cheyenne Depot appears in the upper right on the road to Cheyenne.—*WY State AMH Dept.*

A military band provided welcome entertainment for both the military and civilian communities, a glue that helped bond the communities and encourage the mutual assistance so important in those early days. The provisional government coped in a fashion with most of the town's more pressing problems, but an unruly element common to the end-of-track towns remained beyond its control. The Reverend Joseph Cook noted in his diary for January 23, 1868, one of the many occasions when the military assisted civil authorities in maintaining order. Cook reported shooting in the streets of Cheyenne and a great deal of unrest until the cavalry arrived and restored order.

The Reverend Cook had come to Cheyenne a short time before as a young Episcopalian missionary to establish a church. Post Chaplain E.B. Tuttle, another Episcopalian, suffered ill health and frequently asked the Reverend Cook to conduct services at the post. Cook made many friends

Officers' duplex family houses were completed in February 1868, after the enlisted mens' barracks had been finished. Temporary and ill-suited for the cold Wyoming winters, these houses were occupied by army officers' families for the next thirty years. The post/regimental commander's house is at the left.—*WY State AMH Dept.*

there, including the post trader, J.D. Woolley, and the Cheyenne Depot commander, Captain Elias B. Carling. Woolley and Carling were very helpful to Cook in establishing Cheyenne's St. Mark's Episcopal Church. While Cook held the wife of the post/regimental commander in high esteem, he disliked the colonel because of his penchant for having regimental dress parades on Sunday afternoons. Cook, like most clerics, did not approve of Sunday parades, or any other activity on the Sabbath that was not absolutely necessary. By February, the progress of the post's building program enabled the commander to invite Cheyenneites to drive out on Washington's Birthday and see a grand review and dress parade. Colonel Stevenson hosted a reception a few days later in the newly completed post commander's house for Cheyenne dignitaries and his officers. Not many socially acceptable ladies yet resided in Cheyenne, but there were some officers' wives on post. A total of twenty-five ladies, and

This house was first occupied by post and Thirtieth Infantry regimental commander Colonel John D. Stevenson and his wife. A part of the first floor also served initially as the post/regimental headquarters. The first of the officers' family quarters completed, it served as the site of a grand soiree given for civilian and military dignitaries in the area, such as they were, on Washington's birthday in 1868.—*WY State AMH Dept.*

twice that many gentlemen, were reported to have enjoyed the hospitality of the commander in the beautifully decorated rooms of the new house. Refreshments included "wine superb along with all that epicurean taste could desire." The *Leader* reported: "Long will the occasion be remembered by many who had the good fortune to be present at Fort Russell last evening."

A week later, Stevenson hosted a larger and equally sumptuous affair that inaugurated social life for the military and civilian communities. It was held in a large and spacious post hall set apart by the commander for chapel services, bible classes, and social functions, and the newly acquired regimental band played for the gala occasion. The *Leader*'s editor attended and expressed his approbation the next day with these words: "All . . . sat down at eleven o'clock to a well laid table of choice provisions, and something from France to settle the same." While Colonel Stevenson might not have been popular with the Reverend Joseph Cook, his hospitality in February and March assured him friends in Cheyenne, so long as he kept up the pace.

1. William H. Bisbee, *Through Four American Wars*, (Boston: Meador Publishing Company, 1931), p. 131.

2. *Cheyenne Daily Leader*, October 17, 1867.

3. General W.T. Sherman, *Personal Memoirs of Gen'l W.T. Sherman*, Vol. 2 (New York: Charles L. Webster and Co., 1891), p. 435.

4. Louis L. Simonin, *The Rocky Mountain West In 1867*, (translated from LeGrand-Ouest des Etuts-Unis by Wilson O. Clough), (Lincoln: University of Nebraska Press, 1966), p. 63.

5. Ibid. p. 68.

6. Ibid. p. 71.

Major General Philip H. Sheridan replaced Sherman on the Peace Commission that arrived at Fort D.A. Russell in April 1868, to negotiate a treaty at Fort Laramie with the High Plains Indian tribes. Sheridan succeeded Sherman the next year as commander of the Division of the Missouri. He held that position for the next fourteen years during the most turbulent period of the settlement of the West.

Chapter Three
First Spring Campaign And The Treaty Of 1868

Fort D.A. Russell remained at approximately the same number of companies (eleven) through the first winter. Troops that could be spared labored to improve the living facilities, weather permitting. When the spring prairie grass had greened enough to provide forage for the animals, the post became almost deserted, with troops moving out to guard the railroad and its workers, and to escort the many official parties arriving from the East. Spring grass also meant that the Indian bands would be on the move. In April 1868, six companies consisting of 481 enlisted men and seventeen officers left the post for guard duty along the railroad.

Lack of troop enthusiasm for the coming spring campaign appeared as early as February and March 1868, with an unusually large number of soldiers in the guardhouse (sixty-two and seventy-eight). Desertions also jumped dramatically; twenty-three and twenty-seven "went over the hill" in February and March. While it was never difficult to desert in the western army, it could be dangerous. Two of the three soldiers who tried to desert during a severe snowstorm in March found it wise to return to the post before proceeding very far on foot. The third soldier was found dead several days later, frozen in a snowbank not far away. Usually, deserting soldiers would try to catch a train or take along their horse, saddle, and a firearm. During the spring and summer when the units were busiest campaigning, confinement and desertion fell to almost nothing.

Hoping for a more successful meeting at Fort Laramie with the Indian leaders than had been experienced the previous year, the Peace Commission arrived at Fort D.A. Russell on April 6, 1868. General Phil Sheridan had replaced General W.T. Sherman on the commission. After a review of troops at Fort D.A. Russell the next day, General Sheridan and party set out for Fort Laramie heavily escorted. Several of the Indian leaders arrived late at Fort Laramie, and the commission met intermittently for over a month with mixed results. In mid-May most of the commission members returned to Cheyenne and reported that a treaty had been concluded with the Crows, Brule Sioux, Northern Cheyenne, and Arapaho but not with Red Cloud's Oglala Sioux. General Harney, an old soldier with considerable Indian experience, remained at Fort Laramie to meet with the Oglala chiefs Red Cloud and Man-Afraid-of-His-Horses, who were still expected.

An important provision of the Fort Laramie Treaty of 1868, the army's abandonment of the Bozeman Trail forts Phil Kearny, Reno, and C.F. Smith, created mixed emotions among the military and civilian communities. As a result of the treaty, travel and settlement in the Indian lands would be dangerous and severely restricted. The military would be prevented from entering the ceded Indian territory except for special occasions. In turn, the Indians signing the treaty agreed to keep the peace and settle on reservations north of the North Platte River in the areas later to become the states of Wyoming, Montana, and South Dakota. The government promised to provide them rations, annuity goods, and the white man's culture.

Not much change was noted immediately in the Indians' behavior after the Peace Commission's visit to Fort Laramie, nor should it have been expected. The usual loose tribal leadership, the tendency for young bucks to act independently, lack of communications, and the Indians' faint understanding of the treaty's provisions all contributed to the white mans' frustration when violations occurred.

While Fort D.A. Russell and Cheyenne remained free of any direct attacks, Indians were frequently seen in the immediate area. Raids on livestock by small bands occurred often, and a clash near Cheyenne between four stock herders and a war party caused a great deal of concern in town. A steady harrassment of the railroad working parties by various bands continued to cause casualties and damage, slowing progress and increasing the Union Pacific's demands for more military protection.

While the building program at the post continued at a reduced speed through the spring of 1868, there were some setbacks. A serious one occurred when the stables of Companies I and J, Second Cavalry, burned, killing sixty-five horses. Although fireguards were maintained for early detection of fires, blazes were difficult to contain and extinguish if high winds prevailed. Oil lamps, faulty heating stove flues, wooden buildings with dry shingle roofs, plus large amounts of stored hay and grain all provided ready material for a fire. Nearby water barrels and buckets were kept filled for such emergencies, but these means were quickly exhausted if the fire took hold. The post's horse-drawn fire engine required some time to arrive at the scene of a fire and longer to get up steam that would provide pressure to force water from the hoses to the flames. The source of water also posed a problem. No central water distribution system existed until 1884, sixteen years later. Water pumped from Crow Creek by a steam engine to an elevated wooden tank on the west side of the post provided the storage for a soldier detail to fill the fire engine and a water wagon.

The water wagon could deliver water to a fire, or more often, provide daily deliveries to the barrels located behind the houses, barracks, mess halls, and stables. Mrs. Elizabeth Burt, wife of Captain Andrew Burt, then of the Eighteenth Infantry at Fort Bridger and three times stationed at Fort D.A. Russell, described the system of the time and the lack of amenities typical of all western garrisons:

Bathrooms were an unknown luxury in the Army. My husband was a major who had served twenty years in the Army before we possessed that luxury. At this time water was hauled from the river and emptied into barrels at the kitchen door. Microbes were unheard of in those days, and we drank the water, and what milk we could purchase, with no thought of disaster.[1]

Late spring of 1868 found Fort D.A. Russell's infantry and cavalry units escorting several official parties and guarding the Union Pacific east to Fort Kearney, Nebraska, and west to the Medicine Bow Mountains. Only a caretaker force remained at the post for the summer. This troop deployment pattern remained similar for the next twelve years: troops in the field from spring until late fall while the Indians were active and moving, then a return to winter quarters when the Indians settled down. As commander of the Department of the Platte, General Christopher Augur followed the practice of assigning infantry and cavalry companies to each military post so that a mix of the two could be more effectively employed. Cavalry could patrol between the stations along the railroad while infantry units manned and defended the stations and work parties during the dangerous months.

The closure of the three forts on the Bozeman Trail plus Fort Morgan and Camp Collins in northern Colorado during the spring and summer of 1868 caused some realignment of units in the northern High Plains area. The Fort Laramie Treaty of 1868 and the coming of the railroad had lessened the importance of Fort Morgan and Camp Collins. One hundred wagons pulled by four- and six-mule teams moved the last company of infantry from Fort Morgan to Fort D.A. Russell. The infantry company undoubtedly found a warm welcome and quick employment at Fort D.A. Russell. The demand for troop protection never ceased.

Movement orders for the Thirtieth Infantry arrived in July 1868, only a year after the regiment had first set up camp at Crow Creek Crossing. The regiment had orders to build a new post 150 miles west, Fort Fred Steele, on the line of the railroad near present-day Rawlins, Wyoming. Whether or not Colonel Stevenson's personal business activities in Cheyenne caused the early transfer of his regiment is uncertain.

The Eighteenth Infantry with four companies, commanded by Lieutenant Colonel Henry W. Wessells, arrived from Fort Fetterman in late July, replacing the Thirtieth Infantry. Three companies of the Second Cavalry also arrived to take station. Other companies of both regiments remained at various other points along the railroad. Companies of the Eighteenth Infantry on-post took up the task of continuing the building program started by the Thirtieth Infantry a year earlier. Some rebuilding also had to be done; the post guardhouse had burned down in August. The telegraph line to Fort Laramie also needed attention. It suffered from the Wyoming winds and Indians.

A prime morale builder for a western regiment and a prized possession continued to be a band, and the Eighteenth Infantry had brought along a good one. The 1868 Fourth of July celebration in Cheyenne included a grand parade led by the Eighteenth Infantry band and followed by the regimental commander, staff, and those units of the regiment that happened to be available. Only a year before, in 1867, officials of the Department of the Platte and the Union Pacific had met at Crow Creek Crossing on the Fourth of July to discuss where the settlement and the military reservation would be located. A thriving civilian community had developed in that year and now celebrated the national Independence Day with the help of the military garrison. On a patriotic theme that included the merits of Cheyenne, the *Leader*'s editor also recognized the military's important role in western settlement:

> One of the most important adjuncts to the prosperity of Cheyenne is Fort D.A. Russell, a garrison capable of comfortably quartering fourteen companies of men, and Head Quarters. . . .This post, occupying the position it does, employs a great number of men and teams, and annually expends millions of dollars, all of which operated in favor of this city. . . .Fort Russell is pronounced the best arranged and one of the most important military garrisons in the United States.[2]

Cheyenne's continuing fear of an Indian attack on the town peaked in mid-July 1868. Just at the time when only a caretaker force of soldiers remained at Fort D.A. Russell, the *Leader* reported that a large band of Indians had appeared suddenly and camped: "Yesterday a party of about two hundred Indians of assorted sex and sizes came up Crow Creek to within about three miles of this city where they erected their lodges, and are now ready for anything from matrimony to manslaughter." Much to the relief of Cheyenne, the Indians proved to be friendly. Three days later a follow-up story appeared: "The Indians who are encamped below town appear to be doing a lively business in the sale of bows, arrows, quivers and moccasins. Now is the time to secure Indian trophies. Perhaps a few white mens' scalps may also be for sale by the precious scoundrels.[3]

Visitors of a different type came in late July 1868. General U.S. Grant and party arrived to inspect and review on his visit to selected posts of the western army. Grant served as Commanding General of the United States Army, but he was also campaigning for the presidency of the United States. His party included Generals Sherman and Sheridan, who wished to inspect the garrison's building progress. As was usually the case when these distinguished generals arrived, visits with wartime comrades on the post and in town held a high priority. A large delegation of the Grant for President Club called on Grant at the Ford House in Cheyenne where his party stayed. Accommodations for visiting dignitaries at the post were non-existent until many years later. Military visitors were usually "put up" at the house of a friend on the post, or they "bunked" in Cheyenne.

Activities through August 1868 amounted to normal garrison duty for the small detachment of soldiers holding the fort. Most of the assigned companies were fanned out along the Union Pacific line. A daring and successful Indian raid on the guarded Wells Fargo horse herd south of Cheyenne reminded the townsfolk that there might not be enough military strength on hand to protect them. Meetings were held to organize a militia and defend the town. While the citizens attending the meetings were reported by the newspaper to know exactly what to do with the Indians, the army at Fort D.A. Russell was not so certain. A Department of the Platte directive to all commanding officers advised that Indians had a right to roam and hunt over all the lands ceded to them. It further directed that army units should not go into Indian territory or interfere with their rights unless the Indians committed overt acts or depredations. This policy was terminated, however, when the troublesome raids continued. Criticism from the Congress and the press caused Sherman to direct his commanders to conduct the roaming Indians, or those not complying with the terms of the Fort Laramie Treaty of 1868, to their assigned reservations.

There seemed to be no question in the minds of most western newspaper editors about how to handle the Indians. Few journalists agreed with what they felt had become a very lenient Indian policy foisted on the West by the Johnson administration. The *Leader*'s critical comments on the government's policy and failure to aggressively pursue Indians, or even hold an adequate number of troops at Fort D.A. Russell to protect the Cheyenne community during the "Indian chasing season," continued unabated:

> The other day the 27th Infantry arrived here from Montana and northern Wyoming, and instead of being retained here or in Colorado—a territory destitute of anything like government protection and swarming with Indians—they are ordered to Omaha as a measure of economy . . . but that is the economy of not fighting Indians which the government has so long pursued. The people are about satisfied of its economy, and would now like to see a little effective Indian fighting just for a change.[4]

In the face of such editorials, several of the units being moved from the three closed Bozeman Trail forts were redeployed where needed. Coming from Fort C.F. Smith, the Twenty-seventh Infantry camped several weeks at Fort D.A. Russell on their way to new stations along the Union Pacific line. Captain and Mrs. Andrew Burt had been assigned to Fort Bridger in 1866, Fort C.F. Smith in 1867, and had passed Fort D.A. Russell, or its site, on each move. In the fall of 1868 they were moving again, this time to Ogallala Station in western Nebraska. The Burts considered Fort D.A. Russell and Cheyenne a welcome improvement, except for the wind. Mrs. Burt wrote in her journal: "The wind constantly sweeping the parade ground bare, drove the garrison almost to despair with its monotony."

While the Union Pacific had a passenger train going east and another one west every day, Wells Fargo stagecoaches remained the daily means of traveling between Cheyenne and Denver. Soon they would be replaced by the "iron horse." Strangely enough, stagecoaches generally were unmolested, but depredations reported in the fall of 1868 to the north and south of Cheyenne caused some concern for the safety of the coaches on the Denver road. Two companies of the Second Cavalry, under Major James S. Brisbin, searched extensively for Indians reported to be raiding stock ranches on the Cache La Poudre River in Colorado. No Indians could be found by Major Brisbin during this scout. As usually happened, the fast-moving Indians disappeared before the scouting party arrived. While the stagecoaches between Cheyenne and Denver experienced little difficulty with Indians, railroad working parties were not so fortunate.

The rail line building from Denver to Cheyenne, the Denver Pacific Railroad, largely owned by the Union Pacific, experienced frequent Indian troubles. The grading contractor working just south of Cheyenne threatened to quit if the army did not send troops to protect his workers from the harrassment of hostile Indians. Some urgency was attached to completion of this branch line; it would diminish Denver's isolation, increase Cheyenne's commerce, and decrease the Indians' ability to threaten northern Colorado. Fort D.A. Russell's area of responsibility extended well into Colorado. When reports were received of Indians making mischief there, troops were sent if available and as quickly as possible. The reported troublemakers were almost always on the move and hard to locate. Mounted patrols were considered most effective in chasing hostile bands as well as deterring them from harrassing the railroad workers and the settlers. However, there never seemed to be enough soldiers to satisfy the demands of the railroad and civilian authorities. Limited manpower restricted the number of patrols that could be sent out, and then those patrols had the usual difficulty of locating the troublesome Indians.

A scout from Fort D.A. Russell in September 1868, led by Lieutenant D.D. Norton of the Second Cavalry, demonstrated once more how hard it could be to find moving Indians. Ordered along the road toward Denver after more reports of Indian depredations and harrassment, Lieutenant Norton's scout proved unproductive. Since he could find no Indians, Lieutenant Norton questioned the validity of the many reports received from Colorado of Indian depredations and concluded: "the majority of the reports, so prevelant a short time previous to my departure, are in the main without foundation."[5]

Colorado Governor Hunt was probably not aware of Lieutenant Norton's report when he sent a strong request to General Sherman to send troops to defend Denver from what he perceived to be an immediate threat of Indian attack. His alternative recommendation to Sherman would have federalized the Colorado militia and had them handle the hostile Indians, at government expense of course. Sherman's response contained a touch of rancor and some advice for the governor and the settlers:

> Governor Hunt: I would make no concessions to clamor, but would assure the people of Denver if they want to fight Indians they can have all they want. The great bulk of the Arapahoes have surrendered to General Sheridan at Fort Dodge. He has one column after the Cheyenne on the Cimarron and another toward Beaver Creek. General Grant promises me more cavalry, and now that the Indians are clearly in the wrong, I will not prevent your people from chasing them, if they are really in earnest, but it is more than our small army can do to defend every ranch. . . . The settlers should collect and

defend their own property, leaving the regular troops to go after the Indians.[6]

While the community of Cheyenne considered Indians to be the main threat, another unruly group caused its share of bloodshed. As Cheyenne grew, more lawless white men gathered, and the town could not control them. Their misdeeds encouraged drastic action at times. The presence of such a collection of outlaws required that the horses and warehouses at Fort D.A. Russell and the Cheyenne Depot be closely guarded, but still there were losses. Frontier justice was administered on several occasions during the first year or so. A soldier mail carrier had his horse stolen in late November while in the Cheyenne post office picking up the post mail. A nine-man detachment of the Second Cavalry set out in hot pursuit after the thieves. They captured a reportedly notorious horse thief named Sam Dugan and a cohort at the natural fort, an outcropping of rocks thirteen miles south of Cheyenne. Dugan had the army mail carrier's horse plus several other horses taken from Cheyenne. First jailed in the post guardhouse, Dugan was turned over to a Colorado lawman the next day to be hanged two days later in Denver.

Not all outlaws were handled as precipitously as Dugan was when captured, but Cheyenne had started to take a firmer stand. Earlier the post command had sent help to Cheyenne several times when requested. Then some of the citizens of Cheyenne decided on a more direct recourse to address the problem posed by the outlaws—organization of a small vigilante group. The Reverend Joseph Cook recorded one of the severest of their actions, which occurred on October 16, 1868:

> The Vigilantes started out about service time to clear the town of the worst of the rogues and the whole town was in excitement. They hung three men that night and the next morning in broad daylight they hung another. Two innocent men were shot in the melee and have since died and another is wounded in the arm. It was a fearful night—a perfect reign of terror. But it will tend to quiet the place. It was exceedingly dangerous before with garroting, robbing and shooting.[7]

While violent deaths occurred in the streets of Cheyenne, the Eighteenth Infantry suffered a more natural loss with the sudden death of their commander, Lieutenant Colonel H.W. Wessells, in October 1868. The old soldier died of an incapacitating stroke caused in part by many years of rigorous service plus advanced age. Wessells had graduated from the United States Military Academy at West Point, New York in 1833. He had been expecting a regular promotion to full colonel.

The interim commander, Major James Van Voast, faced the task of handling the Indian depredations that continued on all sides through the fall and well into the winter of 1868-1869. A late and mild winter permitted the Indians to continue to roam, keeping many small army detachments at isolated stations and on patrol, away from winter quarters at Fort D.A. Russell. Some very bold attacks occurred in the late fall in western Nebraska against the Union Pacific. An attack on Alkali Station ninety-four miles east of Cheyenne by a large band of Sioux resulted in torn-up tracks and a derailed train. The Indians were bold enough to linger at the site and unsuccessfully try to capture the troop train sent from Fort D.A. Russell to the scene.

Lieutenant Colonel C.H. Alden served as the first post surgeon at Fort D.A. Russell and assisted post commander Colonel John D. Stevenson in planning the post layout. Alden also prepared the excellent 1870 report for the Surgeon General's office titled "A Report on Barracks and Hospitals" that detailed the conditions and progress made at early Fort D.A. Russell.—*WY State AMH Dept.*

1. Merrill J. Mattes, *Indians, Infants and Infantry: Andrew and Elizabeth Burt on the Frontier*, (Denver: The Old West Publishing Company, 1960), p. 25.
2. *Cheyenne Daily Leader*, July 4, 1868.
3. *Cheyenne Daily Leader*, July 18 and 21, 1868.
4. *Cheyenne Daily Leader*, September 1, 1868.
5. U.S. Army Continental Commands, Department of the Platte Records 1858–1895, (RG533, Roll 117), National Archives (film on file at Coe Library, University of Wyoming, Laramie).
6. *Cheyenne Daily Leader*, September 10, 1868.
7. Joseph W. Cook, *Diary and Letters*, (Laramie: The Laramie Republican Co., 1919), p. 104.

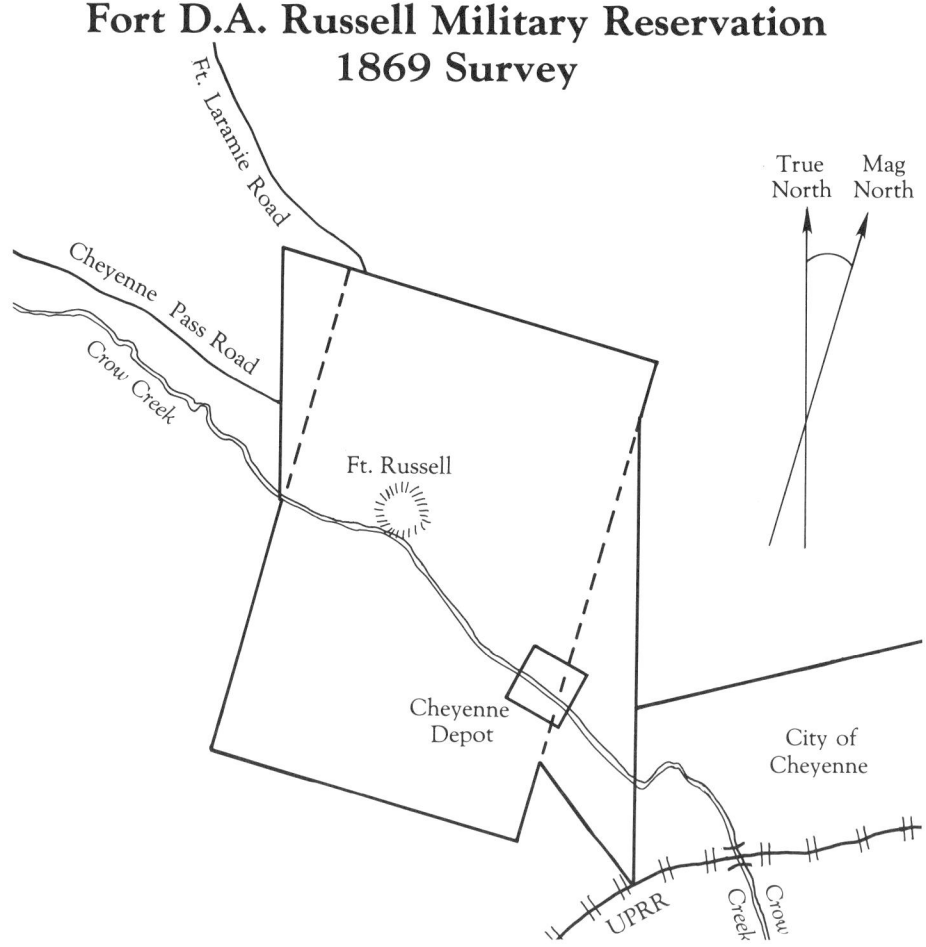

The Fort D.A. Russell military reservation was surveyed in 1867 on a magnetic north axis as a two-mile-wide and three-mile-long parallelogram. In 1869 another survey attempted to align the sides of the reservation with true north section lines by adding land in the northwest and southeast corners. The reservation retained this form for the next thirty-five years.

Chapter Four
The Army And Indian Policy

The long-standing argument about which governmental department, War or Interior, should control Indian affairs heated up with each new Indian depredation reported by the press. Neither General Grant nor General Sherman, nor hardly anyone in the army, liked the post-Civil War Indian policy or the Interior Department's way of handling the Indians. Army leadership felt that vested interests in the Interior Department controlled Indian affairs with the support of eastern "do gooders" who had neither an understanding of the problem nor responsibility for the Indians' actions. In his annual report of 1868, Sherman complained to the War Department that people arrived on the frontier in ever-increasing numbers and traveled without precaution. Further, the army had no control over Indians or settlers, but they bore the blame for everything that went wrong. Sherman strongly recommended that management of Indian affairs be transferred back to the War Department.

This squabble had many supporters on each side of the issue, but it did not help the army's already difficult problem of finding troublesome Indians reported from various sources that were frequently unreliable. One such a report caused a three-week scout to be sent from Fort D.A. Russell on November 3. Captain E.R. Armes of the Second Cavalry led three companies (E, F, and G) that were joined in western Nebraska by a company of Pawnee Scouts. The contingent amounted to four officers and eighty-four men. No hostile Indians could be found as far east as Potter's Station on the Union Pacific in Nebraska and as far north as Chimney Rock on the North Platte River. The only encounter reported during the expedition happened when the Pawnee Scouts caught two Cheyenne tribesmen near Chimney Rock.

The prolonged mild December weather found many Indian bands still roaming. Another cavalry detachment had to ride to Antelope Station east of Cheyenne to deal with a moving band of Sioux. Then in early January 1869, a company of Second Cavalry again made their way to the Cache La Poudre in Colorado to search for Indians reported to be stealing settlers' livestock. Another unit of the Second Cavalry, Company A led by Captain Thomas B. Dervees, scouted west to Sherman Station on the Union Pacific in response to Indians reported there. The scout encountered no Indians, and Captain Dervees concluded that the reports were false. He logically reasoned that the over one thousand railroad workers cutting ties and grading within fifteen miles of Sherman Station would have seen Indians entering the area and raised an alarm.

The cavalry and infantry units at Fort D.A. Russell continued campaigning on a limited scale during the 1868-1869 winter. The weather remained unusually mild, and the reports of Indian activity kept coming in. This suited most of the troops so long as the weather cooperated. Sudden storms and extended periods of low temperatures could be disastrous to a unit if caught out any distance without sufficient food, wood, and forage. Most unit commanders felt more comfortable when Indian activity subsided and permitted the units to withdraw by November to their assigned post and winter quarters. This period served as a respite to repair equipment, get the horses and mules back in shape, participate in training programs, and enjoy whatever delights the local community had to offer. Expeditions could still be launched against any late marauding Indian bands, although a winter expedition usually meant severe hardship on men and animals.

While troops stationed at Fort D.A. Russell the first years spent most of their time patrolling for, guarding from, and fighting Indians as well as putting up buildings on the post and training recruits, they also found time for recreation. Despite a private's low basic pay, which amounted to thirteen dollars a month, paydays were still happy occasions for the soldiers. Paydays occurred only when the paymaster arrived from Omaha at intervals of several months with money for the troops. Most soldiers were broke between visits of the paymaster and thus depended for much of their recreation on the company and regiment they belonged to.

The post trader, J.D. Woolley, provided a recreation facility of sorts in the trader's store located on the east side of the parade ground, but everything there required cash or credit. Outdoor athletics were very popular, being free, but the Wyoming weather posed some restrictions. Good unit commanders still made certain that their athletic programs received a high priority. The long-standing officer/enlisted men non-fraternization policy caused most social activities to be separated, but that did not prevent events from being enjoyable for officers and enlisted men. Theatricals, band concerts, and dances were always well attended. Maids working for officers' families and the company laundresses reigned at the enlisted men's dances and other activities, and were queens for the occasions. Few off-post civilians, men or women, were invited to join the enlisted mens' on-post events until years later. However, regimental non-commissioned staff officers would occasionally organize and sponsor a ball downtown, and these occasions were well received by the military and civilian communities.

Not many enlisted men were married, for the army did not make adequate allowance for wives and families. An old saying, "If the army wanted a soldier to have a wife it would issue him one," served as a part of the traditional philosophy of the time. The prominent role played by the laundresses at each post stemmed from their being an authorized and integral part of each regiment, which they had been since early in the century. As such, they offered a feminine presence for the enlisted men. The lack of other females provided the laundresses a field void of competition, and most acquired a soldier husband before or after becoming a laundress. The combined income of a laundress and soldier husband, along with rations, fuel, and the quarters authorized laundresses, could provide for a family. General C.C. Augur's concern for the regimental laundresses when the Thirtieth Infantry was about to move from Fort Kearney to western Nebraska and then on to Fort D.A. Russell in 1867 prompted him to send this telegram to the commander of Fort Kearney:

> Explain to the laundresses of the 30th Infantry that the regiment is going into the upper country in a few days to be gone all summer, and that they, the laundresses, must be content where they are until fall, when they will join the regiment.[1]

While officers could afford to participate in more varied activities and many were married, their organized social entertainment followed much the same pattern as that of the soldiers. Balls sponsored by military and civilian organizations remained popular affairs. The officers frequently entertained Cheyenne society and received invitations to events in town. The military presence contributed a major influence to the style and taste of Cheyenne's social life.

Downtown activities of any sort helped alleviate the continuing overcrowded conditions at the post. The early part of 1869 saw more shifting of units than usual, with as many as fifteen companies from four regiments assigned in March, far more than could be comfortably accommodated. The garrison included two companies of Fourth Infantry, two companies of Thirtieth Infantry, six companies of Second Cavalry, and five companies of Eighteenth Infantry. The post was considered an Eighteenth Infantry garrison because the post commander, headquarters staff, and band belonged to that regiment.

Being still a part of Dakota Territory, Cheyenne and Fort D.A. Russell could not yet count on civil law enforcement to apprehend or try lawbreakers. Frontier justice prevailed once more on February 12, 1869, when a company commander took action against a man he believed guilty of that most reprehensible of crimes, stealing horses or mules:

> Last night Captain Egan of the 2d Cavalry sent four men to the city to arrest Dick Douglas, accused of being a horse thief. He stole eleven mules from the train which recently accompanied Captain Egan's expedition to the Republican River. Douglas was arrested in a dance hall and taken to Fort Russell.[2]

Four days later the newspaper reported that a "mob" had hung Douglas between Cheyenne Depot and the post. The article did not indicate where the mob came from.

The inauguration of General Ulysses S. Grant as the eighteenth president of the United States on March 4, 1869, gave members of the western army encouragement. Grant and Sherman had become well acquainted with the problems in the West. Sherman replaced Grant as the Commanding General of the Army and pinned on the four stars authorized for that position. Sheridan took Sherman's command of the Division of the Missouri, pinned on the three stars of that position, and moved the headquarters from St. Louis to Chicago. All were graduates of West Point and had known each other for some time. Grant and Sherman had first been friends and schoolmates in 1839. Sherman graduated in 1839, three years earlier than Grant. Much the youngest, Sheridan graduated in 1853. All three had distinguished records as Civil War generals.

The new administration's Indian policy, also known as Grant's Peace Policy, introduced some surprising changes that did not please the western newspapers or the army. The *Leader*'s editor wrote this two weeks after Grant's inauguration:

> President Grant is determined to appoint Quakers for Superintendents of Indian Affairs and for Indian agents. If Quakers possess superior official qualities to the members of any other religious sect, denomination, or society, or even if they possess that reputation, the hunt is a valuable one for office seekers and will probably be promptly acted on by them. We look for a large accession to the Society of Friends.

Many western historians agree with the criticism heaped on Grant's Peace Policy and the people selected to run it. While the "white man" accepted the responsibility for civilizing the wild tribes, the task did not come easily or quickly. The Plains Indians continued to look on hostile activities as a normal way of life and viewed peace efforts as a weakness on the part of the whites.

Military units arriving in the spring of 1869 were badly needed; the Indians were growing ever more hostile and troublesome. Fort D.A. Russell served for a time as a holding station for units going north, away from the railroad. In April 1869, seventeen companies from five different regiments called the post home, but only 294 enlisted men and seventeen officers were present. Lieutenant Colonel Luther P. Bradley arrived in April 1869 with two companies of Twenty-seventh Infantry along with his headquarters staff and band to assume command. Bradley and the Twenty-seventh Infantry replaced the Eighteenth Infantry as the "host" regiment.

There were still six companies of Second Cavalry at Fort D.A. Russell in April, but talk of an impending move could be heard. The prospect sounded so real that sixty-nine men deserted. Rumors of a unit move to an isolated post, or of an extended field campaign, usually caused the desertion rate to rise, sometimes dramatically. Field campaigns that promised to encounter hostile Indians heightened fears of the new and inexperienced soldiers of what might happen to them in battle. The soldiers knew that Plains Indians gave no quarter and ignored surrender signals. If it became impossible to break through when surrounded, or to hole up, those soldiers not killed immediately were tortured.

While the Plains Indians didn't care whether Cheyenne and Fort D.A. Russell lay in Dakota or another territory, the granting of territorial status to Wyoming in April 1869, pleased the small white population. Territorial status offered solutions to many pressing problems inherent in a new land, including enforcement of law and order. The appointment of an Ohioan, John A. Campbell, as Wyoming's first territorial governor proved to be an excellent choice. Cheyenne became the temporary capital, there being no other contenders at the time, and a territorial government came into being. More good news followed when the Central Pacific tracks met the Union Pacific on Promontory Point in Utah at 12:14 P.M. on May 10, 1869. Now a coast-to-coast railroad ran across the nation. There would no longer be a vulnerable end-of-the-track railroad working party for the Indians to harrass. The army's burdensome task of protecting the railroad line, while not over, had begun to ease.

The spring and summer of 1869 saw about ten to twelve companies still assigned to Fort D.A. Russell, with most of them on patrol, escort duty, or detailed to an outpost along the railroad. A major action occurred in July when the Fifth Cavalry and two companies of Pawnee Scouts defeated a sizeable Dog Soldier band of Cheyenne Indians in a battle at Summit Springs in northeast Colorado. The Fifth Cavalry, commanded by Major Eugene Carr, greatly reduced the Cheyenne Indian threat in the northern High Plains.

Six companies of the Fifth Cavalry under the command of Lieutenant Colonel Thomas Duncan took station at Fort D.A. Russell after the summer campaign. The regiment had spent several months on the Republican River in northeast Colorado and southeast Nebraska. Arriving in November with 150 soldiers and over 100 teams and wagons, these six companies were glad to "put up" for the winter. The last unit of Second Cavalry, Company E, left Fort D.A. Russell in early November 1869 for Plum Creek, now Lexington, Nebraska. Other earlier newcomers to the garrison included two companies of the Ninth Infantry with their headquarters staff and band from California. Colonel John King commanded the regiment and assumed command of the post on arrival in July 1869. The remaining ten companies of King's regiment were posted to Fort McPherson, Nebraska, and other garrisons in the department.

In the wake of these new arrivals, the rumor on September 17 of a payday reported in the Cheyenne press received a warm welcome by the entire community. The paymaster had not been seen all summer. Many units were still in the field, but getting paid in the field was considered better than waiting for another four months:

> The soldiers at Russell are to be paid off next week. Four month's pay is now due and the boys are looking for the paymaster with considerable interest. Some of the money will doubtless find its way to the city, and if so, it is presumed nobody will object. Our circulating medium needs recruiting from some source.[3]

Still serving as commander-in-chief of the army, General Ulysses S. Grant visited Fort D.A. Russell in 1868 while campaigning for the presidency. He turned over command of the army to Sherman in March 1868 and became the eighteenth president of the United States, 1877. His "Indian Policy" remained controversial with the army and settlers in the West throughout his administration.—*National Archives*

As the eventful year of 1869 came to a close, Fort D.A. Russell had ten companies in winter quarters from three regiments. They were the Ninth Infantry, Fourth Infantry, and Fifth Cavalry, with a total personnel strength numbering twenty-four officers and 518 enlisted men. These units fitted into the garrison more comfortably than the fifteen companies had a year earlier. John King, colonel of the Ninth Infantry, remained post commander. The building program had added a few structures during the summer, and the post now had twelve barracks, thirty-one officers' quarters, stables and shops, plus a forty-eight-bed hospital. A post cemetery, opened in the early days, numbered twenty-two burials, including two officers, fifteen soldiers known, and five unknown. Despite the cemetery's seemingly high population, the hospital rarely had more than a handful of patients, and the overall health of the post had been better than most other western garrisons.

Measured by any standard, the officers and men that served at Fort D.A. Russell during these first thirty months had served "hardship tours." They played an important role in the completion of the first transcontinental railroad and in the settlement of the West.

1. Records of the War Department, Department of the Platte, Letters sent April 2, 1866–October 30, 1867, (RG98, Roll 7), National Archives, (film on file at Coe Library, University of Wyoming, Laramie).
2. *Cheyenne Daily Leader*, February 12 and 16, 1869.
3. *Cheyenne Daily Leader*, September 17, 1869.

Sketch of Fort D.A. Russell by an unknown artist about 1870. View is north, across Crow Creek. Horse stables are along the creek to the right, and laundresses' houses are to the left. The commander's big house shows on officers row, to the left of the flagpole.—*WY State AMH Dept.*

PART II
INDIAN WAR ON THE HIGH PLAINS
1870–1879

Duplex houses on officer's row, built in 1867–1868, showed improvements in 1870 with trees and board sidewalks in front of the houses. The improvement most desired by army wives, indoor plumbing, would not be forthcoming for another fourteen years.—*WY State AMH Dept.*

Chapter Five
Patrolling And Escorting

Although the buildings and facilities for men and animals in 1870 at Fort D.A. Russell were temporary at best and inadequate by most standards, the post provided an effective base of operations to continue the work of protecting the railroad and settling the frontier. No one knew how long the post, or Cheyenne for that matter, would last, but it seemed clear that the army would be needed on the northern High Plains for some time. Congress gradually reduced the size of the regular army after the Civil War to a skeleton force of about 25,000 men by 1876. It remained at that level for the next twenty-two years. This small force had to be spread across the country, with reconstruction requiring about half of the troops in the southern states. The remainder took care of the "Indian problem" in the West and the potential problem with Maximillian's Mexico along the border.

The practice of assigning both infantry and cavalry companies to western posts resulted in mixing regiments; seldom did a regiment have all of its units together at the same post. Each regiment had ten or twelve companies with a staff and headquarters, but the companies became semi-independent when operating away from their parent organization. The strength of a company seldom exceeded eighty and sometimes fell as low as thirty. An average strength during the 1870s amounted to about fifty. If the company served as home to the men, the regiment served as the parent. In his memoirs, General W.T. Sherman put the nineteenth-century regiment and company in perspective:

> The regiment is the family. The colonel, as the father, should have a personal acquaintance with every officer and man, and should instill a feeling of pride and affection for himself, so that his officers and men would naturally look to him for personal advice and instruction. In war the regiment should never be subdivided, but should always be maintained entire. In peace this is impossible.[1]

Winter quarters at Fort D.A. Russell in 1870 gave the ten companies assigned an opportunity to recover from the season's campaigning. A shaky peace existed, but a widespread Indian uprising could develop in the spring. Officers and men found time to visit Cheyenne when their finances permitted, and paydays were followed by disturbances in the saloons. A shooting at Cheyenne Depot occurred in March when Lieutenant George F. Mason of the Fifth Cavalry challenged A.J. Botsford, a civilian employee of the depot, to a shoot-out. Botsford had insulted Mason in a Cheyenne saloon the night before. Mason rode to Botsford's office the next morning and called him out, demanding an apology. Both men were wounded in the shooting that followed, Botsford slightly and Mason mortally. Mason died later that day and was buried in the post cemetery. Members of the Fifth Cavalry tried to take Botsford from the town jail the next day and hang him but failed in their attempt. A civil court in Cheyenne later acquitted Botsford.

In March 1870, Company B of the Fifth Cavalry pursued an Indian war party east of Cheyenne along the railroad, but little other campaigning occurred until April. A party of fifteen Indians attacked four Cheyenne citizens two miles out of town in early April, a sure indication that the tribes were on the move. The townsfolk luckily escaped with their scalps to Fort D.A. Russell. Most of the assigned units had already moved out from the post to outlying stations or were on patrol. This, like most spring deployment of units, almost emptied the post. Company B of the Fourth Infantry left on April 5 for Camp Brown near South Pass in the western part of Wyoming Territory. Company E of the Fifth Cavalry set out on April 10 to scout the country near Pine Bluffs. Companies G and I of the Ninth Infantry took to the field on April 20 for detached service, Company G for Camp Douglas, Utah Territory, and Company I to Fort Bridger, Wyoming Territory. Company G, Fifth Cavalry, departed the post on April 24 to patrol the country near Hillsdale Station east of Cheyenne. Barely enough manpower remained to garrison the post and perform the essential guard duties.

Since its establishment in 1867, Fort D.A. Russell had often been called on to launch a scouting party or patrol in a hurry in response to some real or imagined need in the area. Patrols and rescue parties were often commanded by a noncommissioned officer. A severe limitation was imposed on the units in April 1870, when a letter from headquarters directed that all scouting parties be accompanied by a commissioned officer. While a captain and two lieutenants were authorized, a company rarely numbered more than two officers assigned and sometimes only one. A colonel, lieutenant colonel, and major were authorized for the regimental headquarters and staff, but they all rarely served together. The lieutenant colonel and major were usually on detached service in other parts of the country, while many of the lieutenants were assigned to recruiting duty in the large cities, or as generals' aides. The limiting headquarters directive caused a revision in the deployment pattern that had been followed by Fort D.A. Russell and all other army posts.

One of the annual spring tasks left to the small force remaining at the post included planting and cultivating the post garden. The railroad could bring in plenty of fruit and vegetables from California now, but the army felt that money could be saved by having a post garden. The army had not reckoned with the arid climate and poor soil, or the periodic hordes of grasshoppers in the area of Fort D.A. Russell. A lack of manpower to tend the garden also hindered production for several summers. Initially the garden was hand watered, but more efficient irrigation ditches were constructed in subsequent years. According to a report by Post Surgeon C.H. Alden of the early gardening attempts, the railroad had to bring in all the fruit and vegetables for the first several years. Still, the annual attempt to grow a garden continued.

The army at Fort D.A. Russell faced a new concern in 1870 that started in February and continued up to late summer. A group of Cheyenne citizens formed an association to explore the mineral resources of the Big Horn Mountains in northern central Wyoming Territory, far from any army protection. By terms of the Fort Laramie Treaty of 1868, the government had agreed to leave that area unsettled. Ignoring the terms of the treaty and in a continuing effort to expedite the settlement of Wyoming Territory, the *Leader* gave this prescient view in the March 3, 1870, edition: "The Indians must stand aside or be overwhelmed by the ever advancing and ever increasing tide of emigration.... If the Indian treaties have gotten into such a tangled knot that they cannot be untied, the sword of the pioneer will sever them."

Named the Big Horn Mining Association, members and investors were attracted from as far away as Chicago. The Big Horn Mountains were reported to be rich in minerals, including gold. Governor J.A. Campbell proceeded to Washington to secure the blessings of the government and a military escort for the expedition. A party was expected to start from Cheyenne for the Big Horn area in April with Fort D.A. Russell providing a military escort. Such a prospect, in addition to all of his other troop committments, must have given the post commander, Colonel John King, some uneasy moments.

With full knowledge of Colonel King's understandable opposition to the idea, President Grant authorized the Big Horn expedition to proceed from Cheyenne, but there were conditions. The Big Horn Mining Association's leadership agreed not to trespass on the reservation of the Shoshoni and not to go north of the Wyoming Territorial boundary line nor east of the Big Horn Mountain Range. The association's leaders were also given to understand that they must not expect any military aid or protection for the settlements they might establish, nor for the mines they opened.

Despite such conditions and some delays, the association continued preparations to launch the expedition. Hostile Indian activity to the north stepped up as the spring progressed, and along the rail line in the near vicinity of Cheyenne. One report told of an attack on an express train in western Nebraska near Ogallala Station. A large party of well-armed Indians attempted to blockade the line by riding their ponies onto the tracks. They expected the train to stop. About thirty ponies and Indians died when the train charged through. The remaining Indians were seen riding off in a northerly direction after the train had passed, fewer in number but wiser.

After repeated warnings and several precautionary delays taken in hope that Indian bands would move out of the area, the Big Horn Mining Association's expedition left Cheyenne on May 20, 1870, with about 150 men and ten teams. Surprisingly enough, the expedition reached its destination in the Big Horns without encountering any Indian opposition. However, they did not find the wealth in minerals expected. Most of the expedition members were back in Cheyenne by August, much the worse for wear and lucky to be alive but with many exciting tales to tell. In October 1870, General C.C. Augur reported to Washington that a troop of cavalry had been sent three months earlier to the Big Horn Basin to bring the members of the Big Horn Mining Association back to Cheyenne before the Indians discovered them in their territory. Augur wrote that the tribesmen were away from that area, so no trouble had occurred. The expedition had been found by the army in the Basin near Greybull in disarray, so the cavalry had left it alone, knowing it would soon fall apart, which it did.

Some other ventures underway at this time fared better. On June 21, 1870, western settlement received a boost with the completion of the last rails of the Denver Pacific Railroad, linking Denver one hundred miles south with the Union Pacific at Cheyenne. Now Cheyenne had better access to Colorado commerce and Fort D.A. Russell could dispatch troops by train quickly when needed there.

The post and town were not increasing so much in size as in importance as a military base of operations and supply center, and as a commercial and financial center for a large area. Such attractions as P.T. Barnum's Circus were now finding their way to Cheyenne. Cattle had caught on, and herds thrived in southeast Wyoming Territory. The Union Pacific provided ready transportation to carry those cattle to eastern markets. The two Indian agencies east of Fort Laramie, Red Cloud and Spotted Tail, also offered good markets for Wyoming cattle, providing the army could keep those tribes peaceful and accepting in their government annuities lots of Wyoming beef.

Heavy demands on Fort D.A. Russell for patrol and escort troops continued throughout the summer. The Indian commissioners going to Fort Laramie in August to negotiate with the Sioux demanded a large escort. A party of thirty students from Yale College, headed by the noted paleontologist Professor O.C. Marsh, could safely explore fossil beds in northwestern Nebraska (now named Agate Fossil Beds National Monument) with a good-sized guard of troopers from Fort D.A. Russell. The few soldiers left at the garrison in August 1870 must have been in Cheyenne soon after the paymaster arrived, for the newspaper reported a few days of "righteous carnival."

The population of Cheyenne declined to 1,450 citizens in 1870, down from about 4,000 two years earlier. Any commotion of blue uniforms in town was quickly noticed by much of the population. Drunken paydays, infrequent as they were, plagued Fort D.A. Russell and Cheyenne for many years even after the town had grown much larger. Brigadier General Christopher C. Augur expressed a common view in a report to the army adjutant general in 1870: "In my opinion, most of the drunkenness among soldiers in the Army, and a large majority of desertions, is due to our system of paying the troops at long intervals. Pay day becomes an event which affords means for its own celebrations, and is almost universally followed by days of drunkenness and disorders and desertions."[2]

Cheyenne newspaper reports supported General Augur's view of soldier behavior on paydays, and it appears that most soldiers coming to Cheyenne on payday carried a gun. But payday for the "soldier boys" provided a welcome event in Cheyenne, and the town tolerated the usual turbulence for a day or so, then proper behavior became the norm. Military police did not exist, and the post commander left control of the unruly troops in Cheyenne for the town authorities to handle. The large majority of soldiers coming to town did not cause problems, but those who did soon had their stories told in the *Leader*, such as this one in October 1870:

> Yesterday afternoon as several intoxicated soldiers were passing along seventeenth street near Eddy, one of them drew his revolver for the purpose of shooting at some hogs feeding in the street. A companion tried to prevent the cruelty and got shot in the thigh as a result, one to the hospital and one to jail.[3]

As the companies returned to winter quarters in the late fall, an uneasy feeling prevailed that Indian troubles, which had not subsided, might very well increase despite the oncoming cold weather. The twelve infantry companies moving into winter quarters at Fort D.A. Russell were prepared to take to the field on short notice. There were six companies of Ninth Infantry, two companies of Fourteenth Infantry, and four companies of Fourth Infantry. A total of twenty-nine officers and 687 men was reported in the January 1871 Post Return. Each of the twelve companies had their own barracks and mess this winter. Even though they might have to leave in a hurry, winter quarters again allowed units time and opportunity to recoup and repair, and for the troops to enjoy such recreational activities as theater and dances.

The post surgeon's report in 1870 declared that the amateur theater program at Fort D.A. Russell almost compared to dances in popularity: "During the past winter a soldier's theater and officers' theater have been kept up, and have afforded much entertainment to the garrison." Organized dances, or "hops," still reigned first in popularity, and the *Leader* on January 10, 1871, reported that a military ball with over 300 ladies and soldiers present enjoyed a "perfect success": "There was plenty of dancing and to the credit of the officers and soldiers at Fort D.A. Russell, there was not a single difficulty or misunderstanding."

Variety theaters were also popular and flourished in Cheyenne from the earliest days. The Theater Comique, the Concert Hall, the Model Concert Hall, and the Gold Room drew full houses. While Cheyenne boasted more than its share of "entertainment places" that offered a variety of attractions, good wholesome entertainment could be found by the soldiers at low or no cost. Some infamous activities also attracted the soldiers. One such unfortunate occasion appeared in the press in March 1871: "Last night at a house of loose architecture a soldier, Sergeant of Company D, 5th Cavalry, was shot by a comrade. Victim is expected to die." The victim, First Sergeant John M. Limeburner, did die from the wound and received a splendid funeral from his comrades in Company D along with the handsomest tombstone in the post cemetery.

Next to the firearms carried by so many, fires continued to be the most worrisome hazard with which soldiers and civilians had to contend. In February 1871, an early-morning fire consumed the barracks occupied by Company B, Fourteenth Infantry. All occupants were able to escape. The cause of this barracks fire was believed to be an overheated stovepipe. Once a fire got underway, fanned by a brisk Wyoming wind, the building and sometimes several buildings went up in smoke.

In an early attempt to make the civilian community more aware of the economic contribution of Fort D.A. Russell, the army released the amount of the payroll, $52,000, soon be paid to the troops by the visiting paymaster. The army wanted the post to be seen as a major economic contributor to the Cheyenne community. The military would continue to periodically remind the civilian community of this significant contribution emanating from Fort D.A. Russell. The low pay of officers and enlisted men still amounted to a good amount when several units were paid. About $30,000 would be paid at isolated Forts Fetterman and Laramie when the paymaster reached there, which also benefited Cheyenne.

The spring of 1871 did not witness the big Indian uprising that had been expected to develop on the northern High Plains. However, the Oglala and Brule Sioux tribes camped at Fort Laramie made noisy demonstrations to obtain more annuities from the government. A large number of patrols and escorts were still operating from Fort D.A. Russell, but the garrison was able to take time to spruce up a bit. Two to three thousand trees were planted. Cottonwood, aspen, and pine were the favorites because they survived better than other species and were readily available in the Pole Mountain area west of the post. The relative calm prevailing among the Indian tribes also encouraged a further increase of cattle herds.

Fort D.A. Russell enjoyed a rare opportunity in 1871, at a time when recruits arrived at regular intervals from the recruiting depots, to release their "marginal" soldiers. One hundred were discharged and were characterized by the local editor as "hospital beats and guard house occupants. Some of these worthless fellows had as high as $100 due them on being discharged, but instead of saving the money and procuring passage to their homes, they distributed it about town last night."[4]

With all the units rid of their less productive soldiers, the Fifth Cavalry must have been in fighting trim when orders arrived in November 1871 to move to Arizona. Units of this regiment had first arrived at Fort D.A. Russell in August 1869 and been very busy most of the time since. The news of their departure appeared in the *Leader*'s social column: "The officers and ladies remaining at Fort Russell are to give a ball sometime this coming week, complimentary to the officers and ladies of the Fifth Cavalry, shortly to leave."

The departure of the Fifth Cavalry left only five companies of Ninth Infantry remaining; no cavalry units remained on the post. The year 1871 closed with a new commander assigned to the Department of the Platte, Brigadier General E.O.C. Ord replacing Brigadier General Christopher C. Augur, who moved to command the Department of Texas. A frequent visitor to Fort D.A. Russell from his Omaha headquarters, Augur had been highly regarded as a vigorous campaigner and had done an excellent job as department commander during a very critical period, 1867-1871.

A replacement regiment for the Fifth Cavalry did not arrive until March 1872, when the Third Cavalry took station at Fort D.A. Russell. Colonel John H. King, colonel of the Ninth Infantry, which still had five companies on post, continued as garrison commander. Judging by the newspaper accounts, King enjoyed a good deal of popularity with both the military and civilian communities.

Soon after arriving, three companies of Third Cavalry under command of Captain Guy V. Henry were ordered to the Red Cloud Agency, then just inside the Nebraska border on the North Platte River. Their mission to quell the Indian unrest there caused Captain Henry's force to march 135 miles in two and a half days in order to reach the agency before serious trouble erupted. The army's presence in force quieted the Indians, and after remaining at the agency three weeks, Captain Henry and his troopers returned to Fort D.A. Russell.

---

1. General W.T. Sherman, *Personal Memoirs of Gen'l W.T. Sherman*, (New York: Charles L. Webster and Co., 1891), p. 385.
2. Records of the War Department, U.S. Army Continental Commands, Department of the Platte, Letters sent April 2, 1858, (RG98), National Archives, (film on file at Coe Library, University of Wyoming, Laramie).
3. *Cheyenne Daily Leader*, October 13, 1870.
4. *Cheyenne Daily Leader*, July 1, 1871.

Colonel Joseph J. Reynolds arrived at Fort D.A. Russell in May 1874 and assumed command of both the Third Cavalry and the post. An 1839 graduate of the U.S. Military Academy at West Point, New York, Reynolds was near sixty years old when he led the regiment north from the post on February 21, 1876, on the ill-fated winter campaign to the Powder River area. Department of the Platte commander Brigadier General George Crook subsequently brought charges against Reynolds for mismanaging the Battle of Powder River.—*WY State AMH Dept.*

Chapter Six
The Peace Policy And Gold In The Black Hills

Captain Guy Henry's experience with the Red Cloud Agency typified the Indians' uncertain mood in the spring and summer of 1872. Yet most of that year followed the peaceful pattern of the previous year, in part because of the concerted efforts of the Peace Commission to reach an accommodation with the hostile tribes. Even though it had made some progress, the Peace Commission still had work to do, and the restraints included in the new peace policy made their work more difficult.

While the military never waivered in support of President Grant's administration, the western army did not support his peace policy. Western congressmen were continuously petitioning for changes that would expedite western settlement. A letter from President Grant to a George H. Stuart appeared in the *Leader* on November 3, 1872, denying reports of a radical change in the policy: "If any change takes place in the Indian policy of the Government while I hold my present office, it will be on the humanitarian side of the question." Civilizing and christianizing were the two main objectives of the policy. While the army leaders at Fort D.A. Russell did not like the peace policy, they did their best to comply with its provisions, in keeping with the best traditions of the regular army.

The peace policy and other concerns of the community were put aside momentarily in September to give a proper sendoff to the very popular post and Ninth Infantry commander, Colonel John King, and his family. King, along with the noncommissioned headquarters staff and band of the Ninth Infantry, had been ordered to Omaha Barracks, Nebraska. Colonel James V. Bomford and the Eighth Infantry, plus the regimental headquarters and band, arrived in October to replace the Ninth Infantry. Colonel Bomford brought with him only two companies of Eighth Infantry. Still, the Post Return for December 1872 reported ten companies from four regiments at Fort D.A. Russell, with twenty-seven officers and 582 men. The year had been relatively quiet, and once more, the Indian uprising earlier predicted had not materialized. Desertions for the month of December were at an all-time low of two. Winter "hops" and theatricals blossomed forth in full bloom.

The post library established in 1867 had not survived, and reading did not contribute much to the winter recreation available to the soldiers.

Money to buy books and magazines, and assignment of qualified persons to operate a library, did not enjoy a high priority. Nor did reading seem to be a favorite pastime of the soldiers. Many could not read, at least in English. Sometimes books and other reading material were available in the company barracks, but keeping a unit library together during seasonal campaigns posed problems. Not until the twentieth century could an established post library be found at Fort D.A. Russell, or at any other western army post.

Winter quarters routine ended in early April 1873 when the Oglala Sioux at the Red Cloud Agency were reported "restless." War parties from that agency were roaming as far east as the Upper Loup River in central Nebraska. An attack on a ranch south of Cheyenne added to the increasing concern at Fort D.A. Russell. The massacre of Brigadier General Edward R.S. Canby and two members of his party by the Modoc Indians during a peace conference in northern California tended to heighten anti-Indian sentiment in the western army.

The aftermath of the Canby massacre saw the Modoc leaders hanged or imprisoned and Fort D.A. Russell being considered as a relocation center for the Modoc tribe. The Modoc affair challenged the wisdom of Grant's Peace Policy more than any other event did before the Battle of the Little Big Horn three years later. Newspaper editors throughout the West used it as evidence that Indians were not ready to be trusted. Public sentiment ran high, and the government planned to move the Modocs from their tribal lands as a form of punishment. Starting eastward by train, they were met in Cheyenne with the pleased announcement that they would not be staying. General Sheridan had ordered them on to Fort McPherson, Nebraska, fifteen miles east of North Platte. The people in North Platte might not have been pleased with this arrangement either. Plains Indian unrest and hostile activity had risen dramatically. The Department of the Platte commander, Brigadier General Ord, warned settlers on the North Platte River in western Nebraska that the Sioux were on the warpath. He promised to send more troops to the area at once.

The Canby massacre and other Indian disturbances in the spring of 1873 did not lessen the Grant administration's determination to implement its Indian policy. The secretary of the interior issued additional guidelines and generally reaffirmed the administration's views on how the Indians should be treated. The secretary proposed to put all Indians on reservations where they could be provided for. He promised that supplies of food and clothing would be available on the reservations for those Indians cooperating, plus other amenities: "The government, by advice of religious organizations, would try to procure competent, upright, faithful, moral and religious agents to care for the Indians and in establishing schools and building churches.[1]

While the controversy waged hot and heavy in the Congress and the press over the administration's Indian policy, the summer of 1873 saw less conflict on the northern High Plains than had been expected. Nevertheless, the threat remained, and there were more than the usual number of war parties on the move committing depredations. Companies at Fort D.A.

Russell continued escorting official parties, some journeying as far as Yellowstone Park in northwest Wyoming Territory. Scouting parties sent from the post on July 1, August 3, and September 3 ranged in size from fourteen to eighty-four men.

Fort D.A. Russell's area of responsibility continued to be long stretches of railroad and stage lines as well as the stations and settlements along those lines. Government land surveyors in western Nebraska and Wyoming, who often found themselves surrounded by parties of roving Indians, were very vulnerable unless escorted by soldiers from the post. The cavalry also watched over the supply trains going north, an undesirable duty because of the wagons' slow progress over the prairie trails. Ox-drawn wagon trains were the slowest of all, making only eight to twelve miles a day; the oxen had a tendency to graze along the way. Mule-drawn wagon trains moved faster and could make up to thirty miles a day, but the cavalry troopers still considered that a slow pace.

Despite the many legitimate requests for army protection from many sources, Fort D.A. Russell found the men and resources to send out hunting parties for recreational and provisioning purposes. These expeditions were very popular with the soldiers, and they sometimes stayed out several days or a week. They invariably brought much-welcomed game back to be divided among the company kitchens. The hunters also scouted the area for Indian sign or activity. The Post Return for September and October 1873 reported two companies led by the post commander on hunting expeditions for short periods west of the post. Colonel Bomford continued to lead hunting parties from the post well into the winter, even though he suffered ill health. December 1, 1873, found eleven companies from three regiments at Fort D.A. Russell, settling in. The post military complement totaled twenty officers and 695 men.

As the cold weather season of 1874 prepared to give way to spring, preparations again began for a major spring campaign against the hostile tribes. Colonel J.J. Reynolds of the Third Cavalry had arrived in February to replace Colonel Bomford as post commander. Continuing ill health had required Colonel Bomford to meet with the retirement board. Major Frank North and a company of Pawnee Scouts again responded to the Department of the Platte's call to campaign against the Sioux, Cheyenne, and Arapaho. They joined the Third Cavalry to reinforce the regulars, a matter of some consequence in view of the call from Congress for further military reductions.

An article appearing in the *Leader* on February 18, 1874, on the proposed troop reduction gave Lieutenant General Phil Sheridan's testimony to a House Committee. Pared down annually after the Civil War in appropriations and manpower, the army had bottomed out with a little more than 25,000 officers and enlisted men. Serving as commander of the Division of the Missouri at the time, Sheridan said that his force of 16,000 men, which had charge of the vast western territory where the wild tribes were scattered, already had become too small for the work at hand. He testified that his troops worked harder than any other soldiers in the world.

Sheridan again recommended that the War Department be given the management of Indian affairs, and he ridiculed moral suasion as an effective means of pacifying the hostile tribes. He also deprecated the frequent legislation picking on the army; he felt it demoralized officers and men. Sheridan was a highly popular and respected commander, and his testimony was read with great interest at Fort D.A. Russell and in Cheyenne.

In the midst of congressional deliberations on army appropriations, eight companies of what became known as the 1874 Sioux Expedition launched the spring campaign when they marched from Fort D.A. Russell during mid-February in below-zero weather. They reached Fort Laramie on February 26 and 27. Four more companies of cavalry were added at Fort Laramie, and in early March the column moved to the area of the Red Cloud and Spotted Tail Indian agencies, now in northwestern Nebraska. Most of the companies remained in this area for several weeks. A new military post, established and adjacent to the Red Cloud Agency in the spring of 1874, took the name Camp Robinson after Lieutenant Levi H. Robinson. The lieutenant had been killed by the Sioux near Fort Laramie a few weeks earlier.

The dangers perceived with the deployment of units to Fort Laramie and other areas in the troubled western Nebraska and northern Wyoming areas during the late winter and spring of 1874 resulted in the desertion of forty-three soldiers. Some officers' wives were also about ready to desert. Martha Summerhayes, an eastern bride of Eighth Infantry Lieutenant John W. Summerhayes, arrived at Fort D.A. Russell shortly before her husband departed to join his company at the Spotted Tail Agency for two months. She described Cheyenne as the wildest sort of place. "Cheyenne in those early days was an amusing but unattractive frontier town; . . . cows, pigs and saloons seemed to be a feature of the place." She also recorded her dislike of the army's practice of "turning out" of quarters the next lower ranking officer, with twenty-four hours to move, as the accepted means for obtaining quarters for a newly arrived officer. The displaced officer would then find the next lower ranking officer to turn out. Her dislike of this practice was shared by most officers' wives. The quarters acquired by Lieutenant and Mrs. Summerhayes had been occupied by a lieutenant whose wife had gone east. The quarters consisted of three rooms and a kitchen, which formed one-half of a double house on the parade.[2] The army wives at Fort D.A. Russell tried hard to appreciate their blessings, particularly those that did not exist at other posts in the West. The wives agreed on one good thing about the post near Cheyenne—a train a day went east.

Reports by the Custer expedition in 1874 of gold in the Black Hills changed the order of things with the Indians in the northern High Plains. This news created a tremendous pressure for opening up that area to settlement and development. Even though the government continued to regard the Black Hills as Indian territory restricted from white settlement and development, miners and developers converged on the area from Sioux

City and Cheyenne. The army received orders to stop them, but there were too many intruders and too few soldiers. A message from General Sheridan in September 1874 spelled out the severe measures to be taken when intruders were apprehended: "Should the companies now organizing a Sioux City and Yankton trespass on the Sioux Indian reservation, you are hereby directed to use the forces at your command to burn the wagon train, destroy the outfit and arrest the leaders, confining them at the nearest military post in Indian Country.[3]

Units sent from Fort D.A. Russell to the Red Cloud and Spotted Tail agencies not only had to keep the Sioux in line but also had to try to round up the white invaders heading for the Black Hills. The soldiers found this duty far from easy, especially with the increased publicity given to the discovery of gold. The task of the military escort for the weekly wagon trains carrying rations and annuities from Cheyenne Depot north to the two Sioux agencies became particularly difficult.

A feature article in the *Leader* on September 4, 1874, advertised Cheyenne as the best departure point on the shortest route to the forbidden mines in the Sioux reservation, the Black Hills, only 220 miles via Fort Laramie and the Red Cloud Agency. Cheyenne was also mentioned as the best place for miners to outfit for such a journey. The article did not mention that the commander at Fort D.A. Russell had been ordered by the War Department to stop all intruders.

There were six companies, three of Third Cavalry and three of Twenty-third Infantry, at Fort D.A. Russell when the year ended, all hoping for a quiet winter respite. Any such reprieve was interrupted early on January 4, 1875, during a prolonged cold spell when another disastrous fire destroyed six sets of officers' quarters on the west side of the parade. The fire started about 4:00 A.M. in the quarters of Lieutenant Julius H. Pardee, Twenty-third Infantry, and spread rapidly along the whole northwest line of houses. Little could be done, according to the *Leader*'s report, to halt the progress of the flames: "Many men distinguished themselves by acts of daring; 1st Sergeant of D Company, 23d Infantry, was badly burned and Private Meyers of Company L, 3d Cavalry, lost his life trying to get Lieutenant Pardee's property out of his house. His charred remains were found in the house. The officers burned out were taken into the quarters of the officers along the east line."

The announcement in March 1875 that Brigadier General George Crook would replace Brigadier General E.O.C. Ord as commander of the Department of the Platte signaled a more aggressive policy toward the hostile northern High Plains Indians. Crook, who assumed command on April 27, 1875, was a veteran Indian compaigner. The press expected Crook to take to the field immediately and drive the hostile bands back to the reservations.

Limited resources in 1875 precluded any extensive offensive against the hostile Indians. Instead, the units at Fort D.A. Russell again scattered in every direction, patrolling, escorting, and guarding salient points along the Union Pacific Railroad. Miners and adventurers encroaching on Sioux territory, the Black Hills, continued to plague the commander of Fort D.A. Russell. After Company H of the Third Cavalry left the post on March 24, 1875, marching north with orders to arrest trespassers in the Black Hills, only two companies remained for garrison and escort duty. Still, a project got underway that summer to rejuvenate the temporary barracks and houses now eight years old and in need of repair. The post hospital received a thorough renovation while the barracks and officers' quarters were treated to lathing, plastering, and liming. These improvements coincided

Captain Anson Mills served as a troop commander in the Third Cavalry at Fort D.A. Russell. He led his company in the winter Powder River campaign of 1876, the later battle on the Rosebud, and was cited for gallantry in action in the late summer Battle of Slim Buttes. Mills developed the woven web ammunition carrier and its accompanying web equipment which replaced the leather cartridge boxes and made him a wealthy man at the end of his military career. His excellent *My Story* published in 1918 provides an interesting account of his career and life in the western army.— Mills, My Story.

with a general recognition of the post's critical role in the region and an urgent need to improve living conditions.

While in the opinion of some federal officials relations with the Sioux were improving, others felt that direct consultations should be undertaken immediately to quiet the unrest on the northern High Plains. Accordingly, a delegation of Sioux led by chiefs Red Cloud and Spotted Tail traveled in early summer to Washington, D.C., for a conference with the secretary of the interior and President Grant. When they arrived at the capital, the Sioux chiefs were asked to give up the Black Hills. No decisions were reached at the conference, and after the ritual ceremonies and banquets had been held, the Indian party returned to their reservations. Soon after, a special commission headed by Iowa Senator William B. Allison traveled to the Red Cloud Agency to continue the discussions, but negotiations soon stalemated. The government faced a dilemma. White men held effective possession of the Black Hills even though they were there illegally. Public demand for an official opening of the coveted territory continued to grow. However, the Black Hills still belonged to the Sioux in a legal sense, and no white man had a right to be there.

As the summer drew to a close, optimism in Cheyenne that the Black Hills would be opened to settlement continued to grow. A general belief prevailed that since Red Cloud and Spotted Tail had sold their tribal hunting rights in the Republican Valley in June 1875 for a monetary consideration, they would most likely do the same with the Black Hills. Then during a visit to Fort D.A. Russell in August 1875, General W.T. Sherman supported that view by predicting the Black Hills and northern Wyoming would be open in a few months.

Despite the optimism in Cheyenne, the Peace Commission failed to make any progress with the Sioux in their negotiations for the Black Hills at their several meetings in the fall. On September 20, 1875, the *Leader* reported that upwards of 25,000 Indians had gathered at the Red Cloud Agency awaiting the outcome of the council negotiations. The *Leader* also reported on September 27 that the commissioners had suffered a severe scare. During the last meeting on September 24, a small hostile group of Sioux aroused by an incensed warrior named Little Big Man surrounded the commissioners and threatened a massacre. After extricating themselves with the help of some friendly chiefs, the commissioners packed up and headed for Cheyenne. Their last attempt was thus noted: "The Commissioners to treat for the Black Hills returned here from Red Cloud today on their way east. The attempt to obtain the Hills was a failure, the Indians holding out for a far greater sum than the country is worth."[4] Another approach seemed necessary now.

1. *Cheyenne Daily Leader*, April 25, 1873.
2. Martha Summerhayes, *Vanquished Arizona: Recollections of My Army Life*, (Philadelphia: J.B. Lippincott Company, 1908), pp. 19–29.
3. *Cheyenne Daily Leader*, September 4, 1874.
4. *Cheyenne Daily Leader*, October 4, 1875.

Colonel Wesley Merritt arrived at Fort D.A. Russell with his Fifth Cavalry Regiment on November 4, 1876, after many months of hard campaigning in the north with Brigadier General Crook. Merritt and the Fifth Cavalry garrisoned Fort D.A. Russell until April 1880 when they moved to Fort Laramie. Merritt later served as superintendent of the U.S. Military Academy at West Point, New York.— *WY State AMH Dept.*

Chapter Seven
Campaigns of 1876

In early January 1876, the Indian Bureau notified their Sioux agents to send runners immediately to all Indian bands in the unceded territory, mainly northern Wyoming and Montana, directing them to move back to their reservations. The bureau gave a deadline of January 31 for the Indians to return to their appointed lands. Those remaining out would be considered hostile, and the army would come after them. The Sioux, Cheyenne, and Arapaho constituted the major northern High Plains Indian tribes that were away from their reserves. These Indians were not inclined to pay much attention to Indian Bureau directives to move under the best of conditions, and even less so in the cold of winter. Realizing its inability to force the issue, the Indian Bureau and Interior Department turned the problem over to the War Department.

While the press expressed enthusiasm for launching a winter attack against the hostile tribes away from their reservations, army commanders knew that cold-weather campaigns took a heavy toll on men and animals. Winter operations could also quickly turn into disasters if severe cold or deep snow were encountered. Thus, the army had not often undertaken extensive winter campaigning in the northern High Plains.

The construction of a modern iron bridge over the North Platte River at Fort Laramie, completed in early January 1876, eased the problem of crossing that river with supply wagons for winter and summer campaigns. Transportation of travelers to the Black Hills over this bridge also started with the newly organized Cheyenne and Black Hills Stage Line. The first coach left the Inter-Ocean Hotel in Cheyenne on February 3, 1876. Daily departures continued thereafter for the next eleven years. The trip initially took five days to reach the brand-new settlement of Custer City in the Black Hills, and seats on the coaches were in great demand.

The officers and ladies of Fort D.A. Russell were not thinking of these changing conditions when they planned a centennial party at the post for the eve of February 22. Costumes were to be in the style of 1776, and everyone looked forward to this party as a relief from the "midwinter dismals." Then it all had to be cancelled. Five companies of Third Cavalry under command of Colonel J.J. Reynolds left the post on February 21 for the north. A winter campaign had been launched to find those Indians away from their reservations. Stopping briefly at Fort Fetterman on the North Platte River, Reynolds picked up five companies of Second Cavalry and two companies of Fourth Infantry. The Reynolds expedition now numbered twelve companies of about 900 men that included officers, enlisted men, and civilian teamsters. The column departed Fort Fetterman north for the Powder River country on March 1. Brigadier General George Crook, commander of the Department of the Platte and Reynold's immediate superior, accompanied the column. Crook was along ostensibly as an observer, but in effect he directed the expedition most of the time.

A winter storm made a misery of the march, but the determined Crook kept the column moving until they found Indians. On March 16, a large Cheyenne village, first thought to be a Sioux band led by Crazy Horse, was discovered on the Powder River. Colonel Reynolds and six companies of cavalry attacked under cover of darkness. With the element of surprise operating in their favor, the attackers drove the Indians into the hills and captured the band's pony herd. The Indians soon counterattacked, forcing Reynolds's cavalry to withdraw from the village, leaving behind two Third Cavalry toopers badly wounded or dead. Before morning the Indians recaptured most of their horses.

The battered column made its painful way back to Fort Fetterman through continued bitter cold, the campaign a failure. The five companies of Third Cavalry continued on to Fort D.A. Russell, arriving on April 4, men and horses badly worn. Company Commander Captain Anson Mills's evaluation of that winter campaign, written many years later, pointed out some problems that existed in the Third Cavalry long before the regiment left Fort D.A. Russell: "Owing to the age and feebleness of Colonel Reynolds, and the bitter feud that existed in the regiment, this attack on the village on Powder River proved a lamentable failure.[1]

Brigadier General Crook returned to his Omaha headquarters to replan the department's offensive against the northern High Plains Indians. He stopped at Fort D.A. Russell long enough to file charges against those he believed responsible for the failure of the attack on the Cheyenne village. They were Colonel J.J. Reynolds and two company commanders, Captain Alexander Moore and Captain Henry C. Noyes. The charges included "misbehavior before the enemy."[2]

The court martial board convened at the Inter-Ocean Hotel in Cheyenne with Brigadier General John Pope presiding. After a long trial full of countercharges and animosity, Colonel Reynolds was found guilty and sentenced to be suspended from rank and command for one year. Captain Moore stood convicted of neglect of duty; he was suspended from command for six months and confined to the limits of the post. The court considered Captain Noyes "guilty of conduct to the prejudice of good order and military discipline" and sentenced him to be reprimanded by the department commander. Lieutenant Colonel William B. Royal assumed command of the Third Cavalry Regiment in the wake of these findings.

During the time that Reynolds and the Third Cavalry were on the Powder River, Lieutenant General Phil Sheridan and his Division of the Missouri staff in Chicago were developing an all-encompassing spring campaign. Sheridan's plan called for a force from the Department of the Dakota, headed by Brigadier General Alfred H. Terry, to proceed west from Fort Abraham Lincoln into Montana. Colonel John Gibbon would lead another element from Fort Ellis in western Montana to the south-central part of Montana. Crook's force would move back north again from Fort D.A. Russell after refitting, into northern Wyoming and southern Montana. The three columns converging from different directions would expect to box in the hostile bands believed to be concentrated in northern Wyoming-southern Montana. The objective: to find the ever-increasing bands of roving Indians and escort them to their assigned reservations.

Even though Chief Red Cloud tried to keep his tribesmen on the reservation, the Oglala Sioux were reported to have left the Red Cloud Agency in large numbers to join the hostile bands. The best efforts of the Indian agent at the Red Cloud Agency also failed to detain the Oglala Sioux.

General Crook's spring-summer expedition did not get away from Fort D.A. Russell gracefully. Sixty-five men from the Second and Third Cavalry were reported absent May 19 at the first halting place on Lodge Pole Creek about twenty-eight miles north. The deserters took along their horses and arms. One deserter soon captured said that the men left because of rumors that the wounded would be left in the hands of Indians, as had happened in March on Powder River. All members of the expedition were well aware of the Indian practice of killing prisoners immediately or subjecting them to torture, death in any case.

Crook's column from Fort D.A. Russell left Fort Fetterman on May 29, marching again up the old Bozeman Trail toward Montana. On reaching Goose Creek in the area where Sheridan, Wyoming, now lies, Crook established a base camp. His force now consisted of ten companies of Third Cavalry, five of which came from Fort D.A. Russell, plus five companies of Second Cavalry, two companies of Fourth Infantry, and three companies of Ninth Infantry, a total of forty-seven officers and 1,000 enlisted men. The supply train for this column totaled 120 wagons and 1,000 pack mules, plus civilian teamsters and packers.

On June 17, 1876, Crook's entire force met a combined band of Sioux and Cheyenne warriors on Rosebud Creek about thirty-five miles north. Crook had been caught in unfavorable terrain, but after six hours of hard fighting, the Indians withdrew from the battlefield. Crook's losses included ten killed, four mortally wounded, ten dangerously wounded, and twenty-six slightly wounded. Crook did not pursue the Indians but limped back to his base camp on Goose Creek to stay until supplies and reinforcements could be sent from the south. Had Crook been able to pursue those Indians encountered on the Rosebud, the fate of the Seventh Cavalry eight days later at the Battle of the Little Big Horn might have been different.

One of the severely wounded at the Rosebud battle on June 17, Captain Guy V. Henry who led Company D of the Third Cavalry, miraculously survived. Struck by a bullet that passed through both cheekbones and broke the bridge of his nose, Henry suffered through a jolting journey of several hundred miles by mule-borne litter and horse-drawn ambulance.

He reached Fort D.A. Russell on July 5 with other Third Cavalry wounded. Henry recovered after an extended convalescence at Fort D.A. Russell and continued a distinguished military career, retiring a brigadier general in 1898.

Soon after the reinforcing Fifth Cavalry arrived at Goose Creek on August 3 from Fort McPherson, Nebraska, Crook broke up his base camp and marched north and east in search of the main body of Indians believed to still be in the area. His command now included twenty-five companies of Second, Third, and Fifth Cavalry regiments plus ten companies of Fourth, Ninth, and Fourteenth Infantry regiments, a total of more than 2,000 officers and men. A pack train carried provisions for fifteen days—the wagons were sent back to Fort D.A. Russell. Moving across southeast Montana and into Dakota Territory, Crook's column finally encountered and defeated a Sioux band at Slim Buttes on September 9. Crook's force, men and animals again badly used, disbanded on reaching Fort Robinson in late October, the units returning to their assigned garrisons.

The five companies of Third Cavalry returning to Fort D.A. Russell stayed only a short time before moving to another western post. Five companies of Fifth Cavalry took station at Fort D.A. Russell on November 2, replacing the Third Cavalry. Colonel Wesley Merritt, commander of the Fifth Cavalry, assumed command of Fort D.A. Russell on November 11, a position he would hold for the next three and a half years. As the year 1876 rolled to a close, fresh army units continued the search in the northern High Plains for the hostile Indian bands still away from the reservations.

Three distinguished commanders, Nelson Miles, Ranald Mackenzie, and George Crook, led three expeditions into the winter campaign of 1876–1877. Soldiers, supplies, and animals at Fort D.A. Russell and Cheyenne Depot were called on throughout the winter to participate in this large-scale operation designed to round up all roaming bands of Indians and return them to their reservations. Winter quarters had become much less of a period for rest and recuperation.

A part of Crook's force in the continuing winter 1876–1877 campaign against the roaming Indians included the Pawnee Scouts still under the command of Major Frank North. Crook's last winter campaign had gotten underway in November 1876 from Fort Laramie with this notice in the Cheyenne press: "On Monday Crook will move from Fort Laramie with twenty companies of infantry and cavalry plus one hundred Pawnee Scouts to look for hostiles in the North."

The Pawnee Scouts had often operated from Fort D.A. Russell and were familiar sights to the military and civilian communities. Recruited and led by Frank North, a pioneer Nebraskan who had a farm near the Pawnee reservation on the Loup River in central Nebraska, the Pawnees responded each spring when the army notified North that he and the Scouts were again needed.

In the spring of 1875, the government had moved the Pawnee tribe from Nebraska to a reservation in Indian Territory, Oklahoma. Yet in 1876, they came back to Fort D.A. Russell to help the army in the summer, fall, and winter campaigns. The Pawnees were widely recognized for their fierce loyalty to Major North and their white leaders. The *Leader* paid them this tribute on December 12, 1876: "By all odds the most reliable of the irregulars. They are duly enlisted, organized and uniformed as a troop of cavalry, and if it were not for their long hair, which they will not consent to part with, would present a very soldierly appearance." Their last active campaign with the army included an important role in Colonel Mackenzie's late November attack against Dull Knife's band of Cheyenne in northern Wyoming. The Scouts took sixty Cheyenne scalps in that battle.

---

1. Anson Mills, *My Story*, (Washington, D.C.: Press of Byron S. Adams, 1918), p. 166.
2. *General George Crook: His Autobiography*, edited by Martin F. Schmitt, (Norman: Oklahoma Press, 1954), p. 192.

Often referred to as the "Gray Wolf," Brigadier General George Crook assumed command of the Department of the Platte with headquarters at Omaha Barracks in 1875 after his successful Apache campaign in the southwest. Crook's leadership in the 1876 campaigns received considerable criticism, particularly his failure to pursue the hostile Indians after the Battle of the Rosebud in June 1876.

Chapter Eight
The Indian Wars Ended, Almost

The winter campaign of 1876-1877 amounted to the last call for the Pawnee Scouts—the services of this unique group of fighting allies were no longer required. During a visit to Fort D.A. Russell in March 1877, General Crook told a reporter that he considered the Indian wars at an end. Any hostile action to follow would only be of short duration, and, according to Crook: "The Indians will soon lay down their arms and remain at peace with the white man."[1]

In March another important event developed when President Grant signed a bill ratifying the Sioux agreement, which, among other things, opened up to settlement the region in northern Wyoming known as the "unceded Indian territory." The purchase of the Black Hills from the Sioux had been negotiated by the federal government a few months earlier.

On June 1, 1877, Major Frank North and his brother, Captain Luther North, were mustered out of the army for the last time. No more would the fighting Pawnee Scouts be seen at Fort D.A. Russell. It was the first time in fourteen years that Frank had been out of government service. Frank and Luther North, plus younger brother James, established a cattle ranch on the Dismal River north of North Platte with their old friend and fellow scout William F. Cody. They named it the Cody and North Ranch. With most of the hostile Indians back on the reservations, cattle ranching expanded rapidly in western Nebraska and Wyoming.

Although band after band of formerly hostile Indians came into the agencies and surrendered in the spring of 1877, there were some holdouts, such as Sitting Bull and his band of Hunkpapa Sioux who had fled to Canada. There were also some hostile bands reported to be west of the Big Horn Mountains in northern Wyoming. The units at Fort D.A. Russell still faced more field campaigning. In March 1877, a Department of the Platte inspector reported that cavalry units at Fort D.A. Russell, men and horses, were in good shape. Companies averaged eighty soldiers assigned, and their training included daily practice in mounted and dismounted cavalry drill.

The Fifth Cavalry was probably as well prepared as ever before when on May 29, 1877, the regiment marched to Fort Fetterman on an extended campaign to the north. Their reported departure from Fort D.A. Russell might have provided a scene for a later movie or a Charles King novel. The

Leader wrote: "Five companies of the 5th Cavalry passed in review . . . tearful eyes and fair hands looked and waved the fond adieus to the parting troops while the band played 'The Girl I Left Behind Me' and the recklessly rollicking 'Garryowen'." According to the post surgeon, it was one of the finest send-offs that he had ever witnessed.

Despite the grand departure ceremony for the regiment, the usual precampaign apprehension could be seen in the monthly Post Return, which listed thirty-nine desertions. On the march north, Company L was detached at Fort Fetterman to escort General Sheridan and party to the area of the Yellowstone River in Montana. The other four companies proceeded to the Big Horn Basin in northern Wyoming, where they encamped and made a thorough reconnaissance looking for reported hostile Indian bands. They discovered no Indians, and in late July, the five companies moved by rail to Omaha and Chicago. The railway strike riots of that summer required army units for guard and patrol duty. The Hayes administration had decided to use federal troops to cope with the wave of railway strikes that marked the country's first large-scale labor disputes. This unhappy task fell to five companies of the Fifth Cavalry for a few weeks, but they were able to return to Fort D.A. Russell by late August.

The Congress had become increasingly tightfisted with the army each year after the Civil War, and 1877 seemed the worst. The Fifty-fourth Congress failed to pass an appropriations bill to pay the army. The paymaster absented himself from Fort D.A. Russell from June until November. A saving factor, the secretary of war authorized food and fuel to be issued on credit to officers and enlisted men with families. Bankers in New York and Philadelphia were reported to be offering to pay the salaries of officers until the Congress passed the appropriations bill, charging a "fair" interest, of course.

As could be expected, hard currency could hardly be found around the post. A fairly normal reaction to the business of no pay appeared in the *Leader*: "Officers bitterly complain about the government stopping their pay. Many frontier officers are disgusted."[2] Still, the army at Fort D.A. Russell functioned effectively and with the belief that there remained responsible members of Congress who would be able to do what had to be done.

Some time passed before the pay issue was resolved, and in the meantime garrison routine continued much as before. An early and longtime resident of Cheyenne, Mrs. Theresa Jenkins, recalled in 1927 her first visit to the fort in the summer of 1877:

> The barracks were partly built of logs; a little polt [sic] of grass in circular form was the parade ground and some cotton wood trees surrounded the drive. Every evening the aristocracy of Cheyenne drove out to the fort in fine carriages. . . . The social life at Fort Russell was always first-class; we always had the military band to play for the dancing; tallow candles by the dozen set in tin reflectors, illuminated the old post hall.[3]

Company F, Fifth Cavalry, manned the post during the spring and summer of 1877 while the rest of the regiment campaigned in northern Wyoming or served on strike duty in Omaha and Chicago. On August 30, Company F departed for Camp Brown in the Wind River Mountains. Company F served as the vangard for the Fifth Cavalry in their attempt to capture Chief Joseph and his band of fugitive Nez Perce as they entered Wyoming Territory in the area of Yellowstone Park. A real concern prevailed that the Nez Perce would move from Idaho through the corner of Wyoming into Montana and join Sitting Bull in Canada. Chief Joseph and most of his followers finally surrendered to a force under Colonel Nelson Miles in northern Montana in early October 1877 after a thousand mile exodus from their Idaho reservation. The Nez Perce had eluded several army regiments, including the Fifth Cavalry, on their trek from Idaho toward Canada. Moved onto a small reserve in Kansas, they were later relocated to Indian Territory in Oklahoma. In 1885, the government permitted them to locate on a reservation in Washington where they had long wanted to be.

The Nez Perce had successfully escaped the army longer than anyone thought possible, which might have encouraged other tribes to try the same thing. The two agents on the Red Cloud and Spotted Tail agencies in northwestern Nebraska expected trouble from their Indians soon after the surrender of Chief Joseph. The government had started moving the Oglala and Brule Sioux north to new reservations on the Missouri River in central Dakota Territory. The Fifth Cavalry rode from Fort D.A. Russell to Fort Laramie so they would be closer to the potential trouble if it developed. However, the dominant tribal chiefs, Red Cloud and Spotted Tail, unexpectedly agreed to relocate and were able to lead their tribes peacefully to the new reserves.

The Fifth Cavalry happily returned to Fort D.A. Russell. At the end of 1877, five companies of the regiment, plus the regimental headquarters and band, were at the home station. The other seven companies were spread wide, with three companies at Fort McKinney, Wyoming Territory, one company at Sidney Barracks, Nebraska, one company at Fort McPherson, Nebraska, and two companies at Camp Brown, Wyoming Territory.

The five companies of Fifth Cavalry back at Fort D.A. Russell represented far fewer troops than usual in winter quarters. While not much had been done during the year in new construction, some internal improvements had occurred that, combined with the fewer number of men, provided improved living conditions for the assigned soldiers. Fort D.A. Russell had finally done away with the two-tier double wooden bunks in the open bay barracks. The men now slept in single iron cots, a tremendous improvement but one that required more floor space. Additionally, each noncommissioned officer above the grade of corporal was authorized a plain wooden chair in the barracks, and six chairs were authorized for every twelve men of lesser grades.

The cavalrymen could not rest long on these seats, however. Even though General Crook had declared the Indian wars ended in 1877, small pockets of resistance continued for another two years. Indeed, the Utes, Cheyennes, Paiutes, and Bannocks were far from settled, and Sitting Bull with his band of Hunkpapa Sioux remained in Canada out of the army's reach. Three companies of the Fifth Cavalry under Major Verling Hart were dispatched to the Ross Fork Agency near Fort Hall in Idaho for three weeks in January 1878 to help round up the disaffected Bannocks there.

In contrast, and much to the relief of the army at Fort D.A. Russell, the Brule and Oglala Sioux accepted the idea of staying on a reservation and living on government annuities. These two tribes did not remain on the Missouri River reservations for long but moved to southwest Dakota Territory just across the border from Nebraska. The Brule agency, formerly named the Spotted Tail Agency after its chief, became known as the Rosebud Agency. The Oglala agency, formerly known as the Red Cloud Agency, became the Pine Ridge Agency. There were still some small bands from these tribes unable to accept reservation life or, in some cases, the location of the new reservations and conditions.

As the Plains Indians began to take up a new way of life in 1878, a venerable army institution, the company laundress, started the disbanding process. Laundresses had been authorized at the rate of four per company since 1802 and carried on company rosters. However, the army decreed that in the future women would not be allowed to accompany troops in this capacity. The question of retaining company laundresses had earlier been considered by the Congressional House Committee on Military Affairs, and there were conflicting views presented. Many old-timers had mixed emotions. Some army officers thought the laundresses served a useful purpose, while others felt they were troublemakers and not worth their expense.

Usually married to enlisted men, laundresses received from the army their quarters, fuel, one daily food ration, and the services of the post surgeon. They did the washing for the company at a fixed price of seventy cents per month for the men and a dollar for officers. The unwritten law demanded that company members square with the laundresses on payday even though they might not be able to square with anyone else. According to one officer who spent many years at frontier posts, the laundresses and women servants were not only respected for the useful services they provided but were often the honored guests at the post dances, theatricals, and, other entertainments given by the men. At many isolated posts, the laundresses made up a sizeable percentage of the female population. At Fort D.A. Russell in 1878, they numbered thirty women.

Most of the laundresses' husbands would soon be gone for the summer. A campaign in northern Wyoming kicked off on May 20, 1878, when Colonel Wesley Merritt and two companies of the Fifth Cavalry left Fort D.A. Russell for Fort McKinney. The *Leader* reported on May 21, 1878, that they were given the usual splendid Fifth Cavalry send-off. Other companies of the regiment joined en route, so that Merritt reached Fort McKinney on June 3 with eight companies of Fifth Cavalry. Their mission was to round up the Indians that had not yet settled on reservations. Fort

D.A. Russell was garrisoned for the summer with little more than the one hundred recruits that had arrived from Jefferson Barracks at St. louis on April 21. By midsummer the recruits, too, had been sent to their companies in the field. Company F, Fourth Infantry, provided a thirty-two-man detached unit to garrison the post until the Fifth Cavalry returned from campaigning.

Four companies of Fifth Cavalry returned by late November 1878, one company arriving from Idaho. Additionally, the fifteen packers who had accompanied the regiment with 200 mules and two wagons were prepared for winter quarters at Cheyenne Depot. As the year ended, the Post Return listed five companies of Fifth Cavalry and one company of Fourth Infantry at Fort D.A. Russell with fourteen officers and 418 enlisted men.

Colonel Wesley Merritt had to leave his command of the post and the Fifth Cavalry temporarily in early January 1879 to serve on the Major Marcus Reno court of inquiry being held in Chicago. Thus the Merritts missed the holiday festivities at Fort D.A. Russell and in town. The long-established practice on army posts of making courtesy calls on New Year's Day had been adopted in Cheyenne. More than fifteen homes of the town's leading citizens, plus those of two senior officers on the post, were listed in the newspaper as open to friends for calls.

The post holiday season of social and recreation events ended abruptly on January 18, 1879, when the Fifth Cavalry received orders to take to the field in northwestern Nebraska. In early January, the Dull Knife band of Cheyenne Indians being held at Fort Robinson awaiting removal to Indian Territory in Oklahoma broke out of their detention facility and killed several soldiers. Another band of Cheyenne under Chief Little Wolf had been in the sandhills of northwestern Nebraska for several weeks evading the soldiers and all attempts to move them to Oklahoma. Both bands wanted to reach Montana, their traditional tribal hunting lands, and possibly to join Sitting Bull in Canada.

Units from Fort Robinson managed to find most of the Dull Knife band and return them to that post within a few days. The members of the Little Wolf band in the Nebraska sandhills were more elusive. The Fifth Cavalry marched some 700 miles in brutal weather without contacting the Little Wolf band. The Indians had worked their way to southeastern Montana and surrendered to a unit of Second Cavalry from Fort Keogh on March 27, 1879. A few years later, the Northern Cheyenne Indian Reservation was established by the government in southern Montana for these Cheyenne tribal members determined not to settle in Oklahoma.

Arriving back from the discomforts of the field on March 28, the sight of the paymaster at Fort D.A. Russell brought happiness to the troops of the Fifth Cavalry as well as to the Cheyenne merchants. Some soldiers had not been paid for five months, and the paymaster, Major R.D. Clark, announced that he had paid out over $30,000. Several days later a mounted patrol was sent to Cheyenne in search of soldiers who had not returned to the post after receiving their money. Yet it seemed some progress had been made in payday behavior. Cheyenne merchants and Fort D.A. Russell soldiers were getting along better on paydays. One positive step had been made when the Cheyenne City Council passed an ordinance making it illegal to carry concealed firearms. The city marshal enforced that ordinance, and the number of payday shootings decreased dramatically.

With the coming of spring and good April weather, regimental dress parades were held every evening except Saturday. The regimental band gave an open-air band concert after the parade starting at 5:30 P.M., and the residents of the post and Cheyenne looked forward to these musical events. The *Leader* noted on July 29, 1879, the popularity of these occasions: "There were thirty-five carriages freighted with our citizens, besides those on horseback, at the fort on Sunday evening to witness the dress parade and hear the band."

In mid-September Secretary of the Interior Carl Schurz and party arrived at Fort D.A. Russell on a tour of the West. His reception received the full attention of the *Leader*, which reported on September 20, 1879, that carriages brought townspeople to the post, where they found the regiment ready and waiting: "The Fifth Cavalry, under the command of General Merritt, were mounted and drawn up in single file, making a long and brilliant line, each company coming to a present sabres as the carriages containing the visitors rolled by." Then the command formed by companies and marched into the post. A reception followed at General Merritt's quarters, and the Fifth Cavalry band "discoursed inspiring music." Adding a feminine touch to the festivities, "Mrs. General Merritt, assisted by a staff of brilliant ladies, dispensed appropriate hospitality." At the conclusion of the gathering, Cheyenne's finest returned to their vehicles and whirled back to the city.

While firing ranges were a part of every army post and marksmanship was considered a prime asset for every soldier, the purchase of ammunition for rifle and revolver target practice had never enjoyed a high priority in the annual budget. The Commanding General of the Army, General W.T. Sherman, changed this, and a great deal of target practice occurred at Fort D.A. Russell in 1879. There had been some improvements made in the army Springfield rifle and ammunition. Competition rifle matches were becoming popular, and a Cheyenne rifle team competed regularly with Fort Russell's Fourth Infantry sharpshooters. The Cheyenne team won regularly with a Sharps rifle, while the Fourth Infantry used the army Springfield, a single-shot breechloader. William F. Cody's Buffalo Bill Show appeared in Cheyenne in August 1879 and included Cody's shooting exhibition using a Freund and modified Sharps rifle. The Freund brothers were Cheyenne gunsmiths with a national reputation for fine rifles. Many Fort D.A. Russell officers sported a Freund rifle, or a Freund modified rifle, acquired at their own expense.

Possibly some of the officers took along their Freund rifles when, after a peaceful summer at Fort D.A. Russell, two companies of Fifth Cavalry were ordered on September 20, 1879, to the troubled White River Ute Indian Agency in northwestern Colorado. Under the command of Captain J.S. Payne, the Fifth Cavalry units traveled by train to Rawlins, where a company of Third Cavalry and units drawn from the Fourth Infantry from Fort Fred Steele near Rawlins joined them. Commanded by Major Thomas T. Thornburgh from Fort Fred Steele, the entire column proceeded south on the morning of September 21 on a 200-mile march to the White River Agency. Thornburgh's force numbered 153 officers and enlisted men, twenty-five civilian teamsters, packers and guides, and thirty-three supply wagons. On September 29, 1879, still some fifteen miles short of the White River Agency, a battle with the Ute Indians occurred on Milk Creek that left eleven soldiers dead, including Major Thornburgh. Another twenty-three, including Captain Payne, were wounded. The Utes kept the column under fire, preventing movement forward or back.

The Utes had long occupied western Colorado between the Rocky Mountains and the Wasatch Range in Utah with about seven separate bands. Two bands had been assigned an agency on the White River in northwestern Colorado, although all the bands roamed the area as they pleased. Attempts of Agent Nathan C. Meeker to acculturate and domesticate the northern Utes in the agricultural ways of the white man created resentment and unrest among the two bands of White River Utes. Meeker had been the agricultural editor of the *New York Tribune* and in 1870 had come west and established as a cooperative enterprise the Union Colony #1, later named Greeley, Colorado. He also established and served as editor of the daily *Greeley Tribune*.

Becoming disillusioned with cooperative progress in the Union Colony, Meeker applied for work with the Indians and was accepted in February 1879. When Meeker first requested that the army send troops to the White River to stem the Ute unrest, he had hoped for the arrest of the leaders. In response to Meeker's request, troops from forts D.A. Russell and Fred Steele had been ordered to march to the White River. Agent Meeker and nine of his employees were killed at the White River Agency while the battle raged at Milk Creek on the afternoon of September 29. Nathan Meeker's wife and children were spared.

When word of the deteriorating situation on Milk Creek reached army headquarters in Omaha and Washington, Colonel Wesley Merritt received word at Fort D.A. Russell to hurry a relief force to Milk Creek. On October 1, he led four companies of the Fifth Cavalry and a large pack train to Rawlins by train, and then marched south. Several companies of the Fourth Infantry, with a large pack train, joined the Fifth Cavalry at Rawlins. Merritt's movement south from Rawlins has been appropriately referred to as the "lightning march," more than 170 miles over rugged terrain in four days. The column arrived at Milk Creek on October 5 and raised the siege, dispersing the hostile Utes to the area of the agency on the White River.

A considerable military force was soon on the scene of the Ute Agency in addition to the Fort D.A. Russell units. After several weeks of negotiations with Ute leaders, the threat of a major uprising and Ute war diminished. Colonel Merritt and six companies of the Fifth Cavalry returned to Fort D.A. Russell on November 29, leaving three companies on detached service at the White River Agency. A military detachment remained there on a

Army pack mules from Cheyenne Depot usually carried a three-hundred-pound load and hauled most of the supplies for the Fifth Cavalry on their march south from Rawlings in 1879 into the rugged mountains to deal with the Ute uprising on Milk River in Colorado. Mule supply trains from Cheyenne Depot were in demand all over the west when an army campaign encountered rough terrain.—*WY State AMH Dept.*

rotation basis to insure that the Utes remained peaceful. The camp became known as the Camp on White River.

The September 29 battle on Milk Creek cost Companies D and F, Fifth Cavalry, eight enlisted men killed. The wounded numbered two officers and fourteen enlisted men. Horses killed or captured by the Indians totaled 110. By mid-October, Fort D.A. Russell's hospital had received the Fifth Cavalry's sixteen wounded officers and enlisted men plus two civilian teamsters, a blacksmith, and an assistant surgeon.

Winter quarters at Fort D.A. Russell offered the six companies of the Fifth Cavalry the prospect of warm, dry barracks for the rest of 1879, a welcome change from campaigning in northwestern Colorado. The three companies left at the Camp on White River lived in tents and experienced a very cold and uncomfortable winter. Not until several years had passed were the Utes considered trustworthy and the military camp closed, with no regrets from any members of the Fifth Cavalry. Life at the post near Cheyenne offered more creature comforts.

1. *Cheyenne Daily Leader*, March 16, 1977.
2. *Cheyenne Daily Leader*, August 15, 1877.
3. Theresa Jenkins, "Fort Russell Scene of the Gayest of Social Functions," *Kemmerer Kamera*, August 27, 1919.

PART III
FORT D.A.

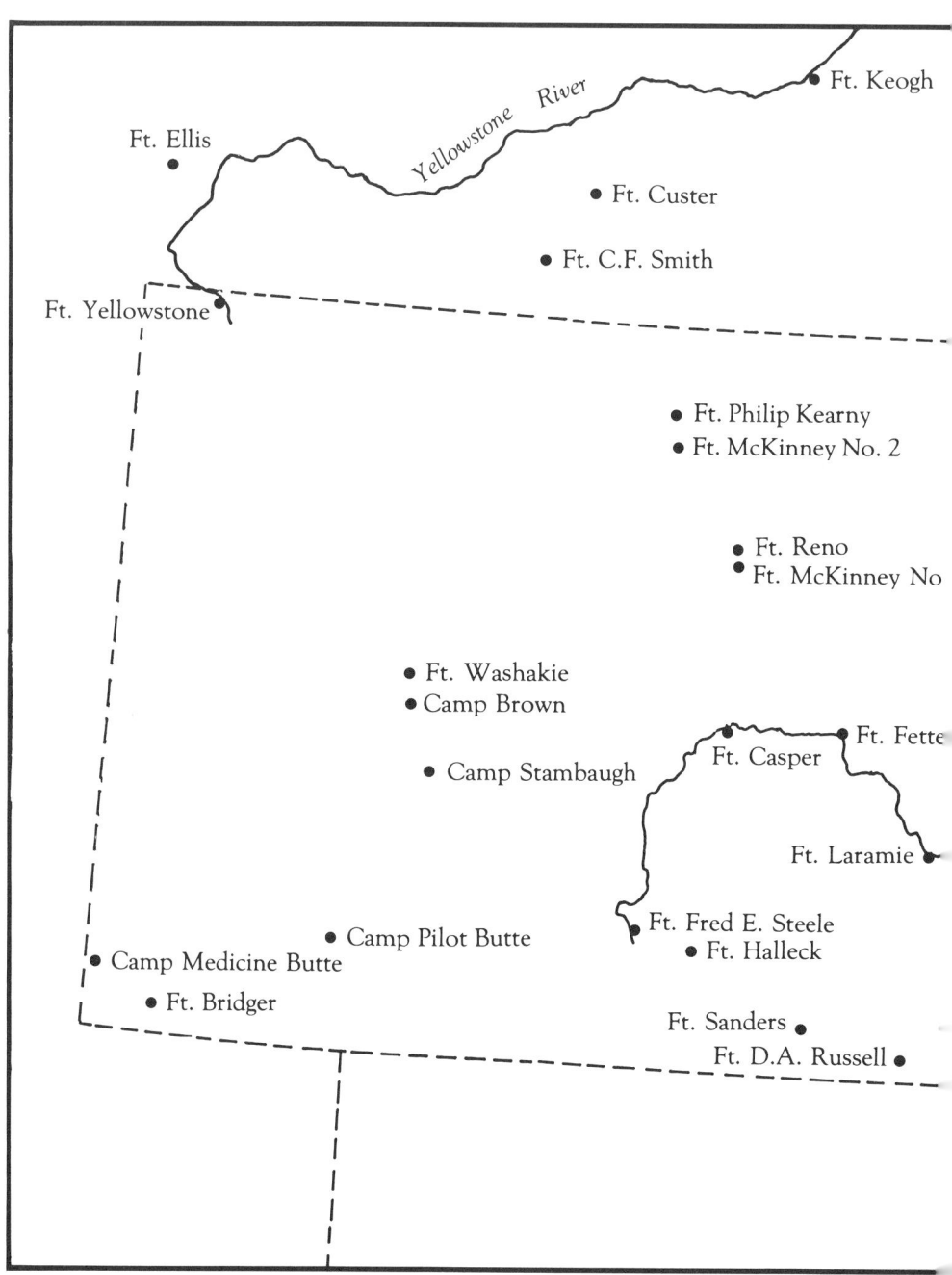

REFURBISHING RUSSELL, 1880-1889

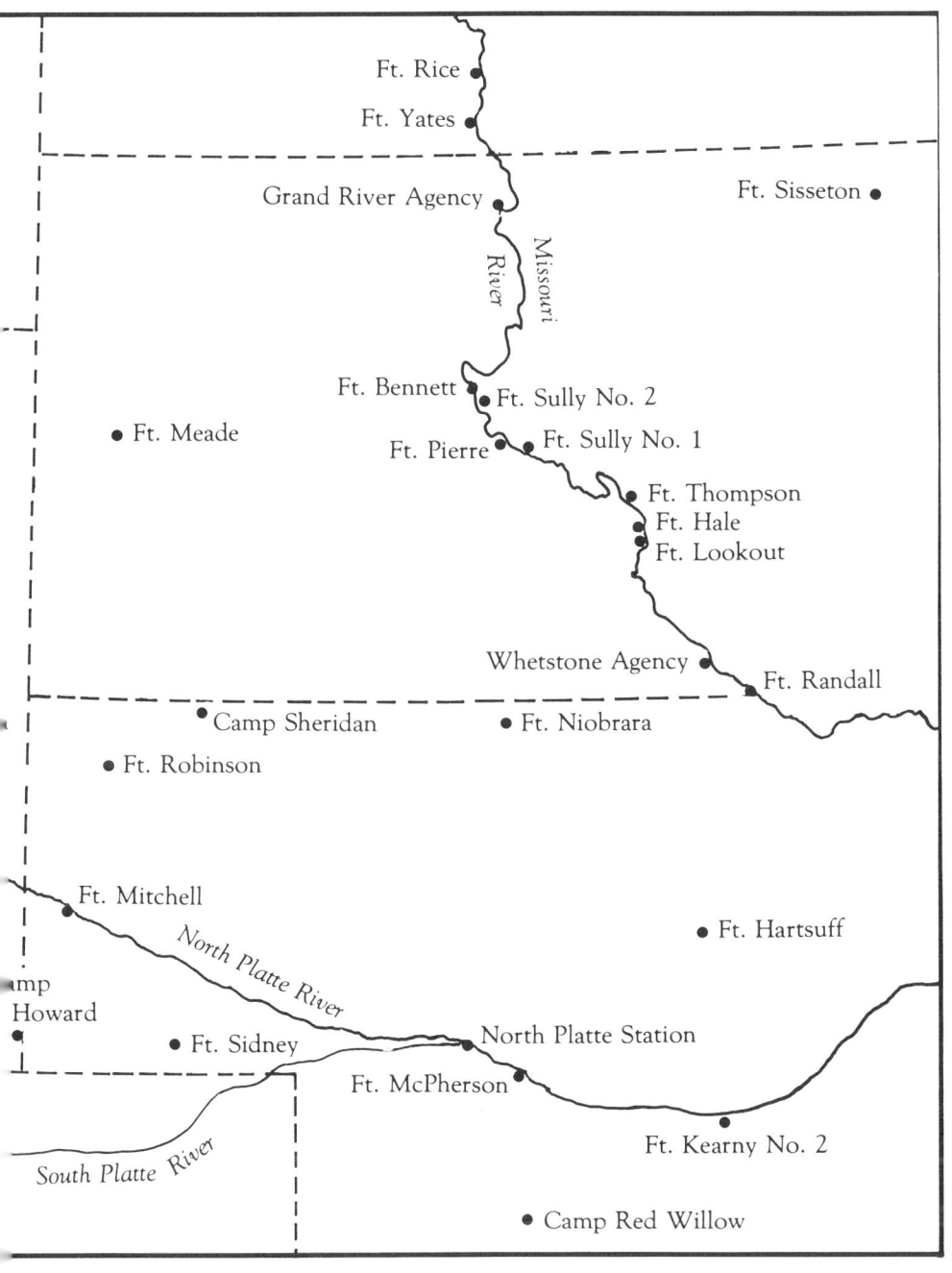

Colonel Albert G. Brackett served as commander of the post and Third Cavalry from May 1880 to May 1882. A very popular commander, Brackett organized many social and recreational activities that provided some change to the usual garrison routine. A group called the Brackett Social Club organized dances for the enlisted men on Friday nights at least every two weeks. Another group that named themselves the Platform Club congregated on the platform of the Union Pacific depot to witness the arrival of the daily train from the east and west.—*Ninetieth SM Wing History Office*

Chapter Nine
Surviving The Cut
Of Posts

In his annual message to Congress in December 1879, President Rutherford B. Hayes (1877-1881) recommended disposing of a large number of military posts in the West. Many of these military installations had been rendered less important by the advance of civilization and settlement. The frontier had continued moving westward, and much progress had been made by the government in establishing reservations for the Indians. Unfriendly neighbors posed no immediate external threat to the national borders, so the attention of the administration and Congress turned to saving money.

In his message, President Hayes expressed satisfaction with the overall peaceful behavior of the western Indian tribes, noting only two exceptions: (1) the 1879 outbreak of the Utes on the White River Reservation in northwestern Colorado, and (2) the Mescalero outbreak in New Mexico. As a result of the generally peaceful trend of the western Indians, many western posts faced the prospect of early closure. A few would be continued and refurbished. The pressing question remained, which few?

For the moment, Fort D.A. Russell paid little attention to these matters. Army life continued much as in the past. Winter quarters and the social season of 1880 opened with several officers' wives announcing their New Year's Day "at home" receptions. Support and rotation of the three Fifth Cavalry companies at the Camp on White River in Ute territory continued. The government announced a treaty with the Utes in March, but the peace remained an uneasy one for the next three years. The wives of the enlisted men gave a Leap Year party at the end of the season, which the *Leader* of March 19, 1880, pronounced a fine success. Colonel and Mrs. Wesley Merritt, along with the staff officers and wives of the regiment, were reported in attendance, and everyone had a jolly good time.

In April 1880, an announced change of station for the Fifth Cavalry sent everyone packing. Nine companies with thirty-four officers and 614 enlisted men marched north ninety miles and took station at Fort Laramie. Many kind words of praise for Colonel Merritt and the men of the Fifth Cavalry appeared in the local press. The regiment had made a good impression in Cheyenne and many fine friends during its almost four-year stay at Fort D.A. Russell. The Third Cavalry returned to Fort D.A. Russell, after having been gone since mid-1876, to replace the Fifth Cavalry.

The Third Cavalry commander, Colonel Albert G. Brackett, assumed command of Fort D.A. Russell on April 29, 1880. Brackett had served at Fort D.A. Russell earlier in 1868 with a Second Cavalry company for a short time. He would leave his mark on the installation with many vigorous programs and good improvements. Cheyenne had grown while the Third Cavalry had been away. It had a reported population of 4,456 in 1880. The military and civilian communities remained optimistic that the fort would remain alive while many of the other western outposts were being closed.

Brackett launched several social and recreational events at Fort D.A. Russell during the summer of 1880 that received high praise from the military and townsfolk alike. As an example, the Fourth of July started with a series of athletic competitions for soldiers. Cash prizes were offered to the winners. The day culminated with each company of the regiment serving their members a special dinner prepared for the occasion, but one company went all out. The commander, staff, and all regimental officers were invited to the dining room of Company G, Third Cavalry, for dinner. Company G served a splendid Fourth of July dinner, delighting all who attended.

Dancing continued to be a very popular part of the program, and "hops" were held frequently. The enlisted men organized a dancing club named the Brackett Social Club, with a "hop" scheduled every two weeks. Officers held dances about as often. The combined opportunities offered many occasions for the military and civilian communities to meet socially. These occasions were very popular, according to the frequent newspaper reports, and usually ended after midnight, sometimes as late as 5:00 A.M..

President Rutherford B. Hayes and party, which included Commander-in-Chief of the Army General W.T. Sherman, visited Cheyenne and Fort D.A. Russell in September on a final swing through the West before the president left office. A joint military and civilian gathering at the fort heard both the president and General Sherman speak. General Sherman recalled his 1866 journey through this area looking over the territory of his new command, the Division of the Missouri:

> My memories cover this country before any of you came here....At that time it was a naked part of the territory. The post and the transportation of government stores which it occasioned was the foundation of your city. If anybody had told me then that within a hundred years a single house of your city would be built, I would have told him he was a fool. I did not believe anybody would live out here of his own choice. Soldiers had to come here because they could not help themselves. But I am glad it turned out otherwise.[1]

At his request and for old times' sake, the general rode back to Cheyenne and the Union Pacific depot in an army ambulance pulled by four mules. Sherman had always enjoyed a good rapport with the reporters in Cheyenne. In response to a question about one of his Washington antagonists, he is said to have responded that he supposed he could now forgive his enemies, for he was more than even with most of them. This was the last of General Sherman's many visits to Fort D.A. Russell, but he continued to be heard. In his annual report to the secretary of war in November 1880, General Sherman mentioned the impact the three transcontinental railroads (Union Pacific, Northern Pacific, and Southern Pacific) had had on pacifying the West:

> These railroads have entirely revolutionized our country in the past few years and imposed on the military an entire change of policy. Hitherto we have been compelled to maintain small posts along the wagon and stage routes of travel. These are no longer needed because they are no longer used, and the settlements which grow up speedily along the new railroads afford the security necessary, and the regular stations built for storage at convenient distances afford shelter for military stores and for men when operating in the neighborhood. We should now abandon many of the smaller posts hitherto necessary, and concentrate at strategic points, generally, near the national frontier where railroads intersect, so as to send out detachments promptly to districts where needed.[2]

The year 1880 wound down with a masquerade ball on Christmas Eve sponsored by the Brackett Social Club. Reported to be a very fine affair, it was attended by a good number of residents from the post and Cheyenne. A comfortable complement of four companies of Third Cavalry, plus one company of Fourth Infantry, took up winter quarters at Fort D.A. Russell with little threat of any Indian disturbance occurring soon on the northern High Plains.

Army troops, however, were expected to take the warpath during the winter when they learned of President Hayes's order prohibiting the sale of intoxicating liquors at military posts. The president's wife, Lucy Webb Hayes, had long been an ardent prohibitionist and darling of the Women's Christian Temperance Union. She refused to serve anything alcoholic in the White House, which earned her the nickname in Washington of "Lemonade Lucy." The War Department expected a noisy reaction from the army.

The response from the soldiers at Fort D.A. Russell to the Hayes prohibition edict turned out to be much different than expected. A letter to the editor of the *Leader* appearing on March 6, 1881, conveyed a petition to the president of the United States signed by more than 200 soldiers at Fort D.A. Russell. The petition requested the continuance of the order proscribing the sale of liquor by post traders on military reservations and gave three reasons: "(1) The sale of liquor by post traders to enlisted men is harmful to them individually and hurts the army, (2) The post trader's store for sale of liquor is divided into two distinct parts, one for officers and one for enlisted men. Officers get decent liquor but men get rot-gut. The enlisted men are penalized severely for drinking, and (3) Post Traders grow rich."

Mr. Charles A. Weidman had replaced the popular J.D. Woolley as post trader at Fort D.A. Russell in the mid-1870s when Woolley sold out and headed for the Black Hills in search of gold. Little is known of Weidman's role as post trader, but the petition indicates that he might not have been popular with the enlisted men. The prohibition of liquor sales by post traders at all military posts remained in effect long past the end of the Hayes administration, and trader profits were severely curtailed as a consequence. The post trader system had evolved from the sutler system of earlier years, a system noted for political influence, fraud, and victimized soldiers. A joint resolution of Congress approved March 30, 1867, pertaining to appointment of post traders, had abolished the army's sutler system. The days of the post trader were now numbered. Congress wielded the ax in the mid-1880s. Its replacement, the post canteen system, proved to be much more equitable and satisfactory.

In addition to their keen interest in prohibition on the post, the local newspapers covered other interesting subjects. For instance, on June 10, 1881, the *Leader* reported on a distinguished gathering in the post hall to hear a lecture by Lieutenant Frederick Schwatka, Third Cavalry. The hall was filled with officers and ladies from the post and Cheyenne Depot, plus a large number of ladies and gentlemen from Cheyenne. The officers were attired in full dress, while the ladies were all arrayed in the height of fashion. Governor J.W. Hoyt sat behind the speaker along with Colonel A.G. Brackett and the regimental staff. Schwatka had been detached from the regiment in 1878 to join an Arctic expedition that had received national recognition. The expedition succeeded in finding part of the remains of the ill-fated Sir John Franklin Expedition lost thirty-five years earlier. Schwatka had been severely injured and returned to his regiment on limited duty. A very capable officer and highly talented speaker, Schwatka had graduated from West Point in 1867 and then acquired degrees in law and medicine while also participating with the regiment in most of the Indian campaigns of the 1870s. The Arctic expedition extracted a heavy physical toll from Lieutenant Schwatka, and he remained on limited duty with the Third Cavalry until 1885, when he resigned his commission for reasons of health.

In the meantime, other members of the regiment also served on detached service away from the post, including several companies of the Third Cavalry at the Camp at White River. Unrest among the Utes at the White River Agency in Colorado continued to require a significant military force there. The troops remaining at Fort D.A. Russell engaged in the "usual garrison duties," which included rifle target practice. Target shooting had become more common and more possible with facilities and time available during the good weather months. No longer were so many companies away from the post escorting, patrolling, and chasing Indians. The introduction of breechloading metallic cartridges after the Civil War increased a unit's firepower considerably if it could maintain a high level of marksmanship. The model 1873 single-shot Springfield rifle (infantry) and carbine (cavalry), caliber .45, continued to be the army's standard weapon for another ten years.

Community relations between the post and town remained at a very high level of cordiality during the summer of 1881 despite a ban on fast driving by Cheyennites through the post. The gates at Fort D.A. Russell were closed as a means of slowing down the speeding carriages and wagons, and they were opened for entry only after the vehicle had come to a halt. Not long after the speed ban appeared, the newspaper came forth with this high compliment for its military neighbor: "Fort Russell is one of the prettiest spots in the neighborhood now and the Sunday afternoon band concerts induce many of our citizens to leave their city behind them for an hour of pleasure there." Much of the population of Cheyenne had been here for most of the fourteen years of its existence, and the yearly tree plantings and other attempts to beautify the post were noted and appreciated. The

Cheyenne stock growers organized the famous Cheyenne Club in 1880 and built a handsome clubhouse the following year. It served as the gathering place for important occasions and people, civilian and military. Officers from Fort D.A. Russell were welcomed without initiation fee upon payment of thirty dollars in dues each six months. The clubhouse boasted of a fine restaurant, bar, billiard room, reading room, and six upstairs sleeping rooms for members and guests. When stockgrowers fell on hard times, the building became the offices for the Industrial Club (1907-1920) later named the Cheyenne Chamber of Commerce (1920-1936). The historic and memorable building was torn down in 1936.—*WY State AMH Dept.*

Lieutenant Colonel Luther P. Bradley, commander of the twenty-seventh Infantry, served as post commander for three months in 1869 while his regiment took station at Fort D.A. Russell. Units of two other infantry and cavalry regiments also served at Fort D.A. Russell during this period, a practice of the western army that continued through the 1870s. Bradley retired in the late 1890s a brigadier general.— *WY State AMH Dept.*

near-pristine view of the garrison described by the reporter was probably not appreciated by some of the community at the post, particularly the wives.

Perhaps the military spouses envied some of the improvements found in the nearby civilian community. Many new innovations were being introduced in Cheyenne during late 1881 and early 1882, including a telephone system and electric lights. It would require more time before these technological marvels were budgeted by the army for Fort D.A. Russell. However, the post received $3,700 to build porches for nine sets of the old barracks, plus fencing for some yards and the parade ground, and a new grain warehouse. This appropriation arrived with no word from the War Department as to whether or not the installation would be closed or kept open.

On the other hand, the departure of the Third Cavalry to Arizona in May 1882 should not have been a surprise, but Cheyenne treated the news as a sad occasion because of the loss of so many old friends. The Third Cavalry had first arrived at Fort D.A. Russell in March 1872, and some units of that regiment had been there most of the time since. Now they were all gone.

The closing of forts Sanders and Fetterman in May 1882 brought units of the Fourth and Ninth Infantry regiments to Fort D.A. Russell as replacement for the Third Cavalry. Hardly had the Fourth Infantry settled in when two companies received orders to open a road from Fort Bridger to Fort Thornburgh in Utah. Then more of the Fourth Infantry transferred to Fort Omaha. This left the Ninth Infantry as the host regiment at Fort D.A. Russell, Major Isaac D. DeRussy commanding. Despite reductions and relocations, the fort had not yet been selected for closure.

Forts D.A. Russell, Laramie, and Robinson served the purpose of monitoring the activities of the Pine Ridge and Rosebud Indian agencies in southwest Dakota, the home of several thousand restless Sioux Indians. The Cheyenne Depot also continued to serve an important role in providing vital supplies to the northern posts and Indian reservations. The *Leader* reported on December 9, 1882, that 300 men were employed at the Cheyenne Depot and that there were about 800 mules on hand to pull the supply wagons. Railroads going north from Cheyenne were another four years in the future, and wagon trains continued to be the prime means of moving freight and passengers.

1. *Cheyenne Daily Leader*, September 5, 1880.
2. *Cheyenne Daily Leader*, November 16, 1880.

The post water tank sat on the high ground above Crow Creek, where it stored water pumped from the creek by a steam engine. A soldier detail-operated water wagon filled the wagon's tank here for delivery to the water barrels behind each of the family houses, laundresses' quarters, barracks and mess halls. Two stoves were required to keep the water from freezing in the winter. Water mains and indoor plumbing made this water tank obsolete in the mid-1880s.—*WY State AMH Dept.*

Chapter Ten
Making The Post Permanent, Finally

The War Department had decided by late 1882 that Fort D.A. Russell would be kept open. Most of the old quarters and barracks built in 1867-1878, and now badly dilapidated, would be torn down, and new brick buildings would be erected on the same site to make a permanent post that would accommodate eight companies. This announcement introduced a building program that would continue into the 1890s and make Fort D.A. Russell a much more pleasant and comfortable station for officers and enlisted men, and for their families. The army's master plan to abandon the smaller garrisons and concentrate the field units at the larger posts, while improving the living conditions at the installations being retained, had gotten underway.

Seven companies of infantry were garrisoned as the year 1882 closed, four companies of Ninth Infantry and three of Seventh Infantry, and for the first time in many years, no cavalry. Target practice, battalion drills, maneuvers, and dress parades now formed the important features of the winter schedule. This constituted significant change from a very few years earlier when only essential minimum activities took place during the cold season. Two officers were also sent to school. Lieutenants John A. Baldwin and Robert A. Lovell of the Ninth Infantry were ordered to report to the School of Application at Fort Leavenworth, Kansas, for the one-year course of instruction. The army in the West now had some breathing space, enough at least to allow time for professional education for the officer corps.

Fort D.A. Russell units had little contact with the Indians during 1883, but some important events occurred in addition to the new building program on the post. An order from the Department of the Platte eliminated the issue of rations to laundresses after June 18, 1883. Terminating this long-standing role of the laundresses required some time and doing. They had become firmly entrenched over the years. termination had been decided by Congress in 1878, but five years later some laundresses still conducted business, even though many of their former perquisites had been taken away. A story in the *Leader* of August 3, 1883, reported that the institution still hung on at Fort D.A. Russell. It told about two pet dogs fighting in front of the laundresses' quarters, the many yelling spectators the dog fight drew, and how the laundresses had to leave their "army pianos" (washboards) to successfully rescue their pets.

The newly arrived commander of Fort D.A. Russell and the Ninth Infantry, Colonel John T. Mason, along with his wife, received a modest reception in June, hosted by the officers of the post and their ladies. Still, it

Colonel John S. Mason served as post and Ninth Infantry commander for three years, 1883–1886, with six to eight companies of the regiment present. Fort D.A. Russell was declared a permanent military installation in 1884, eight-company capacity, with a single regiment serving. Mason, like many of the post–Civil War regimental commanders, had been breveted a general officer during the war. As a courtesy, newspapermen and others continued to use the brevet rank of favorite officers long after, even though the War Department discontinued recognition of brevet ranks in 1870.—*Ninetieth SM Wing History Office*

proved to be the highlight of the social season. An ecstatic newspaper reporter included this: "Never since Fort D.A. Russell was built was there such a brilliant affair. The governor and all the civilian dignitaries were there at 8:30 P.M. when the 9th Infantry band gave a concert. At 9:30 P.M. dancing began and continued until supper at 12. Dancing then continued until the wee small hours."

During this quiet period, President Chester A. Arthur (1881-1885) made a short stop at Cheyenne and Fort D.A. Russell en route to Yellowstone Park. The president and his party were traveling by train to Green River in western Wyoming, then north by wagon train. While every president had visited Cheyenne and Fort D.A. Russell since and including President Grant, President Arthur had been the first to show an interest in the ten-year-old Yellowstone Park. He arrived on August 5, 1883, and a modest military escort accompanied the presidential party from the railhead at Green River. The party proceeded north in three ambulances and a baggage wagon provided by the Cheyenne Depot. The total contingent from Fort D.A. Russell assigned to President Arthur's entourage, gone for more than a month, amounted to thirty-eight men and 178 mules.[1]

For those who remained behind, Cheyenne still offered a variety of theaters and other forms of entertainment. Dress parades at Fort D.A. Russell on Sunday evenings provided the leading attraction. Lillie Langtry's appearance at the Cheyenne Opera House in June 1884 proved to be another leading attraction. She packed the house for all performances. Harry Oelrichs, a New Yorker who headed the Anglo-American Cattle Company, owned a ranch west of the post that Miss Langtry frequently visited. Oelrichs also owned a handsome "tally-ho" carriage, which seated several passengers on top of the vehicle as well as inside. A special friend of Oelrich's, Lillie Langtry loved to travel through Fort D.A. Russell on top of the tally-ho at full gallop on the way to the Oelrichs ranch, giving the troops a special sight of this celebrity.

While new brick buildings went up in January 1885 and a troop detail cut ice at Sloan's Lake to fill the new post ice house, the post trader system came to an end at Fort D.A. Russell. Messrs. Wiedman and Worthington no longer had a franchise. The government appraised and purchased their buildings during the summer and auctioned off the store, bringing to an end the role of the post trader at Fort D.A. Russell. A new and much better system of providing the soldiers such goods and services came into being then, the post canteen.

Another change took place when the new Department of the Platte commander, Brigadier General Oliver O. Howard, announced a plan in May to establish several training camps at different locations to meet two weeks in September. Troops from forts Russell, Laramie, Sidney, and Robinson would march to their camp at a point on the Union Pacific Railroad near Pine Bluffs depot. Before the September encampment, six companies of Ninth Infantry from Fort D.A. Russell were ordered to Cresfield, Kansas, to control the movements of a Cheyenne Indian band trying to move back north from Oklahoma Territory through western Kansas. These units of Ninth Infantry all returned to the post by late August without conflict with the Cheyenne. The training encampment near Pine Bluffs proceeded on schedule, and the department commander pronounced it a success.

The new post waterworks completed in July 1885 probably elicited more joy in the hearts of residents of Fort D.A. Russell than any of the other new facilities. No longer would the daily soldier detail fill the barrels behind each quarters, barracks, and the company kitchen from the water wagon that hauled from the wooden storage tank on the bluff above Crow Creek. The new system consisted of more than 5,000 feet of four-inch pipe laid to encircle the post, with service pipes running to each of the new brick houses, barracks, and mess halls. Nine double-nozzle fire hydrants were also strategically placed on the line for fighting fires, a long-standing problem at this and other frontier garrisons. Water would now be pumped from a large reception well located 200 yards from Crow Creek into a 30,000 gallon elevated metal tank on the bluff above Crow Creek. Gravity created by the elevated tank furnished the pressure.

The first of four new officers' family quarters completed in August, designated captains' quarters, followed completion of the new waterworks. Luxurious by western army standards, they contained nine rooms on two

The Ninth Infantry Regiment is shown lined up for parade in 1885. The large house is the commander quarters just completed in 1885 and still occupied today. The wooden water tower at left stored water pumped from Crow Creek originally for daily delivery to users by a water wagon, but in 1885 water lines extended from the water tower to each of the buildings.—*WY State AMH Dept.*

levals, indoor plumbing, and a wonderful front porch. Fort D.A. Russell would eventually have eleven of these fine houses (seven of them are still in use).

The post commander could now focus his attention on completing the new barracks and houses while the weather remained good and the Indians reasonably peaceful. But trouble of another sort erupted 250 miles west of Fort D.A. Russell in early September 1885.

Bitterness against the Union Pacific Coal Department at Rock Springs, Wyoming, and smoldering racial prejudice had been strong for some time. A riot started by Caucasian miners killed twenty-eight Chinese laborers on September 2, 1885, wounded fifteen others, chased several hundred out of town, and destroyed property valued at $147,000. This incident came to be known in Wyoming as the "Chinese Massacre." Two companies of the Ninth Infantry from Fort D.A. Russell moved to Rock Springs in response to Wyoming Governor Francis E. Warren's request to Washington for federal troops to help restore order. The military camp established at Rock Springs to maintain peace became known as Camp Pilot Butte. Units from Fort D.A. Russell and Fort Douglas, Utah, rotated to Camp Pilot Butte for one- and two-month tours for the next thirteen years, until the Spanish-American War began in 1898, and the camp closed.

Back at Cheyenne, the Ninth Infantry and its personable commander

The English music hall star Lily Langtry appeared in Cheyenne's Opera House several times in the mid-1880s and always to a packed house. When not performing, Miss Langtry loved to ride through the post en route to close friend Harry Oelrich's ranch west of the post sitting atop a tally-ho carriage with the horses at a full gallop. To slow down that lady and other speeders, the post commander had a gate installed that forced all carriages from Cheyenne to stop and then proceed slowly while driving through Fort D.A. Russell.—*WY State AMH Dept.*

A nice day in 1890 brought out some children at Fort D.A. Russell to watch the Seventeenth Infantry Regiment parade and enjoy the occasion. Formed in the background in front of the center house stands a uniformed unit of young Cheyenne ladies, a part of the State Guard, waiting their turn to join the parade. Mustered into service for the Wyoming statehood celebration in 1890, the ladies' organization did not survive long after the celebration activities had wound down.—*WY State AMH Dept.*

took great pains to make a home for the regiment at Fort D.A. Russell and in Cheyenne. Shared social and recreational activities were at an all-time high, such as the Ninth Infantry Dramatic Club's presentation at the Cheyenne Opera House on January 2, 1886. Then, on January 14, 1886, the Dramatic Club gave an entertainment in Garrison Hall on the post and invited the people of Cheyenne. They turned out in goodly number and pronounced it a fine show.

Other improvements introduced by the Ninth Infantry included a regimental reading room equipped with newspapers, periodicals, and books. The new post canteen, next door to the reading room, had a new Brunswick Balke billiard table purchased for the canteen by the Ninth Infantry Literary and Comedy Club. Both the canteen and reading rooms were attractive and popular. The Ninth Infantry became so comfortably ensconced at Fort D.A. Russell that rumors of a pending move were inevitable, and growing stronger.

Capital investments were announced in Cheyenne that encouraged other investments. As an example, the April 10, 1886, edition of the *Leader* outlined plans for a railroad, the Cheyenne and Northern, to build a line north from Cheyenne through Fort D.A. Russell to Wendover on the North Platte River. Largely owned by the Union Pacific, a passenger depot would be located at Fort D.A. Russell to load passengers and supplies that before traveled by wagon, horseback, or on foot. It would be a tremendous

Built soon after Fort D.A. Russell had been declared a permanent post in 1884, this base hospital replaced a very deteriorated wooden structure put up in 1867. Much improved with indoor plumbing and modern operating rooms, the twenty-four bed hospital accommodated the eight-company regiment-size post decreed in 1884. Although boarded up for many years, the structure remains sound.—*WY State AMH Dept.*

asset to the army at Fort D.A. Russell in responding to emergencies and as an improved line of communication with the northern posts of forts Laramie and Robinson. It would also be a great asset to Wyoming in the settlement of its northern land.

Although a feeling of optimism and enthusiasm permeated the air, some long-standing common difficulties continued to plague the military/civilian communities. For instance, loose domestic animals at the fort and in Cheyenne had been a part of the scene since their beginning. Several attempts to round up the stray cattle and impound them did little good. Townsfolk were particularly irate about the cows because they ate the leaves off the few living trees, and about everything else edible. The local editor seemed to be resigned to the animal problem in Cheyenne when he wrote, "It is only by degrees that a town becomes entirely metropolitan in all respects."[2] Horses were kept in stables, but cows, pigs, and goats were penned up somewhere in the rear of the owner's quarters, or they roamed the streets.

Post Surgeon C.H. Alden had reported earlier that a number of cows were kept at the garrison from the beginning, and the hospital had one. Mrs. Elizabeth Burt, wife of Captain Andrew Burt and the mother of a small boy, mentioned in her diary the importance of owning a cow. They took a cow first to Fort Bridger by wagon train in 1866, then to Fort C.F. Smith in 1867, and back to Fort D.A. Russell in 1868, where they sold the animal, now a pet given the name of Susie, to an officer who needed a cow. Fort D.A. Russell also had its share of loose animals, particularly goats, as told in this article under the heading, "Fort Russell Items":

> A billy and nanny goat have been a great annoyance to the garrison people for the past two or three months. It may be very amusing for the billy and nanny to chew up shirts, socks and dry goods in general, and to take their night's lodging on front door stoops and door mats, but it is very annoying to people who own these dry goods and door mats. The boys have attacked them several times with paint brushes, artistically decorated their snowy fleece with elegant monograms, and several shots from a Springfield rifle have been fired at them but all without effect. The owners would confer a great favor by keeping them at home or sending them abroad. Its a fact.[3]

The return of General George Crook as commander of the Department of the Platte with headquarters at Omaha in April 1886 met with enthusiasm at Fort D.A. Russell and in Cheyenne. The post had long played an important role in the Department of the Platte, and the "Gray Wolf" had frequently visited during his earlier tour as commander. He was known as a vigorous campaigner, and the hard feelings evoked by the 1876 campaigns and the Reynolds court martial had gradually faded away. Cheyenne authorities suggested that the department be moved from Omaha to a more central location, such as Cheyenne. The local press always enjoyed easy access to Crook during his visits. Local optimism rose.

When Crook arrived from the Southwest, the long-circulated rumor of

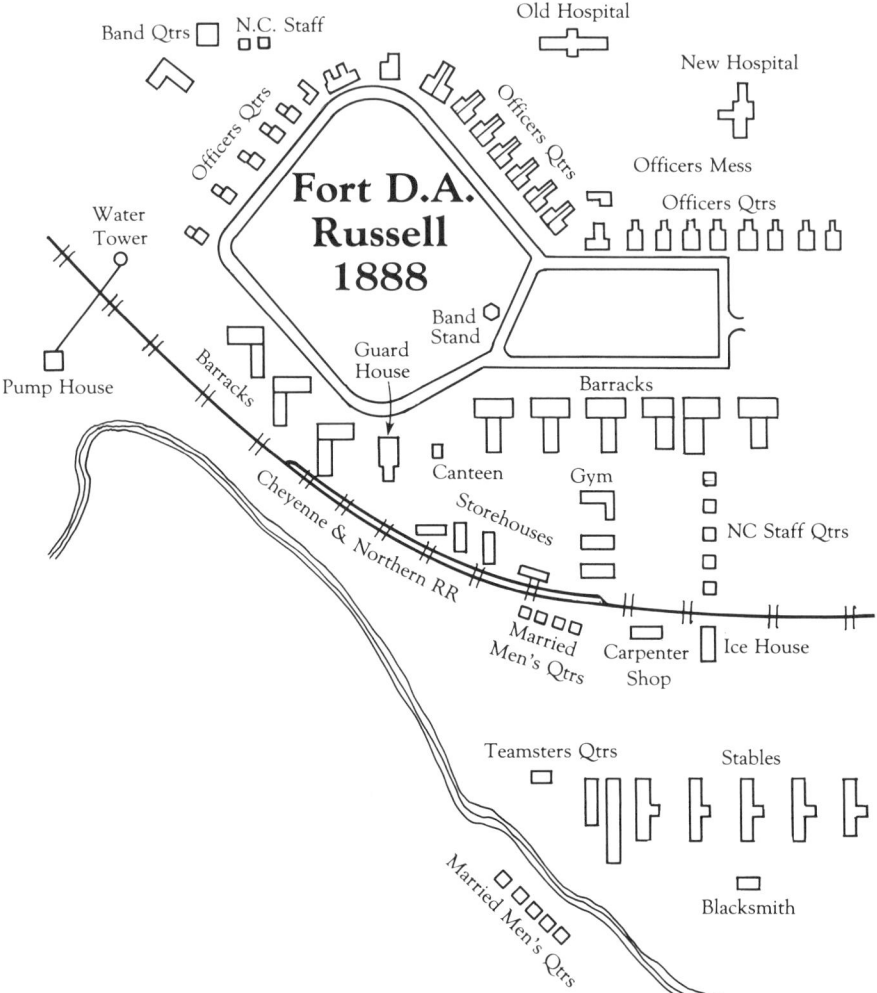

When new permanent brick officers' family houses and enlisted mens' barracks were started in 1884 for an eight company regiment, the new buildings were sited to the south and east of the original parade ground. Most of the old temporary wood buildings, hastily constructed in 1867, were moved or demolished by 1900.

the Ninth Infantry Regiment's move from Fort D.A. Russell became a fact. In July the regiment rotated to Arizona. Their departure from the Cheyenne train station was reported to be a tearful one. No quarters or facilities for families were available in the part of Arizona that the Ninth Infantry was headed for. Wives and children remained in Cheyenne or returned to their hometown and family. The regimental band played the traditional departure piece "The Girl I Left Behind Me" as the troop train pulled out of the station heading for the Arizona border.

1. *Cheyenne Daily Leader*, August 5 and October 5, 1883.
2. *Cheyenne Democratic Leader*, March 3, 1886.
3. *Cheyenne Democratic Leader*, February 11, 1886.

Nine of the eleven newly built captains' quarters are shown in this 1885 photo from the road that ran from Cheyenne through the post to the ranches west of the post. The wire fence in foreground protects the yards of the captains quarters from errant buggies and horsemen.—*WY State AMH Dept.*

Chapter Eleven
Scaling Down To Size:
A Single-Regiment Post

Eight companies of the Ninth Infantry Regiment had been stationed at Fort D.A. Russell for two years in 1886. Indeed, only units of that regiment garrisoned the post for the previous year. The western army's past practice of having companies from two or more different regiments stationed together at one post had finally ended. Henceforth, all the companies of a regiment would be stationed together under their colonel and regimental headquarters, or as many companies of a regiment as a post could possibly accommodate.

Eight companies of the Seventeenth Infantry Regiment, Colonel Alexander Chambers commanding, arrived from the Department of the Dakota in July to replace the Ninth Infantry and remained for the next eight years as the single regiment at Fort D.A. Russell. The people of Cheyenne were delighted to read the announcement soon after the regiment arrived that the band would play every evening except Saturday at six o'clock. A dress parade would follow the band concert, except on Saturdays and Sundays, and everyone was invited.

The outfit barely had time to settle in when Brigadier General Crook arrived in August. Local authorities did not find an opportunity to discuss moving Crook's headquarters from Omaha to Cheyenne. Crook was much more concerned about the continuing unrest among the Ute tribes in Colorado, where he had just visited. The *Leader* printed an interview with Crook on August 29, 1886, in which the veteran campaigner voiced some gloomy views of the situation with the Ute Indians.

Fort D.A. Russell had maintained one or two companies at the Camp on Milk Creek from after the 1879 uprising until 1883, when the camp had been closed. Now it seemed likely that they would be going back again if the six companies in and about the northern Ute territory became hard pressed.

Despite Crook's concerns, political problems in Wyoming Territory were rapidly becoming more important than military problems. Fort D.A. Russell's good friend, Francis E. Warren, had his appointment as territorial governor of Wyoming terminated in November 1886, when President Grover Cleveland (1885-1889 and 1893-1897) appointed Democrat George Baxter to that position. Baxter, an 1877 graduate of West Point, resigned his commission in 1881, while serving as a lieutenant in the Third Cavalry at Fort D.A. Russell, and entered the cattle business. In a short time he gained extensive land and cattle holdings as well as political stature in the Democratic party. His tenure as territorial governor ended after six weeks, when he resigned under pressure. Baxter had been accused of fencing government land, a practice quite common in Wyoming but one that President Cleveland wanted stopped. Thomas Moonlight suceeded Baxter as territorial governor in January 1887. A Democrat from Kansas, Moonlight had attained the rank of colonel and served as commander of Fort Laramie for a short time during the Civil War. He visited Fort D.A. Russell frequently as an official and unofficial guest.

A troop of black cavalry arrived at Fort D.A. Russell from Fort Robinson in June 1887 and camped on Crow Creek between Cheyenne Depot and the post. Their presence created concern in Cheyenne. "Buffalo Soldiers" had not been stationed at Fort D.A. Russell before. They were believed to be there on a fence cutting expedition. Recent press reports had announced that President Cleveland had ordered troops to Cheyenne to open all wire fences in southeast Wyoming that enclosed government land. The black soldiers camped on Crow Creek because Fort D.A. Russell had no room in their barracks for another outfit; the Seventeenth Infantry had eight companies on post, which filled the existing barracks.

Although locals feared the worst, the fence cutting expedition did not materialize. When the cavalry troop departed, the October 19, 1887, edition of the *Leader* carried this tribute:

> The soldiers of the command conducted themselves admirably while camped near and frequently visiting the city. . . . Although every resident of this section had solemnly resolved to hate and detest the colored troops before their arrival, they first tolerated them, but contempt soon turned to respect.

The Cheyenne Depot mule pack train moved the black cavalry troop back to Fort Robinson, taking about three weeks for the round trip. Their departure coincided with the gathering of regiments in the department for summer training, a practice started by a previous department commander, Brigadier General O.O. Howard. The 1887 summer exercises were significantly reduced, with local exercises replacing the large-scale maneuvers. The Seventeenth Infantry marched two companies at a time from Fort D.A. Russell to the Natural Fort seventeen miles south for seven days of maneuvers. Usual garrison duties occupied the eight companies of the Seventeenth Infantry for the remainder of 1887.

The year 1888 started with the sad news of the death of the Seventeenth Infantry commander, Colonel Alexander Chambers, on January 2 in San Antonio, Texas. He had been ailing and was on sick leave. An old-timer, as were most regimental field grade officers, Colonel Chambers had graduated from West Point in 1853 and performed with distinction in Civil War and Indian war campaigns. The new commander, Colonel Henry R. Mizner, also a Civil War veteran, had served in the western army for much of his career. Colonel Mizner would lead the Seventeenth Infantry very ably for two and a half years before he retired.

Shortly after Mizner assumed command, the fort gained its own post office. In January 1887, Mrs. Lucinda Lester, wife of Sergeant Major Lester of the Seventeenth Infantry, received an appointment as postmistress. The army had sent a soldier courier daily, except Sunday, to carry the mail from the Cheyenne post office back to the units at Fort D.A. Russell. This means of acquiring the mail had not been without difficulty. It required four days for a letter from New York to reach Cheyenne, and it could take even longer to be received at Fort D.A. Russell. On one occasion the mail courier had his mount stolen by a Colorado horse thief while collecting the mail from the Cheyenne post office. At other times wagons broke down, horses ran away, soldier mail couriers stopped to have a drink and forgot the mail, all of which contributed to the post's mail delivery problems. Establishing the Fort D.A. Russell post office quickly solved many of the postal problems, and the volume of business soon dictated that a money order office be added.

The new post office fit in nicely with the rebuilding of Fort D.A. Russell. The press inspected the new work at the fort in April 1888 and reported that about twenty new buildings had been completed, all of good brick and stone. Those new buildings included the "best hospital in the department," eight company barracks, seven brick officers' quarters with four more under construction, and some field officers' quarters that the reporter described as large two-story mansions. The Seventeenth Infantry Club, referred to as a canteen or resort for enlisted men, received high marks from the press for providing a pleasant facility and atmosphere. Beer, light wines, and tobaccos (no hard liquor) were sold, and receipts totaled $40,000 over a seventeen-month period. All profits of the club were distributed to the units for the benefit of the enlisted men. The officer's club then, as now, found great difficulty in showing a profit.

Some of the cash flow problems of the officers' club stemmed from an absence of many of the officers for extended periods. Detached service to other parts of the country continued to take away several officers of the regiment. Also summer training and maneuvers absented the officer corps for most of the good weather months. For example, Brigadier General John R. Brooke, who succeeded Crook in Omaha, introduced a summer encampment called the Camp of Instruction at Kearney, Nebraska. The eight companies of the Seventeenth departed Fort D.A. Russell on August 10. They marched 335 miles to Kearney, attended the Camp of Instruction, then marched back, arriving on October 18. The soldiers declared that they had enjoyed the summer camp, but Cheyenne was glad to see them back at the post, particularly the band.

The announcement of General Philip H. Sheridan's death on August 5, 1888, saddened many old-timers at Fort D.A. Russell and in Cheyenne who had campaigned with him during the Civil War and in the Indian wars. Sheridan had always met with his old friends and reporters on his many visits to Fort D.A. Russell, and a full account of his views would appear in print. During his last visit on March 22, 1887, Sheridan had inspected the troops and then attended a reception in his honor given by Colonel Alexander Chambers. All the officers of the regiment and their ladies were there to say hello. He then proceeded to Denver to select the site for a new army post there, Fort Logan. A reporter concluded his account of Sheridan's visit with this observation: "The general is in fair health, but the tide of time begins to show itself and it is plain to be seen that even 'Little Phil' is growing old."[1]

A brighter note reached the garrison in September 1888 with the Department of the Platte's announcement that henceforth troops would be paid monthly, another of the improvements army leaders had been advocating for years. In the late 1860s through the 1870s, paydays were irregular, even though they were supposed to occur at intervals not longer than every three months. Paymasters were sometimes stationed at Fort D.A. Russell and sometimes in Omaha, but the task remained the same. The paymaster drew a considerable amount of currency from headquarters in Omaha and then carried it to all the posts and camps in the department to give each officer and enlisted man the amount due him, by regiment and company. Payday often occurred unexpectedly, but it was always a joyous occasion. Commanders suspended training and nonessential acitivities for a day or so, permitting the soldiers to pay their bills and spend what little money they had been able to retain from the pay table.

Armed mounted escorts were vital for paymasters when traveling from one post to another with bags of money. Numerous road agents and stray Indian bands looked for targets such as paymasters. A disagreement sometimes developed between the paymaster and the escort officer as to who commanded the escort, but in one case it did not matter. The paymaster, Major Daniel N. Bash, and escort stopped for lunch at Antelope Station north of Fort D.A. Russell and left the payroll bag containing $7,500 in the carriage. While they were inside the station, a cowboy identified as Charles Parker dashed up, grabbed the payroll valise, and galloped away. Parker was later apprehended but not with the payroll.

The inauguration of Benjamin Harrison as president of the United States in March 1889 was soon followed by the nomination of Francis E. Warren for governor of Wyoming Territory. The Fort D.A. Russell and Cheyenne communities welcomed the news. Warren's interests were in Wyoming ranching, real estate, and banking. Fort D.A. Russell's interests would be closely guarded for the next forty years by the new territorial governor, sworn in on April 9.

Summer camp for the Seventeenth Infantry in 1889 took place at Camp George Crook located near Fort Robinson, Nebraska, not far from the Oglala Sioux Pine Ridge Indian Reservation. The regiment departed the post in early August, moving part of the way by train and marching the rest of the way where rail lines had not yet been completed. They were joined by other regiments for maneuvers and target practice. In late September, the Seventeenth Infantry returned to Fort D.A. Russell and to the routine of "usual garrison duties."

The building of north-south railroad lines, including the Cheyenne and Northern, greatly decreased the need for a large quartermaster supply depot at Fort D.A. Russell. Rumors had been afloat for months predicting the closing of Cheyenne Depot. A newspaper article in August 1889 proposed making the depot a commercial manufacturing center for military equipment. This article seemed to strengthen the closure of Cheyenne Depot rumors, which soon proved all too true.

1. *Cheyenne Democratic Leader*, March 22, 1888.

Built at the same time as Fort D.A. Russell and with similar temporary wooden structures, Cheyenne Depot in 1886 had deteriorated but continued to provide quartermaster supplies to the northern posts and reservations. The Cheyenne and Northern Railroad began hauling freight to the north that year, greatly reducing the number of wagon trains required by the depot. It was closed, along with many frontier posts, by 1890.—*WY State AMH Dept.*

PART IV
CHEYENNE DEPOT, QUARTERMASTER SUPPLY, 1867-1889

The headquarters of Cheyenne Depot oversaw the supply of upwards of fourteen army posts to the north and west of Fort D.A. Russell, along with various Indian tribes and agencies. The headquarters building shown in mid-1880s was sold and moved into Cheyenne after the depot was deactivated in 1889.

Chapter Twelve
Also Known As
Camp Carling Or Carlin

When Lieutenant General W.T. Sherman directed in the spring of 1867 that a military post and general supply depot be established near the proposed line of the Union Pacific Railroad at the eastern base of the Laramie Mountains, he prophesied the vital role each facility would serve. "From this point for many years all the posts north along the eastern base of the Rocky Mountains will have to be supplied."[1]

In mid-August 1867, a location for the supply depot was selected close to the town on Crow Creek midway between Cheyenne and the parade ground of Fort D.A. Russell. Captain Elias Brown Carling of the Quartermaster Corps, breveted a lieutenant colonel during the Civil War and invariably referred to as Colonel Carling or Carlin, served as the first commander. The depot carried quartermaster supplies, including clothing, equipment, and most everything else needed by the army in the West. Ordnance and subsistence were later added as sub-depots to the Quartermaster Depot.

Captain Carling began immediately to build an organization and facility to provision some fourteen military posts, plus several units operating in the field. As the large warehouses were completed along what would soon be a railroad siding, they housed supplies that arrived by wagon train from the end of the rapidly advancing rail line. When the Union Pacific reached Cheyenne on November 13, 1867, work started immediately on the spur line to the warehouses at the Cheyenne Depot, but another month passed before it would be finished. Then supplies could be unloaded directly from the boxcars into the warehouse.

When the Cheyenne Depot got into full-scale operation at the end of 1867, it proved to be almost as good a source of cash to Cheyenne as the pay of soldiers at Fort D.A. Russell. While the army purchased many items from eastern markets, many commodities such as grain, hay, vegetables, coal, wood, cattle, horses, and other supplies were locally purchased. This not only saved time and transportation costs but procured fresh goods. Deep cellars were dug for storage of potatoes and other vegetables to keep them through the winter. Local purchases by the depot helped build up

Cheyenne Depot, also known as Camp Carling or Carlin after its first commander, served as a quartermaster supply center for the army posts and Indian reservations in the northern High Plains from 1867 to 1889. Supplies arriving from the east on the Union Pacific Railroad would be freighted north by wagon train. The end of the Indian Wars negated the need for the large supply depot.

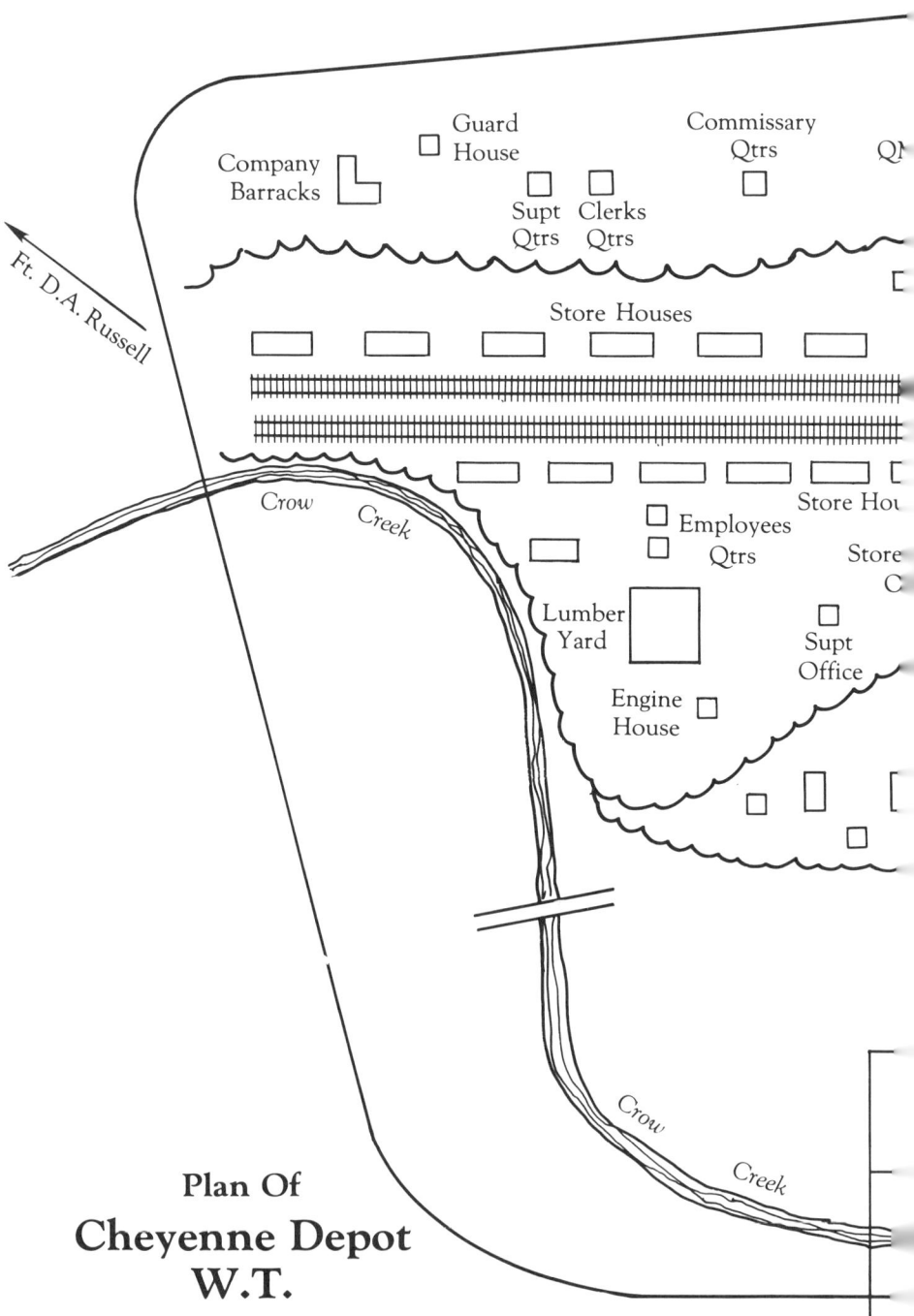

Plan Of
Cheyenne Depot W.T.

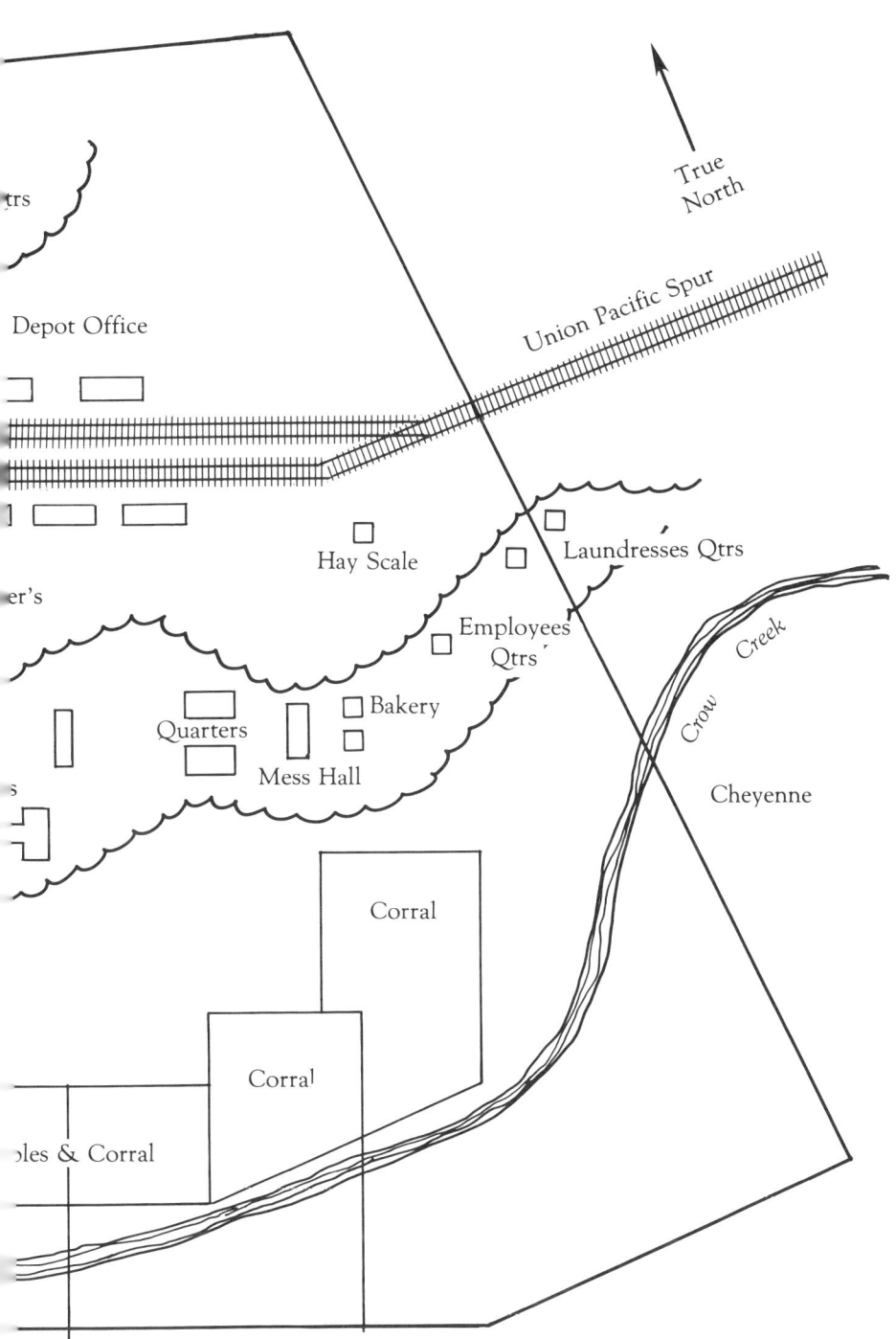

Cheyenne's economy and promoted the sale of agricultural farm products and even small manufactured items. Many of Cheyenne's early citizens appear on the contract registers doing business with the depot in those early days. Not only did the depot quickly become a good market for Cheyenne contractors and merchants, it also provided a good place to see friends. The well-traveled road from Fort D.A. Russell to Cheyenne ran through Cheyenne Depot, a convenient and friendly stopping place.

Wagon trains, usually operated by drayage contractors, hauled the supplies from the Cheyenne Depot north to the military posts and other destinations that included designated Indian agencies. The government's ability to issue annuity goods (food and clothing) offered a strong incentive for Indian tribes to stay on not necessarily friendly terms but not actively hostile terms either.

In order to help keep the tribes calm, these goods were delivered regularly by wagon trains that were usually pulled by oxen, but mules were also used. Even though they were slower, civilian contractors preferred oxen because they could haul heavier loads, needed less grain, and were not likely to stampede from their night pasture. Nor were the oxen as tempting for Indians to steal. An ox team usually had twelve to fourteen yoke to pull three wagons. The front wagon carried 15,000 pounds of cargo, the second 9,000 pounds, and the third wagon carried cooking utensils, tents, and food for the drivers. The tongues of the second and third wagons were cut short and chained to the hind axle of the wagon in front.

A military escort accompanied the loaded wagon trains from Cheyenne Depot for protection from Indian and white raiders. One hundred wagons and five mule pack trains, for the rougher terrain, remained in constant use. Food, ordnance, and military equipment constituted "high value" cargo on the western frontier and would be quickly stolen by various parties if not guarded. Troops from Fort D.A. Russell provided the necessary guard detail for the depot warehouses and wagon trains going north from the depot until 1873. Then a detached company of mounted infantry became a part of the depot's military complement. An infantry or cavalry unit was detailed to Cheyenne Depot until 1882, when the need for close protection diminished. On some early wagon train journeys no military escort could be provided, and then the civilian bullwhackers, or wagon train drivers, had to defend their wagons as best they could. On those occasions they more than earned their pay.

Besides the guard detail, Cheyenne Depot had a military commander and a small cadre of military supervisory personnel. The civilians employed by the Quartermaster Corp performed most of the day-to-day operations of the depot, and that force fluctuated frequently from 500 to as many as 1,000 over the twenty-two years of its existence. The civilians provided the skilled maintenance, supply, and transportation expertise required to operate the largest army supply depot in the West. Maintenance shops in the depot included blacksmith, wheelright, carpenter, saddle and harness, plus others. There were also cook and bunk houses to operate along with wagon sheds, stables, and corrals required for such a supply center. The responsibilities of the Cheyenne Depot were extensive and vital to the army in the northern High Plains. The Quartermaster Corps procured clothing and equipage, erected and maintained all buildings, purchased and shipped all forage and fuel, and saw to the transportation of troops. The Subsistence Department, operating under the quartermaster, purchased all food supplies and prescribed the basic daily rations. The Ordnance Department, also under the quartermaster, developed, tested, and delivered all arms, ammunition, and combat materiel to the fighting forces in the West.

The subsistence sub-depot at Cheyenne Depot supplied forts Russell, Fetterman, and Laramie with fresh vegetables secured from markets near the post and from farmers in Colorado. For example, 450,000 pounds of fresh vegetables were purchased during the first year in operation, 1868. The most common method for supplying fresh beef was to purchase the cattle on the hoof from local ranchers or dealers and drive them to the destination post. Then that military unit would graze the animals near their post until needed.

A lot of supplies were required from the Cheyenne Depot in the mid-1870s to support the army in the field as the Indian campaigns peaked. Supplies left the depot by wagon train for the northern posts on a scheduled basis, and wagon trains also accompanied the military expeditions that took to the field for extended periods. The extensive campaigns of 1876 and 1877 required constant shipping of supplies to a good many posts and units in the field. Supplies were going out by wagon train as fast as they were received by railroad train. The wagon trains always had to be ready to move on short notice.

Indeed, when Colonel J.J. Reynolds led the Third Cavalry from Fort D.A. Russell in late February 1876 toward northern Wyoming in that ill-fated winter campaign, the wagons and pack trains started then from Cheyenne Depot and continued until late fall when the 1876 campaign started to wind down. Without those vital supplies, army units in the field would have soon been helpless against the hostile Indian tribes.

The 1880s saw the building of railroads that could haul supplies and reinforcements rapidly to the north, thus eliminating the need for long-haul wagon trains and the Cheyenne Depot. By the late 1880s most of the northern Indian tribes were living on reservations, and many of the frontier army posts supplied from Cheyenne Depot had been closed. When rumors arose that Cheyenne Depot might also close, a scheme surfaced locally to make the depot a manufacturing center for army equipment and keep it open. This proposal did not receive a warm reception from the army. Consequently, Cheyenne Depot as a quartermaster facility did close in September 1889. Five other army installations in Wyoming Territory had recently suffered the same fate.

Five years after the Cheyenne Depot closed as a quartermaster depot, an 1894 newspaper article revealed that the site had become the central holding area and training ground for the army's mule pack service. Here the men and mules were organized, trained, and dispatched to the areas needing their services. Pack trains were sent to units located throughout the Rocky

Mountain area and to the various army commands in Texas, Arizona, and other areas of the southwest. Thomas Moore, who was designated chief packer of the United States Army and referred to by the reporters as Colonel Moore, headed the pack train service. Reporters liked Thomas Moore and mentioned him frequently. An article in the *Leader* on February 28, 1893, reported that Colonel Thomas Moore, chief packer and master of transportation for the U.S. Army, and his seven assistants, were now back at Camp Carlin after having been away for several months. Moore had served with the army in the West as scout and packer for forty years, and on several occasions with General George Crook, whom he knew well. Moore had lived with his family at Cheyenne Depot for twenty years.

When the Cheyenne Depot closed, the army attached Moore to Fort D.A. Russell, but he continued to work and live at old Cheyenne Depot, or Camp Carlin, with his wife and daughter. Thomas Moore and his pack train served in almost every one of the Indian campaigns between 1870 and 1896 as far away as Arizona, Utah, Idaho, Montana, and the Dakotas.

When Moore died in 1896 at his home at Camp Carlin at the age of sixty-four, his funeral in Cheyenne was reported to be the largest ever seen in the city, with an impressive turn-out from Fort D.A. Russell, including the commander, Colonel James J. Van Horn. Moore lies buried in Lakeview Cemetery, Cheyenne.

Thomas Moore and a white mule named Steamboat are two of the legendary figures that remain an important part of Cheyenne Depot history. According to Mr. Russell L. Tracy, who worked at the depot for several years during the 1880s, "everybody" at Camp Carlin would remember Steamboat. The white mule would, without a driver, bring a buckboard from the stable to the quartermaster's office every morning and stand waiting patiently hour after hour to be used. When the five o'clock bell rang, Steamboat would turn the buckboard, and with head up and tail rising, gallop to the barn and his oats.

Most of the depot buildings were used by Fort D.A. Russell until 1901 when they were sold and moved or torn down. None of the buildings survive today in their original location. Only a stone marker, installed and dedicated in 1927 by the Daughters of the American Revolution with the name "Camp Carlin" inscribed, stands at the former flagpole site as a reminder of Cheyenne Depot.

Another fragment of the depot, the long-forgotten Carlin Cemetery, was discovered in 1935 when workmen uncovered four caskets at 906 Dodge Court in the western edge of Cheyenne when laying a water line. No records could be found of the burials and identification could not be established. The bodies were moved to unmarked graves in Lakeview Cemetery.

Few remains of the old depot can be found today. Nor is it certain when or why the depot became known as "Camp Carling" or "Camp Carlin." In 1867, the army designated the general supply depot at Fort D.A. Russell as Cheyenne Depot. However, the teamsters and other civilian employees were soon calling it Camp Carling or Carlin. The name came from Captain Elias Brown Carling, who served as the first depot commander. Active in early Cheyenne church and civic affairs, his name appeared frequently in the Cheyenne newspaper columns in connection with good causes and the Episcopal Church. It is likely that the name "Camp Carling" or "Carlin" was taken from the popular first commander as an expedient to avoid mixup. Using the name "Cheyenne Depot" or "supply depot" could have sounded similar to the Union Pacific Railroad's train station, also called the "Cheyenne depot."

Although his name stayed on, Captain Elias B. Carling suffered an early and inglorious end. Carling had served at a number of posts after leaving Cheyenne Depot in 1869. He had been assigned to Fort Sanders near Laramie only a short time when this item appeared in the *Leader,* July 1, 1875: "Col. E.B. Carlin, Quartermaster at Fort Sanders, Wyoming, committed suicide last night by cutting his throat from ear to ear. Financial embarrassment and complications of his official affairs are assigned as the cause." More information appeared in the following day's edition:

> Capt. Carlin's Death—The people of Cheyenne will deplore the rash act which terminated the life of Capt. Carlin, late quartermaster at the Cheyenne Depot, which in our early history was called after him, Camp Carlin. Sad stories of late have been circulated in regard to the unfortunate Captain; but as death has cast his mantle over him, we would willingly forget his failings and foibles, and remember only his good qualities while among us.

While it is easy to see that the name "Camp Carling" or "Carlin" came from the original commander, Captain Elias Brown Carling, it is not so easy to see why it would continue to be used after his suicide in 1875. Perhaps the bullwhackers, the many other civilian employees of the depot, and the Cheyenne newspapers are responsible for keeping the name alive, much as they were for adopting it earlier.

A romantic aura has hung over the long-abandoned quartermaster depot. Many of the civilian employees stayed in Cheyenne after the depot closed. A number of those former employees, as well as their children and grandchildren, became prominent Cheyenneites. Perhaps there lies the source of this romanticism.

Regardless of the additional names it acquired, its important twenty-two-year role as a general supply depot gives it a niche in western history, but as a part of the much longer history of Fort D.A. Russell where it happened to be.

---

1. General W.T. Sherman. *Personal Memoirs of Gen'l W.T. Sherman,* Vol. 2 (New York: Charles L. Webster Co., 1891), p. 42.

A group of some fifty "cattlemen" departed from Cheyenne in 1892 for Johnson County in northern Wyoming to take measures designed to protect their cattle against theft. Irate citizens surrounded the "invaders" at the TA Ranch near present-day Buffalo and threatened to eliminate them. A detachment of cavalry from nearby Fort McKinney came to the rescue and forty-three of the invaders were

PART V
CLOSING OUT THE NINETEENTH CENTURY, 1890-1899

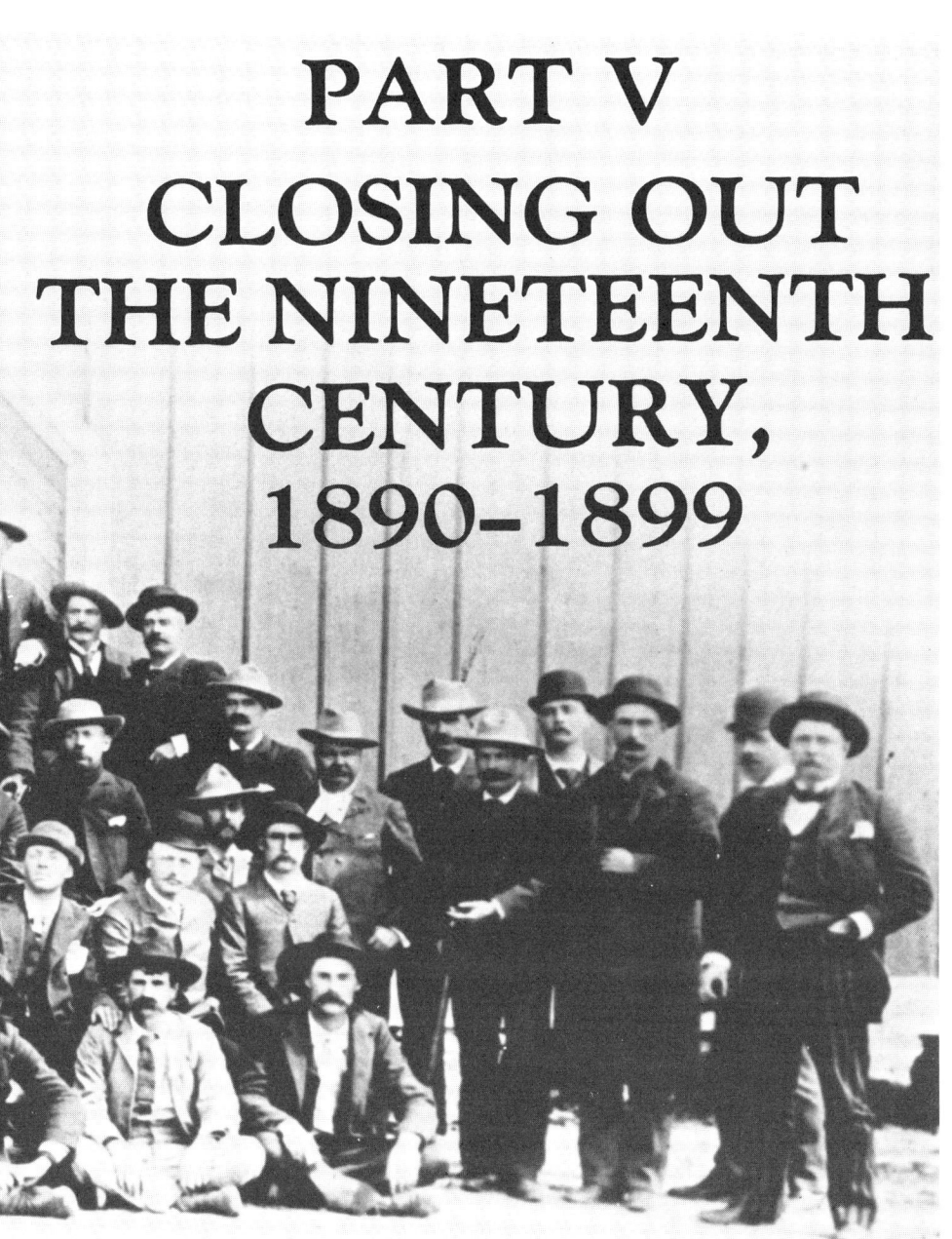

escorted to Fort Russell where they were held for trial. Prominent area ranchers included E.W. Whitcomb (standing fourth from left), expedition leader Frank Wolcott (standing seventh from right), W.E. Guthrie (standing sixth from right), W.C. Irvine (standing fifth from right), and John Tisdale (standing second from right).—*F.E. Warren AFB Base Museum Collection*.

Wyoming rancher and legislator Colonel Jay L. Torrey organized the Second United States Cavalry Volunteer Regiment of 842 mostly Wyoming citizens in 1898 and trained them at Fort D.A. Russell for action against the Spanish. Colonel Torrey sits his horse in front of his headquarters building, now the F.E. Warren AFB Base Museum.—*F.E. Warren AFB Base Museum Collection*

Chapter Thirteen
Wounded Knee, The Johnson County War, And War With Spain

The national census of 1890 declared that a western frontier as such could not be defined. The unsettled area had been so broken up by settlement that a frontier line no longer existed. The very word "frontier" had earlier been difficult to define; it meant different things to different people as the westward settlement proceeded, depending on the period and the purpose. Some considered the frontier as being at the leading edge of the settled territory or the line of settlement, while others looked on it as the start of free land. It was also considered an area by some. Encouraged by the railroads and the Indian move to reservations, continuing settlement of vacant lands had helped to populate the area behind the westward-moving frontier line. However, the Indian problem still remained far from resolved. With the western frontier no longer defined in the minds of the American people, a false sense of having solved "the Western Problem" settled into the halls of Congress. The future of the army in the West was now questioned more sharply than ever.

In his annual report to the secretary of war in 1890, Commander-in-Chief of the Army Major General John M. Schofield (1888-1895) made a number of points that would serve as guidelines for the army in the West for the rest of the decade. First, he said that the Indians now needed wise, just, and humane treatment on their reservations in the presence of such military force as would deter the young and restless among them from imitating the deeds of their ancestors. He also recommended that the army be stationed so that it could respond quickly to any call for its services, including assistance in preparing the militia of the several states for service in time of need. (Cheyenne had shortly before organized a company of militia designated Company B.) Situated as it was on the east-west and north-south railroads, Fort D.A. Russell seemed ideally located to respond to conditions of the 1890s. Its future appeared secure, at least for the time being.

The eight companies of the Seventeenth Infantry stationed at Fort D.A. Russell were mainly occupied with garrison duty. Company B drew the ice detail, or the task of cutting and hauling enough ice from Sloan's Lake to the post ice house to last until the next winter. Other companies participated in the ongoing building renovation program. While many other forts and camps in Wyoming had closed, Fort D.A. Russell's prospects for remaining active looked good. In July 1890, the United States Senate passed a bill providing for the disposal of the abandoned Wyoming military reservations of forts Fetterman, Laramie, Sanders, Steele, and Bridger. The Senate stipulated that military reservation lands would be disposed of under the terms of the Homestead Law, thus making them available to farmer and rancher settlers instead of the land speculators.

For the men who remained at Fort D.A. Russell, no long marches or extended exercises were scheduled during the summer of 1890, except for a sixty-six-mile practice march in September. The Seventeenth Infantry's Company F transplanted trees on the post and repaired the irrigation system that watered the parade ground. The commander of Company F, Captain Clarence E. Bennett, also assumed responsibility for the post garden, while Captain William M. Van Horne, commander of Company A, took charge of the post canteen. The routine of the regiment changed suddenly in mid-December, just when winter had set in and everyone looked forward to Christmas. Orders came to take to the field.

A religious movement among the Indians called the "Messiah Craze" and "Ghost Dance," started by a Paiute Indian in Nevada named Wovoka, had spread to the Sioux in Dakota, where it took on militant overtones. Reports of the northern Sioux bands gathering at the Pine Ridge Reservation of the Oglala Sioux in the early fall brought additional troops to Fort Robinson, Nebraska, near the reservation, as a precautionary measure. The Department of the Platte commander, Brigadier General John R. Brooke, had proceeded to the Pine Ridge Reservation with cavalry in late November and found the Indians very excited. Short Bull, the Sioux prophet of the messiah at Pine Ridge, exhorted the Sioux to not be afraid of anything but to continue the dances.

The mood of the Sioux provided a threatening situation. When Sitting Bull, the Hunkpapa Sioux Chief, was killed by Indian police at the Standing Rock Agency while en route to the Pine Ridge Reservation on December 15, 1890, the situation deteriorated rapidly. The next day, December 16, 1890, the Seventeenth Infantry Regiment at Fort D.A. Russell received orders to proceed to Fort Robinson without delay.

Nine companies of the regiment with twenty-one officers and 237 enlisted men, plus the mule pack train led by Thomas Moore, moved northward on the Cheyenne and Northern Railroad and then east to Fort Robinson over the recently completed Fremont, Elkhorn and Missouri Valley Railroad. The trip took only twenty hours, quite a difference from the weeks previously required by wagon train. Only Company F remained at Fort D.A. Russell to guard the post and perform garrison duty.

After reaching Fort Robinson, units of the Seventeenth Infantry marched north into South Dakota to take positions at various strategic locations. They hoped to divert other Sioux bands away from the Pine Ridge Reservation and prevent them from gathering with Red Cloud's people there. A large group of Minniconjou Sioux under Chief Big Foot was intercepted on Wounded Knee Creek north of Pine Ridge by the Seventh Cavalry from nearby Fort Meade on December 29. A fight erupted when the troopers attempted to disarm the Indians. Casualties included 146 Indians and twenty-five Seventh Cavalry members. This unexpected engagement ended the "Ghost Dance" movement, and the Seventeenth Infantry returned to their barracks at Fort D.A. Russell in early February 1891 without casualty. The Battle of Wounded Knee marked the close of Indian tribal warfare on the northern High Plains.

The sad news of the death of General William T. Sherman in New York on February 15, 1891, seemed to add a note of finality to the era of the Indian wars. Sherman had retired in 1884 as commander-in-chief of the army, having served in the position for fifteen years. A frequent visitor to Fort D.A. Russell in the late 1860s and 1870s when he commanded the Division of the Missouri and then headed the army, he had many army and civilian friends and admirers on the post and in Cheyenne. He last visited Fort D.A. Russell with President Rutherford B. Hayes in September 1880. Sherman had exercised a tremendous influence on the army in the West and on the entire military establishment. That influence would be seen for the next fifty years.

The Seventeenth Infantry commander, Colonel Henry R. Mizner, who rode with Sherman on his march through Georgia to the sea during the Civil War, presided at the memorial service held by the Grand Army of the Republic in Cheyenne. He concluded his remarks with this tribute to his former commander: "Sherman was a great general, a distinguished citizen and a friend true as steel. He was a man, take him all in all; I shall not look upon his like again."

An announcement from Washington in March 1891 caused a stir at Fort D.A. Russell and in Cheyenne. It said that 2,000 Indians would be enlisted in the army immediately. They would make up troop L of each of the cavalry regiments, except the Ninth and Tenth, and Company I of each of the infantry regiments, except the Sixth, Eleventh, Fifteenth, Nineteenth, Twenty-fourth, and Twenty-fifth; fifty-five for each troop and company. English not essential. The Seventeenth Infantry did not receive any Indian recruits or units for reasons not known. This experiment continued for several years with varying degrees of success. No Indian units were ever stationed at Fort D.A. Russell, with the exception of Major Frank North's Pawnee Battalion there for short periods during the twelve years they were used by the army, 1867-1877. Some Indian soldiers belonging to the regiment at Fort Sidney, Nebraska, were reburied in the Fort D.A. Russell cemetery when Fort Sidney closed.

While Fort D.A. Russell could not claim any Indian companies in its ranks, it could count at least one troublesome medic. The post surgeon filed an unusual lawsuit against the post and regimental commander in May 1891. The lawsuit pertained to the long-debated issued of army medical officers practicing medicine in towns near the posts they were assigned. Colonel Mizner had asked for Captain A.H. Appel's removal as post surgeon because he maintained an office and medical practice downtown in Cheyenne. Mizner also charged Appel with showing up late for work at the post hospital, and leaving early. To cap it off, Mizner said Appel was socially acceptable only by virtue of his commission. Mizner retired from the army on August 1, 1891, having reached the mandatory retirement age. The Cheyenne newspaper report did not say what success Captain Appel had with his lawsuit.

Colonel John S. Poland succeeded Mizner as post and regimental commander. His first few months of command were uneventful; in August he led the regiment on a march out Happy Jack Trail to Laramie City, where, at Camp Barber, the Wyoming State Militia Encampment provided summer training. The Seventeenth Infantry joined the state militia in maneuvers for a week and then marched back to Fort D.A. Russell. The regular army's help and encouragement in training newly organized state militia units proved to be a vital ingredient in their success. The fort's well-known mule pack train accompanied the regiment.

After the quiet winter with ten companies of Seventeenth Infantry on the post, the regiment received orders in April 1892 to send a detachment by rail to Douglas, Wyoming, and accept forty-three civilian prisoners, stockmen and their employees. The prisoners had been escorted to Douglas by an Eighth Infantry detachment from Fort McKinney in northern Wyoming. The Seventeenth Infantry detachment picked up the prisoners at Douglas and escorted them to Fort D.A. Russell, arriving on April 24, 1892. Thus ended the stockmens' unsuccessful attempt to control the range, now known as the Johnson County War.

The prisoners were the remains of a well-armed force organized in Cheyenne by the Wyoming Stock Growers Association (WSGA) and sent north to deal with rustlers and others believed to be usurping the stockgrowers' domain. Tabbed the "Invaders," the WSGA force had run into stiff opposition from angry local residents at the TA Ranch a few miles south of Buffalo, Wyoming, and had become besieged. At the behest of the governor of Wyoming and the congressional delegation, President Benjamin Harrison ordered federal troops to intervene. A rescue force from Fort McKinney, led by Colonel James J. Van Horn of the Eighth Infantry, proceeded to the TA Ranch, lifted the siege, and took the Invaders into custody. The stockmen expected a speedy and "proper" resolution to their arrest once they reached Cheyenne.

The prisoners were housed under guard in the post bowling alley at Fort D.A. Russell, with some of the more prominent stockmen being given the freedom of the post. All of the prisoners were allowed visitors. Not until August were they admitted to bail on their own recognizance. A trial date was set and delayed several times. When the prosecuting county declared they were without funds for a trial, the case was dismissed. The Johnson County War and its aftermath had provided some excitement for the communities of Cheyenne and Fort D.A. Russell during a period of the 1890s when little else seemed to be happening. Even such things as the daily routine of the Seventeenth Infantry at Fort D.A. Russell sparked interest when it appeared in the press.

The *Leader* published a letter from a Fort D.A. Russell soldier on April 17, 1892, which presented in some detail the daily schedule and reflected the attitudes and regime of an army enlisted man in the West during the last twenty years of the nineteenth century. Titled "The Daily Doings of a Regular Army Enlisted Man," the introduction included several "old army" cliches that had been around a long time but had never proven to be very trustworthy, including these two: "Quiet men are the best soldiers when there is fighting to do" and "Few hardships in the army for those who do right." The soldier's letter focused on the daily routine at Fort D.A. Russell, which was similar to that at other army posts.

5:45 Morning gun followed by fall-in, reveille roll call. Breakfast follows.

7:30 Surgeon's call is announced and the first sergeants conduct the sick of each company to the post hospital where the attending surgeon examines them.

7:30 Fatigue call is also sounded and the men detailed to fatigue duty (usually two or three from each company) report to the quartermaster sergeant and are assigned to the necessary work such as hauling and delivering coal and forage and other work about the fort.

9:00 Guard mount ceremony; the old guard is relieved by the new. The guard at Fort Russell consists of two officers, four non-commissioned officers and sixteen privates, and the men have to go on only about once in eight or nine nights (seven or eight nights in bed). In day time, only one sentinel is on post but the guard is generally kept busy with the working parties of prisoners. At night five sentinels are on and in stormy weather it is no picnic. The sentries are kept constantly alert calling out the half hours and looking out for the officers who may be around any minute, and woe be to the man caught napping or even not vigilant at his post.

10:30 Drill. If the weather is bad, it is held in quarters.

11:40 First Sergeants' call. First Sergeants report at post headquarters for orders, details for the next day, etc. Recall from fatigue duty sounds just before dinner, which comes at noon. School call notifies the men, mostly recruits, who are required to attend school, that they must report to the school teacher, also enlisted men, and study until 3:30. Attending school is a regular duty and a man can be punished for absence or misconduct, just as for any other military offense. A commissioned officer has general charge of the schools, and there being also one for the children.

1:00 Fatigue call sounds again and the details go out to work till 5 o'clock.

5:15 Supper call.

Sunset Retreat, roll call or dress parade, if the weather is favorable, is at sunset.

10:45 Call to quarters.

11:00 Non-commissioned officer in charge of quarters goes to each man's bunk and sees that all are present and reports absentees to the officer of the day; the long drawn notes of "taps" are sounded by the musician of the guard, and the day is over. Such is the regular routine at this season of the year, but dozens of men are detailed on extra duty as teamsters, carpenters, painters, gardeners, etc., and each company has a cook, clerk, tailor, sometimes a shoemaker and barber. Then there must be men to run the canteen, bakery, printing office, and engine house, help in the commissary and quartermaster store house, serve as clerks at headquarters and elsewhere, and attend to duties too numerous to mention.

The garrison schedule served as a daily habit for most soldiers with little need for a clock to remind them what came next. A full and active schedule served a useful purpose in keeping the soldiers in fighting trim. Army units remained remarkably strong throughout the Indian wars period despite a high desertion rate, epidemics, and hardships that caused most civilians to wonder why a soldier would stay with it. But stay with it many of them did even though pay remained very low and promotions came very slowly. The career soldier, one who had served more than one three- or five-year enlistment, provided the experience and strength of most units. Their off-duty activities or social life formed the part of soldiering that the civilian community found hard to understand. Bachelors formed a majority of the enlisted force, and their social life defied organization at times.

According to one veteran of the Indian wars, Lieutenant Colonel George A. Forsyth, enlisted members of one company seldom sought friends or associates outside of their own company. Members of two regiments on the same post often were comparative strangers to each other, and particularly so if they were infantry and cavalry. The barracks room where the men were quartered represented their home and their most important room; other facilities such as orderly room, the store room, and library were merely adjuncts to the barracks room.

But life outside the post did matter to the soldiers of Fort D.A. Russell; as an example, in mid-August 1894, long-standing grievances against Cheyenne Marshal T. Jeff Carr surfaced. The *Leader* on August 10, 11, and 12, 1894, reported on a growing list of soldier complaints of their treatment in Cheyenne. Soldiers were afraid to come to town for fear of arrest on trivial matters. The newspaper charged, "The troops at Fort Russell, officers and men, have a serious grievance against Cheyenne." The article reported that men were buying civilian clothes to wear when they had to come to Cheyenne to avoid being arrested by Marshal Carr. Soldiers were avoiding the town like a "pest house." The newspaper included a reminder that about $6,000 per month was paid to the enlisted men of the post, the greater part of which stayed in Cheyenne. Marshal Carr denied the *Leader*'s allegations, but the city must have been paying attention; it did not continue his employment for long.

An important part of the "usual garrison duty" when troops were on post included rifle target practice. The recognition of good shooters played an important part in that program, and Fort D.A. Russell always had its share of highly qualified marksmen. In a regimental ceremony in November 1893, Sergeant Park B. Spencer of Company E, Seventeenth Infantry, received the Distinguished Marksman's Badge from the regimental commander, Colonel John S. Poland. The award had been won at the Army Rifle Competition held annually at Fort Sheridan, Illinois, where Sergeant Spencer had represented the regiment.

In the early days at Fort D.A. Russell, target practice with rifle and revolver had a priority, but not a very high one. The heavy escort and patrol demands on assigned units, plus the annual summer campaigns, made it difficult to find the time for target practice. Also, target practice required additional ammunition, which cost money, and military appropriations were sparse after the Civil War. Another consideration, the arms and ammunition in the pre-1890 period were less reliable, and target practice meant earlier failure or wearout of the arms.

In the years shortly after the Civil War, the army converted thousands of the Civil War muzzle loaders to breechloaders, first as a .50 caliber weapon and later as a .45-caliber weapon using a metallic cartridge, with single-shot capability. This Springfield rifle proved to be a significantly improved weapon for both the infantry and cavalry. The horse soldiers usually used the shortened carbine version since it was easier to handle on a horse. The army ultimately selected the .45-caliber cartridge as the most desirable for rifles and pistols. The cavalry troopers carried a rifle and revolver while the infantrymen relied solely on their rifles. The 1889 model of the Springfield rifle embodied the final modification of this single-shot large caliber black powder gun.

In 1893, the army bought a Danish-designed rifle, the Krag-Jorgensen .30-caliber bolt-action piece, which held five cartridges in a magazine. Manufactured at the Springfield Armory in Massachusetts, the Krag had been issued throughout the regular army by the mid-1890s, and it served for the next ten years. A suicide at Fort Russell in April 1895 with a rifle (not an easy thing to do) confirmed that the regiment had been equipped with the Krag.

Although the Indian wars were over for units at Fort D.A. Russell and the new five-shot Krag rifle was not an immediate asset, the mid-1890s found units moving east, west, and south for varying periods to quell domestic turbulence. Four companies of the Seventeenth Infantry were ordered to Green River, Wyoming, in May 1894 to assist federal marshals there in protecting railroad property threatened by the Commonweal Movement, also known as the Commonwealers and Coxyeites. A railroad workers' strike against the Pullman Company in Chicago also erupted in 1894 and quickly spread to include Wyoming and Colorado. The nationwide strike had been called by the American Railway Workers Union, which was headed by Eugene Debs. Most of the strike violence occurred in the Chicago area, but the potential for violence existed in many railroad towns, including those in Wyoming. Two companies of the Seventeenth Infantry were ordered to Pueblo, Colorado, and additional companies went to Rock Springs, Wyoming, and Pocatello, Idaho.

As the labor turmoil intensified, more army units of the Department of the Platte were ordered out to guard the railroad. The commander of the department, Brigadier General John R. Brooke, had orders to keep open the Union Pacific line. Army units were scattered all along the railroad, and soldiers were put aboard all trains. Brooke was considered general manager of the Union Pacific system for the period of this strike. Not until late summer did the rail strike wind down to the point the companies of the Seventeenth Infantry could return to Fort D.A. Russell.

The Seventeenth Infantry had barely found time to unpack when they received change-of-station orders to Columbus Barracks, Ohio. Three companies of the regiment would remain at Fort D.A. Russell for another year and then join the regiment in Ohio. Before leaving for Ohio, the regimental commmander noted in his annual report that the Seventeenth Infantry had been on the western frontier twenty-five of the last twenty-eight years. He also noted that the brick barracks, now barely ten years old, were too small—below standard for space and air per man. Kitchens and dining rooms were old and dilapidated. He said they might last until the post was abandoned. It appeared that Colonel Poland did not have much confidence in the future of Fort D.A. Russell.

The concentration of army units near the big eastern cities, a policy inaugurated by the secretary of war and announced in September 1894, did sound ominous for the future of Fort D.A. Russell. The majority of the army regiments had been located in the West after the reconstruction occupation ended in the South after the Civil War. Now a regional balance was being sought for the peacetime deployment of the nation's small army. Such cities as Washington, D.C., St. Louis, New York, Atlanta, and Columbus, Ohio, were mentioned as recipients. More western posts were to be abandoned, and again Cheyenne's concern arose that the number of soldiers at Fort D.A. Russell might be scaled down or even worse, the post might be closed.

Cheyenne's concern soon lessened when five companies of the Eighth Infantry, plus the headquarters and band, arrived at Fort D.A. Russell in October 1894 from Fort McKinney and settled in for a four-year stay. Colonel James J. Van Horn, who had rescued the Invaders at the TA Ranch in April 1892, still commanded the regiment.

The units at Fort D.A. Russell spent an uneventful winter, with the usual garrison duties. Lieutenant General John M. Schofield, commander-in-chief of the army, and party visited Fort Russell in June three months before his retirement. He received a warm reception at the post and in Cheyenne. Major General Nelson Miles, a distinguished Civil War veteran who had also served for many years in the West, would replace Schofield in

September.

Startling reports began emanating from Jackson Hole in northwest Wyoming in late July, 1895, when 300 Bannock Indians reported to be full of fight showed up on the Hoback River. The Bannocks felt they had a treaty right to hunt in Jackson Hole. The secretary of war ordered the newly appointed commander of the Department of the Platte, Brigadier General Joseph J. Coppinger, to proceed at once to the scene of the trouble and to order such movement of troops as necessary. One newspaper reported sixteen families massacred by the "red devils" in Jackson Hole. Five companies of Fort D.A. Russell's Eighth Infantry, under command of Major William H. Bisbee of the Seventeenth Infantry, were dispatched by railroad to Market Lake, Idaho, and then marched to Jackson Hole. The Fort D.A. Russell pack train with sixty-four mules and escort wagons followed the Eighth Infantry. Some Shoshoni and Lemhi Indians had been reported joining the Bannocks in Jackson Hole. But no confrontations or encounters occurred with the Indians, and in September Coppinger informed the secretary of war that the Indians were not to be blamed for the trouble in Jackson Hole. Not long thereafter, all units of the Eighth Infantry returned to Fort D.A. Russell from Jackson Hole, back in their barracks by mid-November 1895.

The two companies (B and F) of Seventeenth Infantry still at Fort D.A. Russell departed in October for Columbus Barracks, Ohio, to join the regiment. This move permitted the two companies (B and G) of the Eighth Infantry at Fort Niobrara, Nebraska, to join the regiment at Fort D.A. Russell. The usual garrison duties with regular practice marches and target practice occupied the Eighth Infantry at Fort D.A. Russell throughout 1896 and 1897. Detachments of about company strength continued to be dispatched to Camp Pilot Butte at Rock Springs, Wyoming, for one and two months' temporary duty from Fort D.A. Russell and Fort Douglas, Utah.

The army's post canteen system had survived a challenge from the state of Nebraska when the court decided that Fort Robinson had a right to sell liquor to the soldiers through the canteen. Consequently, Fort D.A. Russell's canteen continued to do just fine. The army also started a standardization process of all canteens and changed the name to post exchange, or PX.

With the Indians settled on reservations and a relative quiet prevailing over the nation, the army at Fort D.A. Russell now had time for organized recreation programs. No gymnasium had yet been built, but the multi-purpose "post hall" served as a gym, and also as theater, chapel, and reception hall for social events. Each company now kept a library in their barracks, and the post maintained a library room. The department commander's annual report for 1896 summed up the situation at Fort D.A. Russell by saying that military operations of the year had not been eventful.

The next year found units frequently on the move, and considerable distances were traveled. In September 1897, a detachment of Eighth Infantry, consisting of two officers and twenty-five men, headed by

Lieutenant Colonel George M. Randall, traveled to Saint Michael, Alaska, for temporary duty. One Hotchkiss gun accompanied the detail. Three months later, the pack train, consisting of ten packers and sixty-two mules was ordered to Vancouver Barracks, Washington, from which location they proceeded on to Alaska. The pack train expected to carry supplies forty miles from Dyea, Alaska, to Chilkoot Pass, where supplies would be taken on into Dawson by reindeer. The packs would consist of 300 pounds per mule.

From the frozen north, attention soon turned to the tropics. With the declaration of war with Spain in April 1898, the Eighth Infantry left Fort D.A. Russell on April 20 for Chicamauga Park, Georgia, an assembly point for units to be used in invading Cuba. The Eighth Infantry left one officer, Lieutenant Charles Gerhardt, and nineteen enlisted personnel to man the post for the next four months, until another regular army unit could be assigned. The Eighth Infantry detachment at Camp Pilot Butte was relieved from duty there to join the regiment in Georgia.

In addition to serving as post commander for the next four months, Gerhardt had charge of the Quartermaster Department, the commissary, ordnance, post exchange, and post schools, and acted as post treasurer. This very busy officer also served as range officer, post engineer and signal officer and had charge of post hospital property.

In May 1898, four companies of Wyoming National Guard from four different towns were called up and assembled at Fort D.A. Russell. After a short stay, the four companies moved to San Francisco for further movement in June to the Philippine Islands. There they participated with distinction in the Battle of Manila, which occurred on August 13, 1898, the day after the armistice had officially ended the war.

Another Wyoming outfit, the Second United States Volunteer Cavalry Regiment, was mustered into service at Fort D.A. Russell in May and quartered until June 22, 1898, when it left for Jacksonville, Florida, and thence to Cuba. Commanded by a Wyoming rancher and state legislator, Colonel Jay L. Torrey, the regiment acquired most of the 934 troopers and 656 horses in Wyoming, but some came from Colorado. Misfortune plagued this regiment after it left Wyoming, and it soon became known as a "hard luck" outfit. A train wreck at Tupelo, Mississippi, killed five Wyoming troopers and injured fourteen more, including Colonel Torrey. When the regiment reached Jacksonville, Florida, they went into camp in the swamps and fever struck. They never reached Cuba. Torrey's regiment returned to Fort D.A. Russell soon after the peace declaration in August for "mustering out." Disbandment had been completed by October 1898, two months after the declaration of peace. Six of the regiment's dead—one from the Tupelo train wreck, four from fever in Florida, and one from another illness—were returned to Wyoming in April 1899 for burial in the Fort D.A. Russell Cemetery.

Several histories have been written on the sister regiments, the First and Third United States Volunteer Cavalry regiments, but comparatively little on the Second other than scattered press and periodical articles. Theodore

Roosevelt's leading the First United States Volunteer Cavalry up San Juan Hill has sparked many historical accounts of that regiment.

In September 1898, while the Second still had some mustering out to do before disbanding, a new outfit arrived to garrison the post—four companies of the Twenty-fourth Infantry, a black regiment fresh from action in Cuba. The new commander of the post and the Twenty-fourth Infantry contingent, Captain William H.W. James, was a twenty-six-year veteran of the regiment. Captain James relieved the beleaguered Lieutenant Gerhardt of his many duties in late September. Six companies of the Twenty-fourth Infantry continued on west to Fort Douglas, Utah. Rumors that a black outfit would be assigned to Fort D.A. Russell had preceded the arrival of this unit, and the Cheyenne press had expressed some concern. No black regiments had previously been assigned to Fort D.A. Russell. However, a troop of the black Ninth Cavalry had camped between Cheyenne Depot and Fort D.A. Russell for four months in 1887 and enjoyed a cordial association with Cheyenne. Camp Pilot Butte had been empty for several months, and orders arrived in October for a company of the Twenty-fourth Infantry to move their for temporary duty. Rock Springs felt that they still needed the army to keep the peace between the miners and the Union Pacific, even though it would not be a white unit at the camp.

Although President William McKinley did not sign the peace treaty with Spain until February 10, 1899, the postwar army reduction started immediately after the cessation of hostilities in August. In January and February, 529 soldiers of the Twenty-fourth Infantry at Fort D.A. Russell were discharged, men who had enlisted for the duration of the war. An unusually high sick list prevailed during the winter months, running from 10 to 20 percent of the 400-plus assigned. A part of this rate could be attributed to the various illnesses brought back from Florida and Cuba, and a part to the eagerness for discharge of those who had signed up for the duration.

Replacements for the men discharged in January and February were rapidly procured, and in March two companies (E and I) of Twenty-fourth Infantry at Fort D.A. Russell moved on to the Philippine Islands. A native insurrection there had blossomed into guerilla war against American troops. The two remaining companies (C and F) stayed at Fort D.A. Russell until May, when they were ordered to Mullon Lake, Idaho, for a short time. Indian unrest in Idaho had caused the authorities to call for army units to preserve order there. Those two companies left Idaho and joined their regiment in the Philippines in June.

Troop B of the First Cavalry Regiment arrived at Fort D.A. Russell on June 19, 1899, to garrison the post for the remainder of the nineteenth century. Captain Jacob G. Galbreath, who had joined the First Cavalry in 1873 fresh out of West Point, commanded Troop B and Fort D.A. Russell. One of his lieutenants, Louis Smith, served as post surgeon, and the other one, D. Barkley, functioned as adjutant, signal officer, recruiting officer, post engineer, summary court officer, post commissary officer, and post quartermaster. Additional units were not expected to arrive, because large numbers of army occupation units were needed in Cuba and the Philippines. Now that the most pressing crisis that faced the nation since the Civil War had been resolved, it behooved the nation's civil and military leaders to take stock of the situation and decide how to start the twentieth century.

With the war over, the army and Congress could again critically review the requirements for western army posts. It was expected that the review would take a severe toll in army strength and number of installations. It

Company D, Second United States Cavalry Volunteer Regiment pictured in front of their barracks #209 at Fort D.A. Russell entrained for Florida in June 1898. A train wreck in Mississippi killed five Wyoming troopers and injured many others

must have been a surprise when in March 1899 appropriations for new buildings at Fort D.A. Russell were approved; construction would start in the summer. This decision did much to bolster community morale. The temporary frame officers' residences built in 1867–1868 on the north side of the parade ground would also be torn down and replaced with larger brick quarters. It seemed that Fort D.A. Russell would move into the twentieth century while most of the other Wyoming army posts passed into history.[1]

1. *Cheyenne Daily Leader*, February 21, 1891.

including Colonel Torrey. After many weeks in the Florida swamps, the regiment returned to Fort D.A. Russell and mustered out of service in October 1898.—*F.E. Warren AFB Collection*

Noted Wyoming photographer J.E. Stimson recorded the newly constructed houses on "officers row" in 1908 from the second-story porch of a barracks on Randall Avenue. A parade ground separates the enlisted mens' barracks from the officers row.—*WY State AMH Dept.*

PART VI
THE "NEW" FORT
D.A. RUSSELL,
1900–1909

When President Theodore R. Roosevelt (1901-1909, sixth from left) traveled the west in 1903, Senator Francis E. Warren, (third from left) invited the president to detrain at Laramie and ride the fifty-six miles over the mountains to Fort D.A. Russell on horseback. Departing Laramie early in the morning of May 30, with several prominent Wyomingites, the group paused at the Van Tassel ranch for lunch, then in Telephone Canyon, to have this picture taken. Wyoming Governor Fenimore Chatterton and post commander, Major Harry L. Bailey, Second Cavalry, welcomed the president on the outskirts of Fort D.A. Russell and escorted him to a reception on the post while the artillery saluted with twenty-one guns. Other members of the group on horseback are left to right: W.W. Daley, Otto Gramm, Senator Warren, N.K. Boswell, Joe LeFors, President Roosevelt, Surgeon General Rixey, Frank A. Hadsell, Fred G. Porter, W.L. Park, Seth Bullock, and John Ernest.—WY State AMH Dept.

Chapter Fourteen
The Post Expands
To Brigade Size

The heavy demand for American occupation troops in the Philippine Islands and Cuba after the Spanish-American War ended kept the western army posts low on manpower. Troop B, First Cavalry Regiment, with three officers and 109 men garrisoned the post in January 1900. While new building construction continued as a part of the program started in 1884 (three new brick family officers' quarters were completed in October 1900), the post's future remained uncertain. With the departure of Troop B for China in July and the arrival the next month of two lightly manned companies of the Twenty-third Infantry, the population of Fort D.A. Russell fell lower. Only two officers and seventy-seven men were at the post in September 1900 to receive Vice-president Theodore Roosevelt when he visited Fort D.A. Russell and Cheyenne.

The building construction program continued through 1900, and in July 1901 a sale of most of the old buildings remaining from the 1867 period attracted a good number of buyers from Cheyenne. The sale included eight family houses, the original hospital building, the canteen and canteen ice house, plus other structures. Buyers included such distinguished local citizens as J.M. Carey and L.R. Bresnahan. Most of those buildings were moved to Cheyenne.

In September the Thirteenth Battery of Field Artillery joined the post, the first field artillery unit to be assigned to Fort D.A. Russell. There would be field artillery units on the post most of the time for the next forty years. The two companies of Twenty-third Infantry soon left Fort D.A. Russell, one to take station at Fort Logan, Colorado, and the other to Fort McPherson, Nebraska. Not until October 1901 did the post population grow significantly to around the 500 level with the arrival of four companies of the Eighteenth Infantry, which had spent three years in the Philippines. The regiment and its commander, Colonel James M.J. Ganno, received a warm welcome from Cheyenne on arrival. The regimental band of twenty-seven pieces probably got the best reception of all when they gave a concert on October 23, 1901, at the post bandstand. The band promised to repeat their performance every day that week at 3:30 P.M., weather permitting.

During the rest of 1901 and well into 1902, the manpower level remained at about twenty-two officers and 500 men. The units remained busy with the usual garrison duties, practice marches, target practice, and training the many new recruits received. A renewal of the earlier Hayes administration's prohibition edict appeared in February 1902, when Congress banned the sale of beer and light wines at all post exchanges. In his annual report, the secretary of war expressed his disagreement with that congressional edict. He said it would cause the enlisted men to leave the military posts more often and they would be exposed to bad booze. The secretary apparently did not have much influence with the Congress on this issue, for the beer and wine ban in post exchanges stayed in effect.

The prohibition issue would not matter to Fort D.A. Russell if the post closed. However, a pleasant surprise appeared in February 1902, when a published report revealed that a board of high-ranking military officers charged to consider the future of all military posts had recommended Fort D.A. Russell be designated a permanent post with a full regiment of infantry and a battery of artillery assigned. More good news followed with the announcement that more new family quarters and barracks would be built, including a fine mansion for the post commandant. The newspaper gave full credit to the work of Senator Francis E. Warren, third senior member in the Senate Military Affairs Committee. The article predicted that "stupendous improvements" were going to be made at Fort Russell, making it one of the best military posts in the country.

While the stupendous improvements were yet a promise, the post did soon have a comfortable complement of units assigned. Troop E of the Tenth Cavalry, a black regiment, and the Thirteenth Battery of Field Artillery plus four companies of Eighteenth Infantry "held down the fort" for the summer and fall of 1902. Even though black units of cavalry and infantry had been stationed at Fort D.A. Russell before, Troop E proved to be a particularly popular unit. Having just returned from three years' service in the Philippines, they were pleased to be at Fort D.A. Russell. Borrowing a page from other Wild West shows, the annual Cheyenne Frontier Days celebration at Frontier Park in 1902 had Troop E rescuing a stagecoach being attacked by "redskins." The Indians had been recruited from the Arapaho and Shoshoni tribes on the Wind River Reservation in central Wyoming. Witnesses reported that their performance looked real enough to be frightening.

Two- and three-day practice marches and target practice occupied the Eighteenth Infantry units during the fall of 1902. Most of the marches were made west from the post out Happy Jack Road to the Wood and Timber Reserve, an area in the Laramie Mountains set aside in 1880 for forts Sanders and D.A. Russell, and redesignated the Crow Creek Forest Reserve in 1900.

The Eighteenth Infantry traveled to Fort Riley in October to participate in the large-scale army maneuvers being held there, the most extensive war games in the history of the army, according to one newspaper report. These exercises brought together many regiments for the first time for a two-sided mock engagement with umpires and judges present. Organized and integrated field training for regiments and their staffs could be gained. The army also started bringing state militia/National Guard units into the large-scale field operations to give them experience in working with the regular army units. Large-scale army maneuvers were a new innovation, made possible by a more generous budget from the Congress and a rail transport system that could bring different types of units together quickly, with their equipment, from scattered areas for one to two weeks training. The increased global responsibilities of the United States in the twentieth century made large-scale army maneuvers a prudent part of the nation's new strategy and international image.

The post's uncertain future during the previous two years had contributed to a water dispute with Cheyenne that erupted in late 1902. All new construction work on the post stopped pending arrangements, if possible, for Fort D.A. Russell to receive a satisfactory water supply from the Cheyenne water system. When the difficulty was finally resolved, Cheyenne's mayor-elect M.P. Keefe, who was also a building contractor, received a go-ahead for construction of two artillery barracks at a price of $230,000. Four months later, the quartermaster opened bids for construction of ten new buildings, including officers' and NCO quarters, stables, barracks, a commissary storehouse, and gymnasium. Some facilities included in the new gymnasium were a lunchroom, bowling alley, shooting gallery, and toilets in the basement. The gymnasium would be on the ground floor, and on the third floor would be a reading room, study room, classroom, billiard room, and running track 170 feet in length. The newspaper declared that the Fort D.A. Russell gymnasium would serve as a model for all other army facilities.

Units at Fort D.A. Russell in 1902 were destined to move before they could enjoy the new gymnasium or its attractive facilities. The Eighteenth Infantry's four companies departed for the Philippines in March 1903 and were replaced three months later by four companies of Second Infantry. When the announcement appeared that the new stables would be built on the banks of Crow Creek, angry protests arose from Cheyenne. The feeling prevailed, with good cause, that Crow Creek already carried an overload of animal refuse. In response to the clamor, the army erected the stables some distance from Crow Creek and took other measures to reduce animal refuse from that important stream. A crematorium south of Crow Creek for burning horse manure would be constructed.

Military and civilian leaders alike were anxious to show President Theodore Roosevelt the "new" Fort D.A. Russell in 1903. During a tour of the West, Roosevelt had been invited by the Grand Army of the Republic and the Spanish-American War Veterans in Cheyenne to speak to them. Roosevelt detrained at Laramie on the morning of May 30 and joined a party of prominent Wyoming citizens on horseback for the fifty-mile ride across the Laramie Mountains to Fort D.A. Russell. Arriving at 4:00 P.M., the president was met and welcomed about three miles northwest of the garrison by Wyoming Governor Fenimore Chatterton and Post Commander Major Harry L. Bailey, Second Infantry. A twenty-one-gun salute fired by the Thirteenth Battery of Field Artillery greeted the president as he rode onto the post. The commander, officers, and officers' ladies gave President Roosevelt's party tea and cakes. The president and governor reviewed the troops on horseback and then led the procession for the three-mile march to the speaker's platform in Cheyenne. The president delivered his memorial address to an audience of ten thousand on a vacant quarter block in the center of town.

Undoubtedly the president "learned" during his visit of the plan to enlarge the post's land holdings. Wyoming's Senator Warren had labored hard in Washington to have the Crow Creek Forest Reserve transferred from the Interior Department to the War Department. The forests would still be protected under the Warren plan. The army supported the land acquisition proposal as a future training reserve. Regiments could conduct large-scale maneuvers here in mountainous terrain.

With such plans afoot as the year 1903 neared an end, talk of abandoning Fort D.A. Russell had been replaced by the attention focused on the new construction program. The post had received even more appropriations for several additional buildings. The army's second in command, Major General Henry C. Corbin, visited Fort D.A. Russell in late summer 1903 and declared the progress of new construction satisfactory and the location ideal for the large and growing post.

Nineteen officers and 435 men garrisoned the post as 1904 began. They belonged to Troop E, Tenth Cavalry, the Thirteenth Battery of Field Artillery, and four companies of the Second Infantry. An administrative procedure transferred Fort D.A. Russell from the Department of the Colorado, headquartered at Fort Logan, back to the Department of the Missouri, with its headquarters at Fort Omaha. A reorganization in the 1890s had realigned the military districts and in some cases renamed them, placing Fort D.A. Russell in the Department of the Colorado for a few years.

The eight companies of Eleventh Infantry arriving from the Philippines in March 1904, plus their headquarters staff and band, received a grand welcome by the post and town. The four companies of the Second Cavalry and Troop E of the Tenth Cavalry left Fort D.A. Russell in a change of station soon after the arrival of the Eleventh Infantry. This left the post garrisoned for the rest of 1904 with eight companies of the Eleventh Infantry and the Thirteenth Battery of Field Artillery, a total post complement of about thirty officers and 600 men.

Both infantry and field artillery units held target practice and maneuvers during the summer months on the Crow Creek Forest Reserve, redesignated in 1904 as the Fort D.A. Russell Target and Maneuver Range. Along with the new construction program, more modern utilities appeared; it was announced that "electric rays" would begin to illuminate the streets of Fort D.A. Russell on the evening of December 9, 1904. Although electricity had been installed in the brick family quarters and barracks as early as 1884, oil lamps had continued to be the means of illuminating the streets prior to this time.

Interest in the enlarged Fort D.A. Russell drew the attention of the army chief of staff, Lieutenant General Adna R. Chaffee, and he paid a visit. General Chaffee had served as a junior cavalry officer at several western posts after the Civil War, including Fort D.A. Russell. A public reception at the post hall on August 9, 1904, welcomed General Chaffee. He had many old friends at the fort and in Cheyenne who attended his reception.

General Chaffee had as one of his many goals annual large-scale army maneuvers. However, maneuvers cost a lot of money, and the general had to be satisfied for the time with an every-two-year participation for most regiments. The Eleventh Infantry missed the annual Fort Riley maneuvers in the summer of 1904 but instead engaged in frequent practice marches to the Fort D.A. Russell Target and Maneuver Range and to points as distant as Laramie and Fort Collins.

Pollution of Crow Creek with animal refuse from Fort D.A. Russell had long been a problem to downstream Cheyenne. In 1902 the army constructed a "crematory" on the post south of Crow Creek to burn the refuse from several hundred horses and mules that belonged to the infantry, cavalry and artillery units assigned.—*WY State AMH Dept.*

Participation of military personnel (cavalry preferred) and Indian tribes in Cheyenne's annual Frontier Days celebration has long been an important part of each year's event. Fort D.A. Russell's black horse troop and artillery caissons appeared in the parade and the arena with Indians from the tribe invited by the Frontier Days committee that year to participate. Historically friendly with settlers and the army, the Shoshoni Tribe from the Wind River Reservation in central Wyoming posed for this photograph in Frontier Park in 1902. Other tribes participated in later years to include the Arapaho from the Wind River Reservation and several tribes of Sioux from North and South Dakota reservations.—*WY State AMH Dept.*

The Department of the Missouri commander, a Brigadier General William H. Baldwin, visited the post in late summer and in an interview protested the government's continuing prohibition of wine and beer at post exchanges. He attributed the increased desertion rate to the fact that soldiers had no place on-post to go and buy a beer. He felt that sales of wine and beer would be a great help in alleviating a growing troop morale problem. All the saloons and brothels springing up near the posts ruined good soldiers, according to General Baldwin.

The number of buildings on the post continued to increase, and in late December 1904, the number of troops also rose when an additional company of the Eleventh Infantry arrived from Fort Niobrara, Nebraska, to take station. This made nine companies of that regiment at Fort D.A. Russell. The post had grown beyond the eight-company post so designated in 1884. More new units continued to arrive; in January 1905 the Eighth Battery of Field Artillery transferred from Vancouver Barracks, Washington, to take station. This made two batteries on post, the Eighth and Thirteenth, with six pieces of artillery and 114 horses. In April 1905, Company L, Eleventh Infantry, arrived from Fort Washakie, Wyoming, to join its parent regiment. Fort D.A. Russell now had ten companies of Eleventh Infantry and two field artillery batteries. Later in the year, the two artillery units traveled to Fort Sill, Oklahoma, for firing practice and returned with a new cannon, the 3-inch breechloading field piece that replaced the 2.2-inch gun.

Along with all the barracks, stables, family quarters, and administration buildings being built, the electric (arc) street lights improved the appearance of the post at night. Many other good things enhanced life at Fort D.A. Russell in 1905. The announcement on March 28, 1905, that Senator Francis E. Warren would become chairman of the Senate Committee for Public Buildings and Grounds provided an encouraging sign that the building program would continue. An announcement the next month that a large riding hall would soon be under construction brought forth a declaration by the Cheyenne press that Fort D.A. Russell's facilities would soon exceed those of Fort Myer, Virginia, and Fort Leavenworth, Kansas, recognized as the leading military installations in the United States. Later in the year, Senator Warren became chairman of the Senate Military Affairs Committee, one of the most influential bodies in the Senate and a position he retained for the next twenty-five years.

When the Cheyenne Northern Railroad built north from Cheyenne in 1886 through Fort D.A. Russell, they installed a depot to handle military passengers and freight. The depot survived until after World War II.—*WY State AMH Dept.*

The rare Falcon cannon and Bells of Balangiga, war trophies brought to Fort D.A. Russell by the Eleventh Infantry from the Philippines in 1904, initially rested near the flagpole on the original parade ground. As the post expanded eastward, the trophies and flagpole were moved to a more central location in Trophy Park where they remain.—*National Archives*

Chapter Fifteen
Large-Scale
Summer Maneuvers
At Pole Mountain

In May 1905 when the Eleventh Infantry had been at Fort D.A. Russell a little over a year, this item appeared in the Cheyenne press:

> The parade ground will soon have a new saluting gun and several other relics brought from the Philippine Islands by the regiment, to include the famous bell which gave the signal for the massacre of a whole company. The gun and bells will be placed on a concrete foundation near the flat mast.[1]

The bells and cannon remained on display on the east parade ground until 1925, when they were moved to Trophy Park, more centrally located on the eastward-expanded base. Some seventy-five years after its arrival at Fort D.A. Russell, the "saluting gun" became famous when finally identified as an English Falcon cannon cast by Robert Owen at the Hounsditch Armoury near London in 1557. The cannon bears the escutcheon of Queen Mary I, having been cast during her short reign; it is believed to be the only such cannon extant.

A more modern type of artillery was involved in an unfortunate accident that occurred at the Fort D.A. Russell Target and Maneuver Grounds in August 1905, when the Eleventh Infantry and the two batteries of field artillery, Eighth and Thirteenth, were on maneuvers. A 3.2-inch artillery shell exploded in camp, killing two soldiers and injuring several others. The Eleventh Infantry, under the command of Colonel A.L. Myers, returned to the post soon after the accident, in time for the annual Cheyenne Frontier Days celebration. They staged a sham battle in front of the Frontier Park stands for everyone to see, and their performance proved to be the hit event of the show.

Annual reports to higher headquarters highlighted any fatal accidents that occurred, such as the exploding 3.2-inch artillery shell at the Target and Maneuver Range. But an interesting commentary of a different nature appeared in the 1905 annual report of the commander of the Department of the Missouri, Brigadier General T.J. Windt. It reflected the essence of the life and times of the American soldier in the early twentieth century,

137

including those stationed at Fort D.A. Russell. General Windt did not believe soldiers should marry and sought to discourage army chaplains from performing wedding ceremonies unless the soldier had obtained his commander's permission to marry, not an easy task. The base pay of a soldier had not improved from the thirteen dollars a month set soon after the Civil War. Said General Windt, "The marriage of a soldier after he enlists destroys his status." General Windt represented a dying segment of old-timers who apparently believed in the adage, "if the United States Army wanted a soldier to have a wife, it would issue him one."

The status of families in the army would not improve for many years. The Eleventh Infantry had not been back in the United States long enough to have acquired many wives when early in 1906, the rumor started that the Eleventh Infantry would soon return to the Philippines. This was a distasteful prospect indeed for a regiment that had been home for less than two years. In April the regiment received orders to depart for San Francisco on May 1, and it seemed that the rumor had become a fact. However, these orders turned out to be only temporary duty—San Francisco had been hit by a mighty earthquake. The entire equipage of the unit—including tents, mobile kitchens, and first-aid stations—was moved to San Francisco, where the Eleventh Infantry assisted in distribution of food, policing of the city, providing health care, and many other disaster area tasks. The regiment returned to Fort D.A. Russell on July 9, 1906, in time to take part in the large-scale maneuvers planned for the summer.

The army had long felt that regiments of the infantry, cavalry, and artillery should be brought together periodically for field exercises that would integrate the units and staff. Restrictions on such exercises had been caused by such considerations as funds and land areas that could accommodate such large exercises. Wyoming's Senator Francis E. Warren's fine hand could be seen earlier in the year when a local headline proclaimed, "Senator Warren Has Been Promised a Brigade of Regulars For An Encampment on Crow Creek." The front-page article explained that the Fort D.A. Russell Target and Maneuver Range would be the scene of extensive military maneuvers in the future. Senator Warren had assurances from President Roosevelt and the secretary of war that the next big encampment of troops in the Rocky Mountain country would be here, in southeast Wyoming.

Senator Warren's growing influence could also be seen in the improved prospects of his son-in-law's army career, Captain John J. Pershing. Pershing married Warren's only daughter, Frances, in a gala Washington wedding on January 26, 1905, attended by the president and most of Washington society. A month later speculation in the press had it, and rightly so, that Pershing would soon be promoted from captain to brigadier general over 910 senior army officers.

Senator Warren's popularity and influence also brought a series of high-level visitors to Fort D.A. Russell in 1906, including Secretary of War William Howard Taft. The secretary concurred with Warren's efforts to expand Fort D.A. Russell to a brigade-size post. Such a move would amount to a more than three-fold increase from the eight-company-size post established in 1884 to one with three regiments and upwards of thirty companies. There was even talk in Cheyenne of building a trolley line to this greatly expanded post along a boulevard to be established that would run straight from the capitol to the Fort D.A. Russell front gate.

Despite good intentions and grand schemes, Fort D.A. Russell was virtually empty during the summer of 1906, except for the guard detail left behind. Units of the post were deployed to the Target and Maneuver Range for the scheduled large-scale maneuvers. Also referred to as the Camp of Instruction, National Guard and regular army units were brought together in 1906 for what soon became joint annual summer maneuvers. New types of weapons and uniforms were being issued to the regular army and Guard units. In 1903 the regular army had begun equipping its units with the new and improved .30 caliber bolt-action, magazine-type Springfield rifle.

While it sometimes took years for new issue items to reach posts in the West the Springfield 1903-model rifle had replaced the 1893 Krag-Jorgensen rifle at Fort D.A. Russell by 1907. The *Leader* reported that Sergeant Felix Evans blew off the top of his head with a new "Springfield military rifle." A similar incident had occurred in 1895 at the post with the newly issued Krag-Jorgensen rifle.

When the summer maneuvers were over in late September, Fort D.A. Russell again had a complement of nineteen officers and 486 men. In addition to the twelve lightly manned companies of Eleventh Infantry, there were two batteries of field artillery, the Twelfth and Nineteenth. However, eight companies of Eleventh Infantry left in late fall 1907 for Cuba, where they stayed for the next two years. Only the Third Battalion of Eleventh Infantry with four companies remained at Fort D.A. Russell.

Despite the loss of so many troops, expectations remained high that Fort D.A. Russell would soon be designated a brigade-size post with a brigade headquarters. The army general staff wanted to consolidate units and shut down the smaller outposts, thus establishing as many brigade-size posts as the size of the army would permit.

The building program continued at full speed. There was an announcement in February 1908 that construction on forty-eight more buildings (family quarters, barracks, a new brigade-size hospital, and stables) would start soon. The riding hall was completed in March and proudly proclaimed "the biggest Army building in the West," capable of accommodating a maneuvering squadron of cavalry within its walls. Although Fort D.A. Russell continued to grow, it still had not achieved the status of a brigade-size post.

An item of equal importance to the rank and file at Fort D.A. Russell was a provision in the 1908 army appropriations bill that increased the pay for all ranks. It raised a private's monthly pay from thirteen to twenty-one dollars a month.

Better-paid soldiers were supposed to be happier soldiers. The six batteries of Second Field Artillery Regiment (Mountain) arriving in early summer 1908 should have been happy to be stationed at Fort D.A. Russell.

The third post hospital (100 beds) was completed in 1909 and designed to accommodate a brigade of three regiments. During World War II, the hospital expanded to 300 beds by constructing temporary wooden frame wards in the rear. Replaced in 1977 after sixty-seven years of service with a very modern base hospital, number four, of twenty-four beds, the old hospital building became the headquarters and operating center for the Ninetieth Security Police Group.—*WY State AMH Dept.*

Newly constructed duplex officers' family quarters in 1908 are typical of army-approved architecture of that period. Fifteen different interior designs were employed. The neo-colonial red brick and white columned houses have remained very popular and are much the same except for added street lights, mature trees in the yards, and a paved street that was named Warren Avenue in 1930.—*WY State AMH Dept.*

The indoor riding hall completed in 1907 permitted cavalry units to train men and animals indoors during severe weather. The hall also accommodated the polo teams and children of the post for Saturday morning riding lessons. During World War II the riding hall served as a motor pool and then as the commissary sales store until 1987, when a new commissary was constructed south of Crow Creek. The hall will soon be converted to a recreation facility with tennis courts and a running track.— *WY State AMH Dept.*

The arrival of this unit started the growth of the post complement to brigade size. There were soon artillery, cavalry (two troops of Eighth Cavalry), and infantry (four companies of Eleventh Infantry). With the increase in numbers of artillerymen, off-duty conflict among the branches followed, a not infrequent occurence. The *Leader* reported on May 21, 1908, that the payday had created a lot of excitement in Cheyenne, with a party of artillerymen and infantrymen engaged in a battle royal.

Weekly brigade reviews, that included for the first time infantry, cavalry, and artillery units, became routine in the summer of 1908, much to the delight of people in Cheyenne. The post and Second Field Artillery commander, Colonel Sydney W. Taylor, provided a gracious welcome to all visitors.

Orders from the War Department for summer maneuvers in 1908 at the Fort D.A. Russell Target and Maneuver Range called for the participation of more than 17,000 men. Some of the post complement departed for the maneuvers, but 400 soldiers of the Second Field Artillery and 250 soldiers of the Eleventh Infantry were on hand to receive Senator F.E. Warren when he arrived for a brief visit in June. A "brilliant affair" for the senator at the post hall that evening was hosted by the post commander, Colonel Sydney W. Taylor, with the officers and ladies of the post attending.

Senator Warren may or may not have used his influence to have the streetcar line extended from the outskirts of Cheyenne to the post, but the folks at Fort D.A. Russell were pleased in any case. The Cheyenne Electric Street Railway Company finally extended their line in September 1908 from the western edge of Cheyenne through the post to the western edge of the cantonment area. Frequent trips were made by the enclosed streetcars to and from Cheyenne. The reasonable charge of eight cents, one way, presented a far better alternative to most soldiers than walking to town or trying to catch a ride on an open army horse-drawn wagon.

Still, to some an eight-cent fare seemed too much, and a boycott of the electric streetcars developed when soldiers sought a five-cent fare. An unfortunate accident occurred in June 1909 when an electric car ran over and killed Private Frank M. Wolf on the post while he was participating in the boycott. The motorman was placed in the post guardhouse for his own safety but later released and not held responsible. The Cheyenne Electric Street Railway Company did accede to the troops' demands for a five-cent fare when the soldiers continued to enforce their boycott, but then raised the fare.

While the soldiers were reluctant to pay eight cents for a streetcar ride to town, they were generous enough to spend $500 on a silver loving cup for Senator Francis E. Warren in late December 1908. The cup was presented to the senator in an appropriate ceremony by the Eleventh Infantry's Third Battalion for "His efforts to secure them the recently granted increase of pay."[2] As chairman of the Senate Military Affairs Committee, Senator Warren had been instrumental in obtaining the pay increase for the military services.

The mayor and city council of Cheyenne followed suit the next evening by hosting a banquet in Senator Warren's honor and presenting him with a handsome Moroccan case bearing the Warren coat of arms in silver and enamel. Mayor P.S. Cook made the presentation to Warren as a token of thanks for his efforts in securing from the War Department an appropriation of $400,000 for improvements to the Cheyenne water system. Senator Warren probably deserved all the recognition he received on that occasion, for largely through his efforts, Fort D.A. Russell had been firmly established as a permanent post of brigade size. Some $350,000 per year in construction contracts at Fort D.A. Russell had been received for the six years starting in 1902, for a total of more than $1,882,869—quite an economic benefit to the city of Cheyenne.

The return of the two battalions (eight companies) of the Eleventh Infantry from Cuba in April 1909 brought all twelve companies of that regiment together again. The paymaster distributed over $31,000 in March, the largest monthly payroll ever paid at the post up to that time.

Another cause for celebration came with the arrival of Brigadier General Frederick A. Smith in April as the new brigade and post commander. This provided the occasion for a big reception for the general and the officers of Fort D.A. Russell. Hosted by the Industrial Club of Cheyenne, the event was held at the Industrial Club House. On the same day, the Eleventh Infantry commander, Colonel Richard T. Yeatman, received an "elaborate" retirement farewell. He had first seen service at Fort D.A.

Above: Still the most handsome structure on the post and little changed general officer's quarters #92 was completed on May 5, 1910 at a cost of $126,522.05. **Lower left:** Gen. Frederick A. Smith, the first general officer assigned to Ft. Russell. **Lower right:** Brig. Gen. Ralph Hoyt, first occupant of Bldg. 92.—*WY State AMH Dept.*

Stimson also photographed the enlisted mens' barracks in 1908 with a ball game in progress in front of the barracks. The newly completed buildings had not yet been complemented with shrubs and trees.—*WY State AMH Dept.*

Russell in 1872 as a young lieutenant fresh out of West Point. His thirty-seven-year military career started and ended at the same post in Wyoming.

While some things had changed in the garrison's routine in recent years, most events had just become more routine and firmly embedded in the schedule. For instance, brigade reviews had settled down to monthly events by mid-1909, either on the post parade ground or at the Fort D.A. Russell Target and Maneuver Range, now also referred to by the press as the Pole Mountain Maneuver Area. An attempt to cope with one of the perennial hazards to mounted troops at brigade reviews appeared in a local newspaper:

> Troops at Fort Russell are now waging a campaign against ungentlemanly and indiscreet dogs. Canines are interfering with mounted officers during parades and an order for their deportation has been issued. Two dozen dogs gave chase to every mounted officer that let his horse go faster than a slow walk during the review a few days ago at the post. The officers were greatly annoyed.[3]

The new post/brigade commander had been on the job hardly six months when, in late November, he addressed the Cheyenne Industrial

Club. General Smith shared the platform with two illustrious speakers, Senator Warren and Joseph M. Carey, former U.S. senator and soon to be governor.

Smith took the occasion to tell that group of Cheyenne's leading citizens that while Fort D.A. Russell owed a lot to Senator Warren, the military installation served as a valuable asset to the community and should be treated as such. He pointed out that the government and its servants were considered legitimate prey to extortion. Tradesmen had one price for people of Cheyenne and another for those of the "new" Fort Russell. All the army asked, said Smith, was a fair and square deal. General Smith concluded his critical speech with these pacifying remarks, all of which were reportedly well received:

> The Industrial Club is the motive power of your city and is doing most credible work. I can see its influence for good in every direction. . . . Unlike myself, not practical enough to go into business—not diplomatic enough for the ministry—not quarrelsome enough for the law—not suitable for any ordinary career, except the Army.[4]

As the year ended and a new decade began, the building program continued and more appropriations were announced for Fort D.A. Russell by Senator Warren's Washington office. The senator had again obtained additional appropriations for the post despite the announced tight

Within two years the appearance of officers' row, now Warren Avenue, had improved with the planting of trees and shrubs and the installation of sidewalks and street lights.—*WY State AMH Dept.*

economic policy of the new Taft administration that had declared no expenditures for public buildings. Senator Warren also told the Cheyenne press that he thought he could obtain appropriations to cover the expense of holding military maneuvers at the Fort D.A. Russell Target and Maneuver Range for the coming summer.

The "new" Fort D.A. Russell had become a major army post in the decade just passed. New construction had increased the number of

buildings to accommodate a brigade that numbered more than 2,000 officers and men. Community relations with Cheyenne were cordial, and the post had an important and effective patron, Wyoming's Senator Francis E. Warren. He would continue to be an enthusiastic supporter of the army and the post.

1. *Cheyenne Daily Leader*, May 16, 1905.
2. *Cheyenne Daily Leader*, December 29–30, 1908.
3. *Cheyenne State Leader*, September 2, 1909.
4. *Cheyenne State Leader*, November 24, 1909.

Guard mount for the Ninth Cavalry in front of the regimental guard house on a late summer afternoon in 1910 attracted a good number of spectators from the post and Cheyenne. One of two all-black cavalry regiments in the army, the Ninth Cavalry left Fort D.A. Russell the following year for duty on the Mexican border, along with other army regiments, after a series of incidents there.—*WY State AMH Dept.*

PART VII
MEXICAN TROUBLES AND A WAR IN EUROPE, 1910–1919

Battery F, Fourth Field Artillery Regiment, posed on their barracks porch in 1911 still wearing blue uniforms. The army had started converting to khaki uniforms soon after 1900, but it took many years to complete the change. Battery F had arrived at Fort D.A. Russell in 1909 and departed in March 1913 for the Mexican border.—*WY State AMH Dept.*

Chapter Sixteen
The Brigade Seeks Good Relations With Cheyenne –Most Of The Time

The Taft administration (1909-1913) significantly reduced the level of military appropriations set by the Roosevelt administration right after the Spanish-American War. Cutbacks included funds intended for further expanding the "new" Fort D.A. Russell. Some construction did continue, but the big building program had already been approved or completed by 1910. A great deal of uncertainty existed in the army during the early part of the decade for several reasons, including the Taft administration's vacillation in developing a national strategy. The most notable aspect of this period was the frequent movement of regiments. When moved, units were not soon replaced, leaving the post with only a caretaker force for long periods. While rotating regiments to Cuba and the Philippines, the United States also found itself frequently involved with its southern neighbor, Mexico.

After more than forty years of relative stability, a lasting Mexican revolution started in 1911. Over the next ten years violence occurred on this side of the border in the states of Texas, Arizona, and New Mexico. Border incursions by rebel Mexican bands posed a danger to communities north of the Rio Grande and a threat to peace between the two countries. Units at Fort D.A. Russell were deployed to the border when violations occurred, and the military population of the post varied from more than 2,700 on January 1, 1910, to less than two officers and thirty-six enlisted men in August 1916.

Still, expectations for peace were high in 1910. No immediate dangers threatened our national security. Regiments brought together in good housing conditions at Fort D.A. Russell performed routine peacetime duties and enjoyed garrison life. Good relations with the nearby civilian community were enjoyed during this quiet time. Brigadier General Frederick Smith had in mind improving community relations even more when, on a "spirited charger" in March 1910, he led the brigade of more than 2,500 officers and men, plus 2,000 horses and mules, in a Saturday parade through town. A Cheyenne newspaper reported that the whole town turned out for this two-mile-long parade, which included the Ninth Cavalry, Eleventh Infantry, and the Fourth Field Artillery regiments. Each regiment had at the lead its colonel and regimental band. The animal refuse left on the streets by 2,000 horses and mules must have posed a problem for the street department, but the people of Cheyenne loved that parade.

Although the building program had been greatly reduced throughout the army, and at Fort D.A. Russell, it had not been discontinued. Contracts were awarded in March 1910 for ten buildings, including a post laundry, that had been earlier authorized. New units continued to arrive, including Company I, Signal Corps, which took station in April 1910 with two officers and seventy-two men plus horses and mules. This was the first signal corps company to be assigned to Fort D.A. Russell. Now the post had most of the branches of the service; infantry, cavalry, field artillery, medical, quartermaster, and signal corps.

In looking about for a brigade/post headquarters, since no suitable

Regimental bands provided much of the entertainment for the post and the nearby community when playing for the daily retreat ceremony as well as the weekly parades, scheduled dances, and frequent concerts. The Ninth Cavalry band proved to be particularly popular during that regiment's two year stay at Fort D.A. Russell, 1910-1912. Chief musician Wade H. Hammond sits in the center.—*WY State AMH Dept.*

building had been included in the building program, Brigadier General Frederick Smith selected a two-story brick barracks completed in 1909 for the medical corps. Occupied by the enlisted corpsmen of Company A, Hospital Corps, the structure had been poorly located in the officers' housing area, but the medical corps disliked the idea of giving it up. The disagreement went all the way to the surgeon general in Washington. General Smith gained the quartermaster general's support and a favorable decision when he agreed that building #156 would house several functions, including the brigade/post headquarters, a telephone communications center, an officers' assembly hall, and schoolrooms.

A "Post/Brigade Headquarters" sign soon appeared over the front entrance of building #156, now numbered #65. It continued to serve as a headquarters, until August 1988, and the telephone switchboard still operates twenty-four hours a day. Another dormitory was later built for the hospital corpsmen closer to their workplace in the hospital. The medical caduceus remains in stone over the front entrance of building #65 as a reminder of the first occupants in 1909.

The second floor of the new headquarters immediately became the locale for dances and other types of social affairs; it had the largest and nicest ballroom on the post. Each of the three regiments continued to maintain their own separate officers' clubs (the Eleventh Infantry in quarters #2) until 1913. Then a single officers' club in the headquarters building served all three regiments. A grand and formal reception dedicated the club on February 22, 1913. Many a resident of Cheyenne can recall with fond memories attending activities at that officers' club, particularly members of senior high school classes who often held their dances there. The officers' club remained in the headquarters building until World War II.

The officers club was just one of many facilities that the brigade commander improved for officers and enlisted men during his three-year tour at Fort D.A. Russell, while all the time cultivating relations with the civilian community. When General Smith received orders transferring him to Omaha as commander of the Department of the Missouri, the Cheyenne Industrial Club hosted a farewell that spoke well of his and the army's relationship with Cheyenne. He and Senator Warren had early formed a fast friendship. General Smith's popularity remained high with the community despite his habit of speaking frankly. Senator Warren took the occasion to announce that more buildings would be added to Fort D.A. Russell despite the spending freeze imposed by the Taft administration.

While Cheyenne welcomed a full complement of troops at the post, it did not welcome the frequent conflicts that occurred in town between the different branches. With the stationing of infantry, cavalry, and artillery units at Fort D.A. Russell, the propensity for friction manifested itself on West 18th Street in Cheyenne. Paydays had always posed potential trouble, but now the threat of violence occurred more frequently between paydays. One of a series of incidents took place in May 1910 when a riot and pitched battle was reported in the "tenderloin district." The fight started between artillerymen and infantrymen but evolved to a battle between the Cheyenne police and the soldiers. Four soldiers were reported wounded. A part of the cause of this disturbance and the turning against the police supposedly had to do with the soldiers being angry at law enforcement personnel for killing Private Frank Carrol in the Cheyenne jail a few days earlier.

A great deal of soldier resentment continued toward the Cheyenne police, particularly Police Chief Manewal, until the post adjutant filed charges of murder against a Cheyenne policeman. Tension eased somewhat when the murdered man's outfit, Battery C of the Fourth Field Artillery, left in June for the Philippines. The annual summer deployment to the Target and Maneuver Range's Camp of Instruction at Pole Mountain in late June helped to keep Cheyenne's "tenderloin district" cool for the rest of the year.

Relations between Fort D.A. Russell and Cheyenne remained tenuous at best for the rest of 1910 and into 1911, for several reasons. The soldiers called another boycott of the electric streetcar line in January 1911 in an effort to get the fare reduced again to five cents. A boycott two years earlier had been successful for a short while. This last boycott generated more widespread support among the military, and after a week, the company agreed to try a five-cent fare for soldiers for three weeks. Civilians still had to pay a dime to ride from Cheyenne to the post. The Cheyenne press credited General Smith's speech to the Industrial Club two months earlier as being partly responsible for the settlement.

The issue of the streetcar fares became largely moot in March 1911 and remained so for the next five months, during which time the post's military population dropped from about 3,000 men to slightly more than 300. President Taft had decreed that patrols along the Mexican border be significantly increased. The Mexican Revolution had gotten underway with the overthrow of President Porfirio Diaz, who had ruled a politically stable Mexico for more than a third of a century. The Eleventh Infantry, Ninth Cavalry, and Fourth Field Artillery all departed Fort D.A. Russell in March 1911 for the Texas border. The situation with Mexico seemed to stabilize after a few months, and most of the infantry, cavalry, and field artillery men were back at Fort D.A. Russell by mid-July 1911, in time to participate in the annual Cheyenne Frontier Days parade and show.

While most of the units of Fort D.A. Russell had been in Texas, Cheyenne decided to do something about the town's red light district. The district contained more than a dozen houses in the West End, rented for "immoral purposes." The newly formed West Side Improvement Association announced the closing of all "houses" in the district. However, four months later, business as usual was reported in that part of town when cavalry and field artillery men rioted there. Soldiers from the post were called in by the Cheyenne police to help break up the fray. Then, in November 1911, a big fight erupted about two o'clock one morning there between members of the hospital corps and field artillery armed with guns and knives. Peace prevailed for six months or so, then another riot occurred at 1007 West Eighteenth Street. The Cheyenne police handled this disturbance and arrested several soldiers and a woman. One fatality occurred in this fracas: a soldier from the Fourth Field Artillery was kicked to death. By September 1912, the town fathers had taken another tack and decided that Cheyenne should share in some of the "West End" profits. Accordingly, an ordinance required that West End property owners be assessed monthly at the following rate: house owners, $50 (several sixteen-room houses were in that area); keepers, $200; and all prostitutes were to pay a fine of $10 per month. There were some thirty "houses" in the segregated district.

Many local reformers actively campaigned to clean up the town, but it proved to be easier said than done. Cheyenne's and Fort D.A. Russell's political patron, Senator Francis E. Warren, maintained a benevolent attitude. His support was necessary for any kind of a reform movement in Cheyenne, and he did not put a high priority on reform. Despite his lack of enthusiasm for changing some bad habits of the local citizens, his national political influence remained as strong as his local popularity. Whenever the president, or any other important national political or military figure, considered a trip west, a stop in Cheyenne figured large in their schedule. On a political swing through the region in October 1911, President Taft paid the mandatory visit to Fort D.A. Russell and Cheyenne. His arrival did not spark the usual amount of extra activities or arouse a great deal of excitement, but he stood with Senator Warren for a "march-by" review of the three regiments. About 2,500 military personnel were on hand in October for the parade.

While the president was yet in Cheyenne, the troops at Fort D.A. Russell were again voicing their displeasure with the streetcar owners. The infantry, cavalry, and field artillery had been on the Mexican border during the spring of 1911 when the Cheyenne Electric Street Railway Company raised the fare for soldiers back to the original ten cents. The troops did not take kindly to this increase in price, and the *Leader* announced their reaction in the September 9, 1911, edition: "SOLDIERS TO BOYCOTT ALL CITY MERCHANTS." The newspaper wrote that the men were determined to spend no more money in Cheyenne until the five-cent fare returned. While the brigade commander and senior officers remained discreetly silent on the issue, the soldiers voiced their opinion that the merchants of Cheyenne had failed to support their strike against the streetcar company. To make their point, a committee of soldiers arranged for a special train to Denver right after payday. And true to their strike plan, 700 soldiers entrained for Denver following the mid-September payday. The newspaper report of that occasion touched the heart of the matter with this comment: "They no doubt left much money in Denver."[1]

In an effort to introduce some competition to the streetcar service, if only temporarily, an auto livery service began operating between the post and Cheyenne with four large cars owned by the Loveland-Estes Park Auto Service. The auto service enjoyed a thriving business at ten cents a passenger. Soon after the New Year, a negotiated settlement provided for a streetcar fare of five cents, tickets to be purchased at the post exchange. The cash fare remained at ten cents. The *Leader* called it the most remarkable boycott in the history of the nation. Successful by all counts, it lasted for a year without any violence. The efforts of both state and local leaders were instrumental in settling the strike, and the streetcars were packed again with soldiers soon after the settlement became known.

In early winter 1911, two officers arrived at Fort D.A. Russell for assignment who would become nationally known, but for different reasons and at different times. They were Lieutenant Frank Bloom and Captain William Mitchell. Lieutenant Bloom's posting to the Fourth Field Artillery created some curiosity at the fort and in town. The son of the post tailor at Fort Myer, Virginia, Bloom had received national attention when Fort Myer's commander wrote on Bloom's exam papers that he was "undesirable socially and as an officer because he was a Hebrew." Press attention caused President Taft to rebuke the post commander and give Bloom another chance. Bloom then passed his examinations, got his commission in the army, and an assignment to Fort D.A. Russell.

Captain "Billy" Mitchell's arrival in January 1912 at Fort D.A. Russell did not receive much attention. Having enlisted in an infantry regiment at age eighteen when the United States declared war on Spain and been commissioned seven days later, Mitchell served in Cuba and the Philippines. Son of a wealthy and politically prominent Wisconsin family, Mitchell transferred to the Signal Corps after the war and served with distinction in Alaska, the Philippines again, and Washington, D.C., before coming to Fort D.A. Russell as commander of Company I, Signal Corps. He was recognized as an excellent polo player, a game very popular at most army posts, and he dominated polo play for the season. In September 1912, his signal company, along with the Ninth Cavalry, entrained for the Mexican border where a great many other army units were again gathering.

Mitchell's association with military aviation did not start until 1916, when he became deputy chief of the Signal Corps Aviation Division. During World War I as a brigadier general, he commanded all American combat aviation on the western front and then became assistant chief of the postwar Army Air Service. From that point until his death in 1935, Billy Mitchell served as military aviation's most steadfast supporter and vocal advocate.

Before leaving Fort D.A. Russell, Mitchell and his signal corps company had spent the summer participating in the annual maneuvers at Pole Mountain. Regular army and National Guard regiments had joined the maneuvers at different times during the summer. Included among them were twelve companies of the Third Infantry, Wyoming National Guard, commanded by Colonel Verling K. Hart. A particularly important visitor, Secretary of War Henry Stimson, who visited the post and the maneuver area as an observer for several days, expressed his satisfaction with the readiness of the units he had seen.

The secretary seemed to have little awareness of events that sparked some startling articles appearing in national publications in September 1912. A charge of wrongdoing had been leveled against Wyoming Senator Francis E. Warren. An article written by C.P. Connolly appearing in *Collier's* weekly magazine, August 31, 1912, accused Senator Warren of buying land in the Pole Mountain area to sell to the government for the Fort D.A. Russell Target and Maneuver Reservation. Even the *Leader* repeated one of the charges leveled against the senator on August 30, 1912, in an article titled, "How Senator Warren Used Members of His Family to Loot the United States Treasury." An article two days later declared that Warren should be impeached if even half of the charges made in the *Collier's* article were true. Senator Robert M. LaFollette of Wisconsin, no friend of Warren's politically or socially, said of Warren, "He is a Great Shepherd, not only of sheep but of Special Privileges, Subsidies and Tariff Outrages."[2] A Washington, D.C., newspaper demanded an investigation to answer the charges made in the *Collier's* article.

The charges did not seem to bother Senator Warren's Wyoming constituency, and Fort D.A. Russell continued to receive appropriations for more buildings. Even though the state and national Republican parties were badly divided and warring with Senator Warren, the Wyoming legislature re-elected him handily in a January 1913 joint session.

Senator Warren's interests and influence remained much the same throughout his career as a United States senator. He was an astute tactician and parliamentarian, and his interests and those of Wyoming and Fort D.A. Russell were intertwined. But the press became suspicious of his every move for a while after the unfavorable publicity. They accused him of adding a "joker" to a 1912 appropriations bill that would have removed Army Chief of Staff Major General Leonard Wood from his position because he had not served ten years as a line officer. If Wood had been removed, reasoned the press, the series of changes following would have made it possible for Warren's son-in-law, Brigadier General John J. Pershing, to replace Wood as army chief of staff. When General Wood made an inspection tour of western army posts in October 1912, he did not visit Fort D.A. Russell or Cheyenne even though it would have been convenient for him and he was expected to do so. Instead, he issued a press release from Sheridan, Wyoming, after visiting nearby Fort Mackenzie. General Wood must have had the Wyoming senator in mind when he said, "the Army could not afford to abandon Fort D.A. Russell, even if it was desireable to do so."[3]

Another flare-up in Mexico that started with a military coup in Mexico City in February 1913 altered the course of the Mexican Revolution and gave the United States increasing cause for concern. Fort D.A. Russell units were started for the border almost immediately. The Eleventh Infantry and Fourth Field Artillery, with animals and equipment, departed for Texas City on the Gulf Coast. When President Woodrow Wilson assumed office on March 4, 1913, he increased troop strength on the border and naval forces in the Gulf. He also warned all Americans to leave Mexico.

The departure of the infantry and artillery units left the post almost deserted. The Ninth Cavalry had departed for Douglas, Arizona, and the border the previous September. There were five officers and 130 men on the post assigned to the Quartermaster Detachment, the Field Hospital

Company #1 and Ambulance Company #1 to perform the usual garrison duties. The next month Troops E and H, Twelfth Cavalry, arrived from Fort Robinson, Nebraska, to help guard and maintain the garrison. Their arrival temporarily raised the military strength to almost 200. These two cavalry troops were dispatched to Canon City, Colorado, a year later in April 1914 when a mine strike there required federal troops to maintain order. They remained in the Canon City area until January 1915, when they returned to Fort D.A. Russell. One or two companies of the Twelfth Cavalry were garrisoned at the fort periodically during brief intervals for the next three years, leaving the post with a military strength of less than 100 men for extended periods.

So few troops on station caused the merchants of Cheyenne to feel a strong negative economic impact. With Christmas approaching in 1914, social activities on the post were expected to be very limited. Then Brigadier General John J. Pershing arrived at Fort D.A. Russell for a short leave. His wife and four children had occupied quarters #2 while the general compaigned on the border and in Mexico. Captain Samuel B. Pearson, post commander and head of the Quartermaster Detachment, ushered in the holidays with a gala open house at his quarters in honor of the Pershings. Assigned officers and their ladies were invited to call and pay their respects, with officers in full dress uniform. Friends of the Pershings from Cheyenne who wished to call were also invited to the open house. General and Mrs. Pershing entertained at dinner at the Plains Hotel in Cheyenne the next evening, with dancing after dinner.

General Pershing soon returned to his command on the border, and his family moved to the Presidio in San Francisco, California. In August 1915, while General Pershing still served on the border, Mrs. Pershing and her three daughters died in a late-night fire in their Presidio quarters. Small son Warren, sleeping in another part of the house, escaped with minor burns. Mrs. Pershing and her daughters were buried in Cheyenne's Lakeview Cemetery. The funeral procession included many dignitaries and two troops of Twelfth Cavalry from Fort D.A. Russell. Reported to be one of the larger services in recent memory, the procession extended through town for more than a half mile.

The new year of 1916 brought with it news that the Twenty-fourth Infantry, a black regiment coming from the Philippines, would report for duty in February. The post's military population jumped from slightly more than 100 to more than 2,000 when the regiment arrived. Even though a Wyoming winter offered a traumatic change in climate, members of the Twenty-fourth Infantry were glad to be back in the United States. They were also looking forward to a quiet two- or three-year tour of duty at Fort D.A. Russell. The *Leader* discreetly noted that the regiment's payroll on March 15, 1916, with more soldiers in town than at any time in the past four years, totaled more than $30,000. However, the regiment's stay proved to be a short one. The Twenty-fourth Infantry proceeded to the border the next month, in late March, leaving the post again virtually empty. Little more than one hundred military personnel were left, all quartermaster and hospital corps members. President Wilson had ordered a punitive expedition into Mexico to capture or kill the bandits who had raided Columbus, New Mexico, and other American border settlements.

The post's military population went even lower in June 1916, when further withdrawals were made, leaving only two officers and thirty-eight enlisted men. Field Hospital Company #1 and Ambulance Company #1 had been dispatched to El Paso, Texas, with duty on the Mexican border. One of the two officers left at Fort D.A. Russell, Captain Samuel A. Smoke of the Quartermaster Corps, had earlier retired and now acted as post commander. He signed the monthly Post Returns for the next year as "On Duty at Post." The other officer assigned was a medical officer in charge of the hospital. Captain Smoke also had the task of commanding the Quartermaster Detachment as well as serving as engineer, signal, and ordnance officer. The low point occurred in September when the Post Return reported two officers and thirty-six enlisted men, a very small number to guard and maintain a post as large as Fort D.A. Russell had become.

Captain Smoke's relations with Cheyenne were minimal during this period because his duties kept him fully occupied. He did take time to send a letter to the newspaper threatening to prosecute all motorists exceeding the post's speed limit of sixteen miles per hour.

When Mexican border troubles grew in 1916, the Congress increased the nation's regular army and National Guard preparedness levels, and called to active duty a part of the guard. The Wyoming National Guard mobilized fifty-four officers and 598 enlisted men in June at Fort D.A. Russell. Apparently bureaucratic red tape precluded putting National Guard troops in empty regular army barracks, so a tent city arose to house the guard regiment. It was named Camp Kendrick after Wyoming's Governor John B. Kendrick. Governor Kendrick, soon to be a U.S. senator, held a review of Wyoming's National Guard units at Camp Kendrick soon after they were settled and declared them a fine-looking body of men. The Wyoming National Guard units were ordered to Deming, New Mexico, in early summer and then on to the border in mid-September.

Increased tension with Germany, and some lessening of border tension with Mexico, resulted in the recall in 1917 of the Wyoming guard and their return to Fort D.A. Russell in early March 1917, for what turned out to be a short release from federal service. Although efforts to capture Pancho Villa had not been completely successful, the intensive training received by the regular army and National Guard troops had been invaluable. During the chase, relations between the United States and Germany reached a critical stage, and President Woodrow Wilson had no alternative but to withdraw the punitive expedition from Mexico. The post military population remained at less than fifty until April and May 1917, when the international situation and that at Fort D.A. Russell changed considerably.

1. *Cheyenne State Leader*, September 9, 10, and 16, 1911.
2. *Cheyenne State Leader*, September 15, 1912.
3. *Cheyenne State Leader*, October 11, 1912.

World War I introduced the airplane as an important weapon of war and the maneuvers of ground troops after the war were usually accompanied by bomber or observation planes. The twin-engine bi-plane Glenn Martin bombers were the latest thing in 1920. The Fort D.A. Russell flying field, established in 1919, was closed in mid-1920 and aircraft participating in the summer maneuvers at Pole Mountain used the Cheyenne Municipal airport.—WY *State AMH Dept.*

Chapter Seventeen
War, Demobilization, And The Aviation Era

The United States' declaration of war on Germany on April 6, 1917, set the entire nation to work preparing units to go overseas. National Guard units were mobilized, and most of the regular army regiments were recalled from the border and expanded with newly conscripted recruits, who were quickly gotten ready to head for France and "fight the Boche." A Selective Service Act obligated all males twenty-one to thirty years old, later extended to eighteen to forty-five, to register, which enabled the army to expand to more than three and a half million men. The army was restructured by the act into three segments: (1) the regular army, (2) the National Guard, and (3) a national army, also called a volunteer army. Much was made of these three segments initially in the war, but soon distinctions were largely lost as enlistees and draftees alike were absorbed in all units. In mid-1918, the War Department changed the designation of all the land forces to one "United States Army."

Partly because of his leadership of the punitive expedition into Mexico, Major General John J. Pershing received the coveted appointment as commander of the American Expeditionary Force to France. Pershing soon received the four stars of a full general, the same rank that had a short time earlier again been authorized the army chief of staff. This marked the first occasion in the twentieth century that Congress had allowed the army a rank above the two stars of a major general.

In preparing for war, Cheyenne hoped that Fort D.A. Russell would serve as a recruiting and training station for cavalry. After all, it had the facilities, and Wyoming could furnish the army the finest cavalry horses anywhere. One newspaper report estimated that forty to fifty thousand men would soon be at Fort D.A. Russell.

War preparations began in earnest in May 1917 with the arrival from the border of the First Cavalry Regiment, 1,600 strong, which increased the base military population considerably from the two officers and forty-three men there the previous month. The First Cavalry had orders to organize two additional cavalry regiments at Fort D.A. Russell, the Twenty-fourth and Twenty-fifth. For the next three months recruits and horses arrived in a steady stream to be trained. The military population soon totaled more than 5,000, plus 3,252 horses.

The Third Infantry Regiment, Wyoming National Guard, which again mobilized in a tent city at Fort D.A. Russell in July 1917, hoped to convert their infantry regiment to a cavalry regiment. They were sorely disappointed when the War Department declared that additional cavalry units would not be raised for war service and some units already formed would be redesignated. In August 1917, the newly organized Twenty-fourth and Twenty-fifth Cavalry Regiments at Fort D.A. Russell became the Twenty-fourth and Twenty-fifth Provisional Artillery regiments. Eight cavalry outfits were to be converted to field artillery. The hard-pressed Allies in Europe wanted infantry and artillery units from the Americans, plus large quantities of food and war supplies, but no more horse cavalry units.

Further training of the new artillery organizations also came to a halt at Fort D.A. Russell in late 1917, and those units, along with the First Cavalry, were shipped to Texas. Again the post had been depopulated; five officers and 100 enlisted men remained. In February 1918, the mayor of Cheyenne sent a telegram to Senators Warren and Kendrick asking if the War Department intended to permanently vacate Fort D.A. Russell. Senator Warren's quick response assured the mayor that cavalry and medical troops would soon be assigned in considerable number.

True to his promise, units began arriving about six weeks later. The arriving troops were chagrined to find their new home a "dry" one. The exclusion by Congress of spirits from the army post exchanges in the early part of the twentieth century, an exclusion long since decried by army leaders, continued. To reinforce that earlier ban, President Woodrow Wilson signed a wartime law banning liquor not only at military camps but also at all civilian establishments for a certain distance around those camps. The law also authorized federal authorities to regulate or shut down saloons and "bawdy" houses in the vicinity of military camps. In an effort to support the law, the Cheyenne Literary Club adopted the following resolution: "The City must see that saloons observe the law on selling to soldiers." As far as the saloonkeepers were concerned, the law was not sufficiently clear, and they continued business as usual. Then a meeting of a Cheyenne women's club passed a resolution demanding that saloons and the "District" be closed to soldiers. A few Cheyenne saloonkeepers began to pay attention to the federal law, but for the most part, it remained business as usual in Cheyenne.

Another matter of some importance brought the Cheyenne Literary Club back to the attention of the press. Early in the war the *Leader* started referring to all American soldiers as "sammies," an acronym for Uncle Sam's soldiers. In reporting on a forthcoming pay raise, the newspaper wrote on December 16, 1917, that a private "sammie" would soon be receiving thirty-three dollars per month plus 20 percent extra for overseas duty, up from twenty-one dollars per month for a private. After six months, the Cheyenne Literary Club passed a resolution asking the local news writers to stop calling American soldiers "sammies." They felt the name was objectionable to men in service and appeared meaningless and distasteful. The world "sammie" did not appear afterward in the Cheyenne newspapers when referring to American soldiers.

While it was never clear what kind of soldiers the press referred to with the term "sammies," it seemed unlikely they meant cavalrymen. Horses and soldiers meant cavalry to Cheyenne, and they liked both. After seeing Fort D.A. Russell manned with only a minimum caretaker force for three months, the announcement in March 1918, that a full 315th Cavalry Regiment, plus a squadron of the 312th Cavalry Regiment, would be formed was welcome news. The decision nine months earlier that no more cavalry units would be needed had been overturned for one reason or another. The local press gave credit to Senators Warren and Kendrick for persuading the War Department to use Fort D.A. Russell, and for forming more cavalry regiments.

Other welcome news arrived from Europe's western front in April 1918. American units were at last assuming a major role in the Allied offensive, with General John J. Pershing commanding the American forces. At the same time, the Third Liberty Loan Drive got underway throughout the nation to finance the war effort. Cheyenne and Fort D.A. Russell both exceeded their assigned quotas of bonds sold, a remarkable achievement for a post filled with newly arrived citizen soldiers paid thirty-three dollars a month. The Fourth Liberty Loan Drive took off in October 1918 with similar results. A final Liberty Loan Drive was held after the war, in the spring of 1919.

A lot of war bonds would need to be sold to pay for the many new units being formed to send to the front. The newly formed 315th Cavalry Regiment, commanded by Colonel Walter C. Short, had fifty-one officers and 1,305 men by June 1918 and a full training schedule for all the new recruits still arriving. Equitation classes were held daily, along with a school for noncommissioned officers, stable sergeants, clerks, and blacksmiths. The regiment appeared in the annual Cheyenne Frontier Days parade in July, but without their mounts. Horses and mules were still arriving and being "broken" as quickly as possible. Colonel Short asked Cheyenne motorists driving on the post to do so carefully, for there were many "green" animals who spooked easily. Short earlier had enhanced his standing with Cheyenne when he announced that a daily parade of one mounted squadron would be held at 6:00 P.M., and the people of Cheyenne were invited. The band of the Second Regiment of California National Guard provided the music.

Startling orders arrived in late July 1918, converting the 315th Cavalry Regiment at Fort D.A. Russell to a field artillery regiment, and without delay. The officers and noncommissioned officers were reported to be very unhappy with this turn of events, but convert they did to the Forty-first Field Artillery. In September 1918, all the newly formed field artillery units at Fort D.A. Russell transferred to Camp Jackson, South Carolina, and West Point, Kentucky, leaving the post again with only a small housekeeping cadre of hospital and quartermaster troops. Colonel Walter C. Short left the garrison in September to assume command of the Eighth

Infantry Regiment. A temporary creation of the war known as the United States Guards (Company C, Twenty-third Battalion) arrived in October 1918 from the Presidio at San Francisco. The company totaled four officers and 147 men, not enough but more than some earlier times, to guard and maintain the post for the remainder of 1918.

The armistice of November 11, 1918, ended the war and opened a new era of uncertainty for the future of Fort D.A. Russell. There were less than 250 military personnel at the post in December 1918. The United States Guards company departed for the West Coast, and Companies E and F, Twenty-first Infantry, arrived to take station. More companies of the Twenty-first Infantry soon came in along with Brigadier General P.W. Davison. Davison served as post commander and head of the demobilization station being set up at Fort D.A. Russell.

The fort was designated a postwar demobilization point for a five-state area in mid-February 1919, and soldiers started streaming in for discharge. In order to muster out three million men as rapidly and equitably as possible, while at the same time maintaining an effective military force for occupation and other postwar committments, the War Department discharged men by units. Thirty demobilization centers were selected at strategic locations throughout the country. Units were brought back from overseas as rapidly as shipping space permitted and sent by train to a designated demobilization station. Nine months after the war ended, 3,250,000 men had been mustered out without desrupting the army's mission or the nation's economy.

The plan at Fort D.A. Russell provided for units to arrive in contingents of 2,000 and be demobilized at the rate of 150 men per day. The initial concept was greatly accelerated, and by mid-March 1919, over 1,000 men a week were reported to be moving through Fort D.A. Russell. The record shows that 6,906 soldiers were received for discharge at Fort D.A. Russell in April 1919, and 6,906 soldiers were discharged. The 384th Field Artillery Regiment chose to parade on April 19, 1919, at 5:30 P.M., the evening prior to its discharge. A grand turnout from Cheyenne witnessed their final parade. It had been the first parade with a band at Fort D.A. Russell for many months.

While the demobilization program proceeded smoothly at Fort D.A. Russell, the long-standing problem with Cheyenne saloons and the federal law erupted again. Even though there had existed some sympathy for Prohibition in Wyoming, the legislature did not enact the necessary measures to go into effect until July 1, 1919, long after surrounding states had restricted the sale of liquor. The night before July 1 has been described as one of the wildest in Cheyenne history.

Two months prior to the July deadline for the state to go dry, the *Leader* printed this warning headline: "PURGE CHEYENNE OR LOOSE SOLDIERS—WHICH?" The newspaper explained that only two days remained to clean up Cheyenne, otherwise the War Department would do the job by closing saloons and prosecuting all prostitutes found. The alternative: a quarantine of the town with loss of millions of dollars to

Cheyenne. Major H.C. Frazer, head of law enforcement at Fort D.A. Russell, reported to Cheyenne Mayor E.W. Stone on April 22 that Cheyenne had fifteen houses of "ill-fame," with fifty to seventy-five prostitutes, many of them soliciting on the streets. Major Frazer also told the mayor that eighteen of twenty-four saloons visited would serve a man in uniform all the liquor he wanted. Major Frazer continued with a further charge: "Cheyenne is the worst demobilization point in the West. The troop trains are met by bootleggers and prostitutes.[1]

Cheyenne businessmen were reported to be quite indignant at Major Frazer's charges. The following day, April 23, Major Frazer received orders transferring him to a new assignment in Kansas City. A specially selected committee of the Cheyenne Rotary Club, after a thorough investigation and careful consideration, declared the following month that prostitution and bootlegging were no worse in Cheyenne than in any other town of comparable size. An inspection of the Cheyenne community by the army in July 1919 provided a clean bill of health. A letter to the mayor stated that Cheyenne had been one of the best demobilization points in the United States. In any case, the army sounded happy and the town's indignation had diminished, so it was once again business as usual in "old Cheyenne."

The airplane appeared in the Wyoming skies in numbers not long after the war ended. The army's Far West Flying Circus arrived at Fort D.A. Russell on May 1, 1919, via the Union Pacific Railroad, to put on an air show and promote the sale of Liberty War Bonds as a part of a nationwide Victory Loan Drive. The Circus had sixteen American, British, French, and German airplanes that arrived disassembled and crated. The planes were quickly unloaded from the boxcars and assembled after the morning arrival at the Fort D.A. Russell railhead, then flown that afternoon from a level patch of prairie near the main gate. Commanded by Major Carl A. Spaatz, the Flying Circus put on a great "bombing of Cheyenne" demonstration that ended with stunts and an exhibition dog fight. The air show was a particular hit with the hundreds of soldiers at the post waiting to be demobilized, plus the thousands of Cheyenneites out for the show. This aerial demonstration marked the first time most in Cheyenne and at Fort D.A. Russell had seen an airplane, and they saw sixteen planes flown in spectacular maneuvers by combat pilots just returned from Europe. The entire affair, including the bond drive, enjoyed a great success.

The post continued as a primary demobilization point throughout the summer of 1919. The 148th Field Artillery Regiment, a Wyoming National Guard unit formerly designated the Third Infantry, arrived from France for demobilization in June. Many Cheyenne boys were included in the ranks of the regiment. A huge crowd greeted their train, and a parade proceeded through town to the steps of the capitol, where Governor Robert Carey welcomed the regiment home. Some 8,858 soldiers were demobilized at Fort D.A. Russell in June, including the Wyoming regiment.

The month of June also saw the arrival of the Fifteenth Cavalry from France and another warm welcome from Cheyenne. This regiment came to Fort D.A. Russell not for demobilization but to take station. The regiment had left France with fifty-one French brides, the first of the many war brides introduced to Cheyenne in the next sixty some years and three more wars. The announcement that the Fifteenth Cavalry would remain at Fort D.A. Russell for at least three years came as particularly good news to Cheyenne. The gnawing uncertainty of what would happen to the post when demobilization ended had risen again. With the regiment tentatively committed to Fort D.A. Russell for three years, army recruiting could encourage the young men of Wyoming to enlist in the Fifteenth Cavalry, where they could stay in their home territory.

An immediate concern of the Cheyenne Frontier Days Committee arose soon after the Fifteenth Cavalry came to the area; would they be mounted in time for the annual parade in July? Cheyenne wanted to see this regular

Fort D.A. Russell served as a regional demobilization point for discharging servicemen at the end of World War I. This 1919 post hospital scene shows patients enjoying an afternoon respite while waiting to have their current medical problems cured before discharge or a medical evaluation for the record.—*WY State AMH Dept.*

army cavalry regiment, fresh from France, in the parade and mounted. Fortunately, 500 horses arrived from the remount station at Reno, Nevada, in early July, and the Fifteenth Cavalry rode in grand style, the hit of the parade.

The last of the Victory Bond drives occurred in August, and a flight of five army DH-4 biplanes flew in to put on an air show as a part of the bond sale promotion. This occasion marked the second visit of army airplanes and a good reason to expect another good air show. However, those expectations were not to be realized. The rough ground at the Fort D.A. Russell flying field caused the flight commander, Lieutenant Clifford M. Nutt, to cancel the exhibition and move on to the next scheduled performance at Fort Morgan, Colorado. The post commander, Brigadier General J.P. O'Neil, had entertained hopes of establishing Fort D.A. Russell as a recognized flying field, and Lieutenant Nutt's early departure seemed a setback in that plan. The prairie dog holes in the flying field were quickly filled, and other improvements were made, but not soon enough to hold the lieutenants flight of airplanes. Some civilian aircraft began to show up in the succeeding months and were encouraged to use the field, the only one in southeast Wyoming.

A new post commander, Brigadier General Benjamin Poore, arrived in September, and he too reasoned that Fort D.A. Russell should have a good flying field. Military and civilian aviation were growing rapidly, and both Cheyenne and Fort D.A. Russell needed a flying field. A joint municipal–military airfield at Fort D.A. Russell had been considered and might provide a solution.

Demobilizing the volunteer "doughboys" and selling Victory Bonds held high priorities in the government throughout the year after the war ended, 1919. The release program continued at a rapid pace throughout the summer, and Fort D.A. Russell ceased to be a demobilization point at the end of September 1919. More than 35,000 soldiers had been processed into civilian status there in eight months. With the completion of this mission, the post came under the control of the Western Military Department with headquarters at San Francisco. The schedule would henceforth consist mostly of routine peacetime garrison duty that could still be interesting and exciting.

President Woodrow Wilson visited during the last stages of the demobilization and received a tremendous welcome from both the military and civilian communities. His stewardship of the nation through the difficult three years, 1916–1919, had received good marks. Wilson was on a national tour to mobilize public support for the League of Nations. A few days later he collapsed in Pueblo, Colorado, and then suffered a stroke that invalided him for the remainder of his presidency.

A few weeks after the president's visit, aviation on a large scale came back to Fort D.A. Russell, and quite unexpectedly. It was announced that a Transcontinental Reliability Test would launch seventy planes, mainly United States Army but also some British and French, from the East Coast and sixteen from the West Coast on October 8 to fly round trips between

Several hundred DH-4 biplanes were manufactured in the United States during World War I under contract with the English DeHaviland Company and served as the backbone of the newly developed Air Service branch of the Army Signal Corps. Considered marginal for combat operations, it still served the United States Army after the war ended and well into the 1930s. The DH-4 shown ready for takeoff in 1920 had landed at the Cheyenne airport. The flying field at Fort D.A. Russell closed in mid-1920 and the military afterwards used the Cheyenne Municipal Airport.—*WY State AMH Dept.*

Governor Nellie Taylor Ross took the first shovel of dirt to launch construction of the new hangars at Cheyenne Municipal Airport for the air mail service. Mrs. Ross was the first woman governor to take office in the U.S. (1925-1927).—*WY State AMH Dept.*

New York and San Francisco. The planes were mainly single-engine DH-4s, with a few French Spads, English SE-5s, and German Fokkers, plus three of the new twin-engine Martin bombers. Contestants were to be judged on the basis of speed and endurance. Fort D.A. Russell's "flying field" was designated as a control point where each contestant was required to land, report, and refuel. The flying field was a hotbed of activity for several days while planes going both directions arrived and departed with a minimum of ground time. The Red Cross, YMCA, Knights of Columbus, and the Industrial Club offered hot coffee and all manner of hospitality and assistance from tents set up on the flying field.

Although there were no fatal crashes at Fort D.A. Russell during the Transcontinental Reliability Test, there were a number of landing accidents caused by the ever-present Wyoming wind. A fatal crash occurred in the Medicine Bow Range seventy-five miles west when Lieutenant Edward Wales, en route to Fort D.A. Russell piloting a DH-4 in bad weather, hit a mountain. Fortunately most of the other contestants were more successful. The best time, east to west, fell to a DH-4 flown by Lieutenant Melvin Maynard: twenty-four hours and fifty-nine minutes flying time over the course of three days. Maynard averaged a ground speed of 109.5 miles per hour for the 2,626 mile race, a remarkable pace for the state of aviation in 1919. The first Trans-continental Reliability Test provided the army with a wealth of data and experience for its rapidly growing air service. It also gave the local military and civilian communities two weeks of exciting aviation activity along with a vastly increased awareness of aviation's potential.

As the military garrison prepared to settle down for the winter after the hectic and exciting aviation activities of October, an extensive strike hit the coal mines of Wyoming and some other Rocky Mountain mining states. Post Commander Brigadier General Benjamin Poore placed all coal mines in Wyoming under federal control. Members of the Fifteenth Cavalry were dispatched to Rock Springs, Hanna, Sheridan, Thermopolis, and Hudson to maintain law and order and to keep the mines operating. By mid-December the strike had been settled and all members of the Fifteenth Cavalry had been withdrawn from the coal camps, happy to return to the barracks of Fort D.A. Russell. Never popular with regular army soldiers, watching over this domestic labor disturbance proved to be no exception with the Fifteenth Cavalry.

The army and Fort D.A. Russell both had to find their postwar mission and niche, in keeping with the country's new role in international affairs and its ability to finance that role. It would take awhile, into the next decade, for these missions and niches to be developed and made discernable to the ever watchful Congress as well as to the communities of Fort D.A. Russell and Cheyenne.

1. *Cheyenne State Leader*, April 22, 1919.

A machine gun company passes in review during a brigade parade on the Argonne parade field in the late 1920s. The army mule remained the favorite animal for pulling gun carriages well into the next decade.—*WY State AMH Dept.*

PART VIII
THE POSTWAR ARMY AT FORT D.A. RUSSELL, 1920–1929

General John J. Pershing, commander-in-chief of the American Expeditionary Force in Europe, is pictured in January 1920 on his first visit to Cheyenne and Fort D.A. Russell after the end of World War I. Pershing first visited the graves of his wife and three daughters in Lakeview Cemetery and then spent two weeks with his father-in-law, Senator Francis E. Warren, and family. Pershing let it be known while in Cheyenne that he was not interested in the White House or becoming a presidential candidate in the coming election. He became chief of staff of the army in 1921. Pictured to General Pershing's right are Mr. A.D. Kelly, Dr. Strader, Judge John A. Riner, Governor Robert A. Carey, and Mr. P.S. Cook.—*WY State AMH Dept.*

Chapter Eighteen
The Flying Field Moves To Cheyenne

The decade of the twenties proved to be the most stable and peaceful period that Fort D.A. Russell had yet enjoyed. It was a period during which the terms "garrison duty" and "post improvement program" gained a meaningful and pleasant connotation. The National Defense Act of June 4, 1920, revised the army of the United States and established it with three components. They were the professional regular army, with 200,000 authorized but manned initially at 150,000, the civilian National Guard, and the civilian Organized Reserves (Officers and Enlisted Reserve Corps). The training of civilian components now became a major peacetime task of the regular army at every post throughout the country. The National Defense Act of 1920 also implemented other major changes, including adding a new branch, the Air Service, to be independent of the Signal Corps.

Although the requirement for rapid deployment of regiments to the Mexican border had been greatly reduced, some army units continued to guard the border when the periodic revolutionary disturbances erupted. The army also maintained a 15,000-man force in the army of occupation in Germany until 1923, and a 1,000-man garrison in Tientsin, China, until 1938. Otherwise, the army served "at home" on garrison duty and other assignments.

The reception of General John J. Pershing in early 1920 was both sad and joyous. This was his first return since the end of the war in Europe. After arrival, Pershing first visited the graves at Lakeview Cemetery of his wife and three daughters killed in the Presidio fire at San Francisco in 1915. He then made an inspection of Fort D.A. Russell. Pershing remained in Cheyenne for about two weeks with his in-laws, the Francis E. Warren family, and fully participated in the whirl of social activity that invariably accompanied his visits. A much-rumored potential presidential candidate, Pershing made it known while in Cheyenne that he was not interested in becoming a resident of the White House.

The Fifteenth Cavalry Regiment, commanded by Colonel T.B. Dugan, was about the only unit available for General Pershing to inspect during his visit. It garrisoned the post for the next eighteen months with an average of fifty officers and 600 men. Colonel Dugan also served as post commander, and as such, established a very close relationship with Cheyenne civic clubs, particularly the chamber of commerce and the Frontier Days Committee. News of the death in New Jersey of an earlier (1919) post commander, Brigadier General Peter W. Davison, recalled a project he had undertaken. Visible projects at the post provided an easy means for Cheyenneites to remember past popular and unpopular post commanders. Davison had made Randall Avenue, the road from the post into Cheyenne, an auto drive that remained "a joy to all motorists."[1]

The announcement that four troops of Utah and Idaho National Guard cavalry would attend summer camp at Fort D.A. Russell began a practice that continued for the next decade and more. However, the big excitement focused on the proposed airfield, a joint military/civilian facility to be located near the eastern main entrance to the post, the same landing area used the previous year. The *Wyoming State Tribune* reported that work would start soon to enlarge the airfield. All would be ready for the transcontinental Air Mail Service flights scheduled to start in early September. The air mail route would follow a Chicago-to-San Francisco track, with Omaha, Cheyenne, and Salt Lake City serving as major centers for the new Air Mail Service. Fort D.A. Russell was particularly excited about this opportunity to participate in and contribute to a new service of the air age.

A rude awakening occurred in July 1920, when it seemed that all parts of the joint airfield venture had come together. Secretary of War Newton Baker, in a telegram to Senator Warren, vetoed the plan to make a joint military/civilian airfield at Fort D.A. Russell. Baker felt that the military might need the area for future expansion of the post. With that news in hand, Cheyenne started the search for a new landing site, which had to be found and prepared in little more than thirty days. The Air Mail Service began operation on September 8. Fortunately, some level land north of town became available. Work started there immediately after the secretary of war's surprising message arrived. That airfield still serves, greatly expanded, as Cheyenne's municipal airport.

Two new planes of the Air Mail Service arrived at Fort D.A. Russell's flying field in August piloted by two distinguished aviators, Captain Eddie Rickenbacker and Bert Acosta. They were scouting the air mail route and the proposed landing sites. The planes were Larson single-engine all-metal monoplanes carrying a pilot, mechanic, and three passengers, the latest thing in aviation. Rickenbacker returned the next year in a DH-4, a World War I single-engine wood and fabric utility biplane used by the Air Mail Service. Attempting to set a cross-country speed record, Rickenbacker landed at the Cheyenne airport after dark with embarrassing results. It had been agreed that the landing area and direction would be marked for his after-dark landing with lighted oil drums. But some confusion existed as to which way the arrow should point, with the wind or into the wind. In any case, it pointed the wrong way for "Captain Eddie's" understanding, and he overshot. Soon after touchdown he hit a depression on the eastern edge of the field that had earlier been the Cheyenne-to-Deadwood stage road. His aircraft overturned when he hit the road, there ending his cross-country speed record attempt.

Unwilling to stay and enjoy the hospitality of Fort D.A. Russell and Cheyenne, Richenbacker left the next day as a passenger in the cramped mail compartment of a DH-4 going east, a frustrated record seeker. If he had stayed a few days, he certainly would have been entertained at the officers' club located on the second floor of the post headquarters building #65. Most social activities of the post now occurred there and in the new clubhouse just completed at the polo field on the east side of the base. Sunday afternoon polo teas were favorite occasions, particularly when a hotly contested polo game was on the docket. The Fifteenth Cavalry Regiment had long fielded a very good polo team. They won the Big Eight polo tournament in August, defeating such favorites as the Denver and Colorado Springs teams.

A return visit of General John Pershing and his son Warren in September, as guests of Senator and Mrs. Francis E. Warren, sparked another "grand reception and ball" for sixty couples, hosted by Colonel T.B. Dugan at the officers' club. General Pershing was reported to be a "splendid dancer" and divided his time with the many ladies present. Pershing became chief of staff of the army the following year.

The long-awaited coast-to-coast air mail service started September 8, 1920, right on schedule, using the newly established Cheyenne airport. While local army authorities were disappointed that the joint military/civilian airfield proposal had not been approved, they were confident that the post would soon have a flying field. Periodic attempts followed, but the convenient and excellent facilities of Cheyenne's municipal airport have encouraged military aviation (air force, Wyoming Air National Guard, and army) to use the Cheyenne airport for more than sixty years.

While army aviation and the fledgling Air Mail Service continued to capture the imagination of the American public, the Fifteenth Cavalry and its popular commander, Colonel Thomas B. Dugan, had some good ideas of great benefit. The regiment expected to grow to its authorized strength by signing up from 800 to more than a 1,000 recruits. A very laudatory article in the *Tribune* on November 15, 1920, reported that Colonel Dugan had succeeded in infusing new life into the post with his recruiting and his other innovative programs. The training program paid close attention to ethics, discipline, and maneuvers, but recreational and social activities also received a high priority in the schedule. Polo, marksmanship, horse racing, hunting, and indoor social events were all popular. An exemplary and very successful social event of the season, hosted by Colonel and Mrs. Dugan and called "Follies en Cabaret," included the social set of Cheyenne. Heading the guest list were such luminaries as Senator and Mrs. Francis E. Warren and State Adjutant General and Mrs. Timothy J. McCoy. McCoy went on to fame in the 1930s as a leading Cowboy actor in western movies. Army Relief benefited by $500 from the follies performance.

Colonel Dugan's recruiting program proved successful from the start, and the garrison's population grew to about forty-three officers and 1,000 enlisted men by the end of 1920, mostly recruits in the Fifteenth Cavalry. While that unit continued to grow, Fort D.A. Russell remained a single-regiment post with many empty barracks. The post could acommodate two more regiments, a full brigade. The Utah National Guard had occupied many of the empty barracks during their two-week summer encampment in 1920, but such temporary usage could hardly help maintain the buildings. Earlier in the year, Colonel Dugan had endeared himself to Cheyenne by offering the empty barracks to the Frontier Days Committee to house the rodeo performers, meals to be furnished at cost.

While the army continued to reorganize and retrench, 1921 found the Fifteenth Cavalry, the single regiment at Fort D.A. Russell, relegated to the inactive list. The specter of a closed Fort D.A. Russell again appeared, and the letters and telegrams flew thick and fast to Senator Francis E. Warren. Cheyenne breathed a sigh of relief when the Thirteenth Cavalry Regiment arrived from Fort Clark, Texas, in September 1921 to take station. The Thirteenth Cavalry incorporated those members of the Fifteenth Cavalry not already transferred away, and then settled down to a six-year stay. Colonel Roy B. Harper commanded the newly arrived Thirteenth Cavalry and the post, while the very popular Colonel Thomas B. Dugan proceeded to Fort Howard, Maryland, for reassignment.

The arrival of the Thirteenth Cavalry lessened, but did not eliminate, the fear that the army might have to abandon Fort D.A. Russell. A newspaper headline expressed some new-found optimism when it proclaimed, "FORT RUSSELL NOT AMONG THOSE TO BE SOLD BY WAR DEPARTMENT." The article explained that as a part of the army's postwar economy, more than seventy military installations across the country had been selected to be sold at auction.

Cheyenne's optimism received another boost in the fall not long after the arrival of the Thirteenth Cavalry when the Fifty-third Infantry, commanded by Colonel McCook, arrived to take station. A local reporter suggested that the Thirteenth Cavalry and Fifty-third Infantry now at Fort D.A. Russell might soon be joined by another regiment, rounding out the number of units for a full brigade. Such a welcome prospect received a hearty reception in Cheyenne even though it seemed too good to be true— such a far cry from the gloomy outlook just a few months before.

One of the first tasks handed the Thirteenth Cavalry was to provide a one-man escort home for each of the bodies of Wyoming men who had died on foreign soil during the war in Europe. Mostly buried in American cemeteries in France during the war, the bodies were shipped to the United States after the war if their families desired for interment in their home state. Fort D.A. Russell served as the focal point for reshipment to the deceased's home town.

Now that the makings of a brigade were again at Fort D.A. Russell, a general officer might be assigned, even though the mission seemed to be one of "escorting remains and conducting burial ceremonies." True to the rumors gaining momentum daily, Brigadier General W.G. Sage arrived in mid-October 1921. An eleven-gun salute signaled the assumption of command for the new post commander. A post "hop" was held two nights later to welcome Brigadier General and Mrs. Sage. Post personnel looked forward to getting acquainted with the new commander and his wife, and a winter of stability and social activities. Extracurricular activities had been largely forgone for many years. The Thirteenth Cavalry set up their officers' mess in quarters #79, ready for business.

General Sage's tenure at Fort D.A. Russell proved to be a short one—he died six months after arrival, at age sixty-three, in Omaha while en route to the army's Walter Reed Hospital in Washington, D.C. He was replaced by Brigadier General Edmund Wittenmyer. The unexpected change of commanders and a midwinter influenza epidemic that grew to serious proportions doomed all social activities for the winter. All gatherings of more than six people were forbidden. Not until mid-March did the epidemic start to abate so that the quarantine could be lifted, just in time for spring.

A visit of the newly appointed chief of chaplains, Colonel John T. Acton, in early 1922 did not help the influenza epidemic but did highlight the growing need for a base chapel. The position of chief of chaplains had been created by the Army Reorganization Act of 1920. Lacking a dedicated religious facility, services had been held in any vacant or available room or building if they were held at all. Chaplain Acton declared that Fort D.A. Russell badly needed a chapel. At the time of his visit, Protestant services and Sunday school classes met in the room set aside for court-martials, busy most weekdays. A Catholic priest from Cheyenne came to the post and said mass on Sunday in a ward of the old (1884) hospital building, which also served as the Red Cross facility. The soldiers' weekly "song service" had to be held at the Service Club, in whatever room or space could be obtained at the time. Before continuing on his visit of western posts, the newspaper reported that Chaplain Acton encouraged a more "mutual feeling" of cooperation between the post and community. Neither the chaplain nor the newspaper offered a further explanation. Despite the chaplain's plea, it would be many years before the army would build a chapel at Fort D.A. Russell.

Aside from the lack of any notable progress in the army's religious activities, 1922 did see progress in many programs. With a few minor burbles, the year began almost eighteen years of relative stability for units and personnel, something quite uncommon during the previous eighteen years. Maneuvers and training exercises were of short duration (two to three weeks) and on a regularly scheduled annual basis. The social and recreational programs provided an attractive and busy part of service life at Fort D.A. Russell. Almost every company had a baseball and basketball team, with regimental teams drawn from the best players in the companies. The Thirteenth Cavalry had four polo teams.

A further reduction in army appropriations ruled out the integrated large-scale regular army maneuvers for several years. Posts such as Fort D.A. Russell held their training exercises and maneuvers on a battalion or regimental scale. The regular army posts also hosted and provided training cadres for state National Guard units as well as training camps for College ROTC and Citizens Military Training Camps (CMTC). The National Guard became the largest component of the army of the United States between the wars. While not comparable to active army units in readiness for war, the National Guard became an important element in the nation's defense. More than a thousand National Guard troops from Utah, Colorado, and Wyoming trained at Fort D.A. Russell during the summer of 1922. Southeast Wyoming provided an excellent locale for such training, and Fort D.A. Russell had the facility.

Summer training camps also offered an excellent occasion for staff visits from higher headquarters to view the level of training, equipment, leadership, readiness, etc. Visits of higher headquarters commanders, usually of only about a day's duration but packed with activities for the commander to see and judge, were particularly useful. Occasionally one of these general officers had been stationed at Fort D.A. Russell as a young lieutenant and had memories to keep, or share, of the early days. Chief of Cavalry Major General W.A. Holbrook accepted an invitation to address the Cheyenne Rotarians when he visited Fort D.A. Russell in May 1922. His staff visit was soon followed by those of the chiefs of infantry and field artillery. A staff visit by the chief of field artillery set the rumor mills to running, since field artillery units had been absent from Fort D.A. Russell for several years.

As was often the case, the rumors had some basis. The post and community felt that things were returning to normal when in June 1922, a part of the Seventy-sixth Field Artillery Regiment arrived from Camp Lewis, Washington, to take station at Fort D.A. Russell. Now the Fourth Brigade at Fort D.A. Russell had a cavalry regiment, the Thirteenth, an infantry regiment, the Fifty-third, and part of a field artillery regiment. It seemed a special favor had been bestowed in view of the recent announcement that appropriations could accommodate only a 125,000-man regular army. The post had finally been raised to brigade strength again, indeed an important occasion.

Along with a vigorous summer training program, infantry, cavalry, and field artillery units found time to participate in the post's busy summer polo schedule. The Thirteenth Cavalry Polo and Hunt Club hosted a week-long Wyoming-Colorado Polo Tournament in July 1922 at Fort D.A. Russell. The tournament opened on a Sunday with a ten-event horse show and nine polo matches. Tea and refreshments were served from the Polo Club House on the championship field at the east side of the post. Weekday games started daily at 3:00 P.M. The Thirteenth Cavalry team ultimately reigned by defeating the Diamond Ranch Team, from near Chugwater, Wyoming, for the championship. The regimental commander, Colonel Ray B. Harper, presented the coveted team trophy to the Thirteenth Cavalry Team, and the individual member cups.

The entire post had been saddened at the start of the tournament when a misfortune cost the Thirteenth Cavalry a distinguished officer and polo player. Lieutenant Colonel James Longstreet, son of the famous

Confederate Corps commander, led his command of the Second Squadron (three troops) in a Saturday morning review of the regiment. Longstreet's squadron had passed the reviewing stand at a walk, then turned at the end of the field and come back at a full charge. Longstreet apparently suffered a stroke in front of the reviewing stand. Without warning or any indication of distress, he pitched headlong from his galloping horse. A very popular and well-known bachelor officer fifty-seven years of age, Longstreet was survived by his mother and a brother in Gainesville, Georgia.

A simple funeral ceremony two days later was "solemnized" in Colonel Longstreet's quarters by Base Chaplain Joseph Garrison. The house was filled with floral tributes from organizations and friends at the post. A military cortege escorted the body to Cheyenne's Union Pacific depot for transport to Arlington National Cemetery. The Cheyenne press provided an excellent account of the occasion. The procession included the full brigade, headed by the regimental band with muffled drums sounding the measured beat of a funeral march. The Second Squadron followed in escort, the sabres of officers and men bearing knots of black crepe. Then came the caisson bearing the casket with Colonel Longstreet's remains. Flanking the casket rode the eight senior sergeants of the regiment. Longstreet's mount followed the caisson in "full mourning caparison," boots strapped to the saddle with heels to the front, led by a walking cavalryman. The eight senior captains of the regiment, as pallbearers, came next, followed by the remainder of the regiment. The Fifty-third Infantry followed, and the Seventy-sixth Field Artillery brought up the rear. The occasion constituted a proper tribute to a senior officer of the regiment and a name distinguished in American military history.

While the units at Fort D.A. Russell enjoyed a summer of garrison activity, labor troubles threatened to disrupt that routine. Widespread unrest in the railroad and mine labor organizations during the summer of 1922 evoked a new national attitude; only in the direst of circumstances would federal troops be used in domestic disturbances. Wyoming Governor Robert Carey did not call for National Guard or regular army troops even though considerable unrest had developed throughout the state. However, several western states did call in their National Guard units in 1922. Illinois and Indiana were two states that requested both National Guard and regular army units, but the use of troops by states against their citizens had begun a significant decline. This trend had the full support of the military, both regular army and National Guard.

The continuing decline of the nation's regular army strength finally leveled off toward the end of 1922 at 125,000 enlisted men and 12,000 officers, not including the 7,000 or so members of the Philippine Scouts. The army stabilized at this number until 1936, and War Department appropriations leveled off at about $300 million per year. A reduction in the number of regiments—infantry reduced to thirty-seven and cavalry to fourteen—resulted in the inactivation of the Fifty-third Infantry Regiment in September 1922, after only a year at Fort D.A. Russell. Personnel of the Fifty-third Infantry were assigned to Fort Logan, at Denver, and Fort

A 1922 aerial view of Fort D.A. Russell looking east toward Cheyenne shows the original diamond-shaped parade ground. Also shown are the base hospital at #1, brigade headquarters building and officers club in building #65 at #2, cemetery at #3, Randall Avenue at #4, the riding hall at #5, and the 1884 barracks 209, which

had just burned, at #6. Three years later next-door barracks 208 also burned to the ground. In 1932, a two-story two-company brick barracks was erected (building 208) to replace the two burned buildings, now occupied by the Base Contracting Division.—*WY State AMH Dept.*

Douglas, at Salt Lake City, leaving about a thousand cavalry and field artillery personnel at Fort D.A. Russell.

One of the many immediate concerns with the latest troop reduction at Fort D.A. Russell arose with the reassignment of Chaplain Joseph G. Garrison to the Chaplains' School at Fort Wayne, Michigan. Chaplains were authorized at the rate of one for every thousand enlisted men assigned to a post. With Fort D.A. Russell's strength reduced to about the one thousand level, the assignment of a replacement chaplain seemed uncertain. However, a Catholic chaplain, Father Connelly, did arrive in a few months to fill the position. He was the first military Catholic chaplain to be assigned to the post on a full-time basis.

The Thirteenth Cavalry started the winter season of 1923 by holding the first of a series of winter horse shows in the post riding hall with all of Cheyenne invited. The series culminated in March with a Saint Patrick's Day gymkhana offering all sorts of riding events. Post Commander Brigadier General Edmund Wittenmeyer, along with the officers and enlisted men, invited the people of Cheyenne to be their guests at this largest and most spectacular of horse shows. The press announcement of the event reminded readers how easily they could get to the post riding hall at Fort D.A. Russell; it was only a block from the Randall Avenue streetcar line.

The reduced Fort D.A. Russell brigade settled down to a garrison routine in the winter and spring of 1923, a routine that followed a similar pattern for the next sixteen years, or until the approach of World War II. The schedule included a busy athletic and social program, with some regimental maneuvers in the local area, target practice and supervised training camps for National Guard units, Reserve Officer Training Corps (ROTC) detachments, and the Citizens' Military Training Camps (CMTC). CMTC offered "summer vacations free" for young men between the ages of seventeen and twenty-four with all expenses paid. Being the only complete regiment on the post, the Thirteenth Cavalry had their hands full with the various summer training programs. National Guard units—about a thousand cavalrymen—from Wyoming, Utah, Idaho, and Washington also attended summer camp at Fort D.A. Russell, occupying barracks on the western half of the post that had been emptied by the deactivation of the Fifty-third Infantry.

A visit by President Warren G. Harding in June 1923 turned out to be a bit different than previous presidential visits. In the past these had been festive occasions with pomp and ceremony. However, this visit proved to be a bit of a disappointment. The short stop of one hour and a half allowed for only the very necessary formalities and did not include a visit to Fort D.A. Russell, the first presidential visit to omit the post. The closest thing to a ceremony occurred when the Air Mail Service DH-4 planes from Cheyenne escorted the presidential train from the Colorado-Wyoming border to town. It was neither customary nor comfortable for airplanes to escort railroad trains, even those carrying presidents; still, it could not have been a difficult task in 1923. The cruising speed of a DH-4 was not much more than the train's normal speed.

Harding spoke from the rear of the train at the Union Pacific depot in Cheyenne and then moved to the Plains Hotel a block away for a brief reception. The presidential party proceeded from Cheyenne on west to the coast and Alaska. On the return trip, Harding died in San Francisco of a heart attack. Harding's second visit to Cheyenne did not take any more time than the first. The funeral train carrying the body of the former president to Washington, D.C., stopped briefly in Cheyenne. Included in the escorting party were Senators Francis E. Warren of Wyoming and Borah of Idaho, as well as General John H. Pershing.

A month after the Harding funeral train passed through, a new post commander, Brigadier General John M. Jenkins, arrived from San Francisco and moved into quarters #92, designated for the senior commander. General Jenkins would stay at Fort D.A. Russell for almost four years, ending the past tendency of short tours for post commanders. He left a very favorable imprint on the history of the post. As a part of General Jenkins's welcome, Senator Warren took the occasion to tell a meeting of the Cheyenne Rotary Club that the permanency of Fort D.A. Russell was never better assured, and the prospects for an early increase in troop strength at the post were bright. The American Legion Post in Cheyenne had earlier petitioned the secretary of war to "adequately garrison" Fort D.A. Russell. Certainly the Wyoming congressional delegation had been pressuring the Coolidge administration for more troops at Fort D.A. Russell, and Senator Francis E. Warren led that drive.

Despite the high hopes of the Wyoming delegation, a letter from Secretary of War Jolink Weeks warned that reduced army appropriations had caused a reduction in manpower at many army posts, and more reductions might follow. Secretary Weeks's, letter concluded that it did not seem practical to increase strength at Fort D.A. Russell in the forseeable future. This left a continuing degree of uncertainty about Fort D.A. Russell, but no uncertainty about any support the secretary might contribute.

1. *Wyoming State Tribune*, February 13, 1920.

Automotive power did not come to the infantry, cavalry and artillery units at Fort D.A. Russell until the mid-1930s. Horses and mules remained an important part of the tactical ground unit. In 1927, building 330 pictured served as one of thirty stables. Remaining in much the same exterior configuration, it now serves as a warehouse.)—*WY State AMH Dept.*

Chapter Nineteen
A Community Relations Committee Is Born

Summer camps at Fort D.A. Russell for 1924 included many Coloradans, Colorado State University's ROTC detachment, and 200 National Guardsmen. A particularly festive "hop" was hosted by the post officers and ladies at headquarters for the officers of the Colorado National Guard with Brigadier General and Mrs. John M. Jenkins presiding. The newspaper report told of the beautiful decorations in the ballroom, including regimental standards, masses of lillies, and many gay Chinese lanterns. A reception preceded the dancing, with music provided by the Seventy-sixth Field Artillery orchestra. Supper was served at 11:00 P.M. in the dining room.

A former polo player and avid fan, General Jenkins had arrived in time to preside over the annual Fort D.A. Russell Polo Tournament. Sponsored by the Thirteenth Cavalry Polo and Hunt Club, six highly rated and touted teams from the Rocky Mountain area entered, all hoping to take home the "silver." Much to the surprise of everyone, a little-known Colorado Springs team emerged victorious and garnered all the glory of the 1924 tournament.

A month later, during the annual Frontier Days celebration in Cheyenne, the ladies' clubs of the post put on a Carnival Ball at the post headquarters for two big nights of fun and frolic, admission one dollar for the benefit of the newly organized Army Relief. There were also booths in front of the post headquarters, an area known as Headquarters Park, where "anybody could buy anything." Reported to be a big success with lots of fun for everyone, the Carnival Ball complemented Cheyenne's big event.

Cheyenne's Frontier Days celebration enjoyed a record crowd in 1924. Fort D.A. Russell units were well represented in the parade and other events. The Cheyenne press made this report:

> The Thirteenth Cavalry from Fort D.A. Russell presented a striking scene. Sabers flashed as the horses hoofs beat a tatoo on the pavement. The Seventy-Sixth Field Artillery, the big guns and caissons drawn by six horses each, rolling with the deep rumble always associated with artillery. The Army mule, historic and much

written about, came next drawing field wagons and medical outfits. All slicked up, the mules showed no sign of their reputed cussedness.[1]

After the Cheyenne Frontier Days celebration had been ended and the town tidied up, the troops at Fort D.A. Russell received the news that streetcar service from Cheyenne to Fort D.A. Russell would be replaced by motor bus service. The streetcar track would be removed from Carey Avenue. The Cheyenne Motor Bus Company, operated by local businessman W.E. Dineen, promised to provide a forty-minute schedule for the round trip, with the last departure from downtown at midnight. Although the fare of ten cents remained the same, motor buses did not sound as reliable as streetcars in the minds of the soldiers. The army had not yet moved far toward automotive means of transportation, but Cheyenne businessmen wanted to give it a try.

The arrival of General John Pershing in late August on a final inspection trip of western posts before retirement as army chief of staff signaled the end of an era, the last of the Indian wars veterans to serve as head of the army. General Pershing's inspection of Fort D.A. Russell and the Pole Mountain Target and Maneuver Reserve were given all the attention and respect the occasion deserved. Brigadier General and Mrs. Jenkins hosted General Pershing and his party at a gala dinner in the post commanders quarters. Guests for the occasion included General Pershing's father-in-law, Senator Francis E. Warren, Wyoming Governor and Mrs. William B. Ross, the commander of the Thirteenth Cavalry, Colonel and Mrs. John J. Boniface, and the commander of the Seventy-sixth Field Artillery, Colonel and Mrs. Alden F. Brewster.

Francis E. Warren was not only a good partygoer but a good representative of his constituency. Good news, not unexpected and in keeping with past promises, came with the arrival in October 1924 of half of the Fourth Cavalry Regiment commanded by Colonel T.Q. Donaldson. The Second Squadron, consisting of Troops E, F, G, Band, and Service Troop, 300 strong, came from Fort McIntosh, Texas, to take station at Fort D.A. Russell. The other half of the Fourth Cavalry Regiment had previously been sent to Fort Meade, South Dakota. Fort D.A. Russell now boasted three regimental bands on post, a situation bound to delight the people of Cheyenne. As the year 1924 closed, Fort D.A. Russell had one full cavalry regiment plus one squadron of another. The battalion of field artillery made a total strength of about sixty-eight officers and 1,500 enlisted men. There were also some 1,180 horses for riding and draft, and 260 mules. The garrison covered 5,920 acres and had approximately 210 buildings, 120 of which were officers' quarters, and 45 of which were barracks, guardhouses, canteens, regimental headquarters, and so forth. The remaining 40 of the 210 buildings were used as stables, gun sheds, and storage.

A Cheyenne newspaper article in December 1924 pointed out the opportunity soldiers at Fort D.A. Russell now had for self-improvement and recreation. Six mornings a week they devoted to military instruction and schoolwork, but the afternoons were usually their own time for athletics and recreation. Many practical skills were learned in addition to their military instruction. There were also classes in grade and high school subjects. For recreation, a variety of activities were available to soldiers at the Service Club. The club maintained a large library, a reading room, a gymnasium with running track, and a pool room. Three motion picture shows ran each week with a small admission charge. Also, the non-commissioned officers' club and a commissioned officers club were functioning and were considered purely social organizations.

The military school system at Fort D.A. Russell, producing such good results, had been a product of the Army Reorganization Act of 1920. The act called for a vocational training system that would give the soldier a vocation or trade useful to the army and also useful to the soldier when he left the army. Fort D.A. Russell had four types of schools in 1925. They were post schools proper attended by all men of the post; unit schools conducted by the regiments to train specialists in particular arms such as infantry, cavalry, and field artillery; noncommissioned officers' school in which military subjects were taught by the captain of the company, troop, or battery for the NCOs; and the officers' schools conducted within the regiment for the instruction of regimental officers in military subjects. Six post schools for enlisted men included clerk's school (typewriting and clerical work taught by the post adjutant), saddlery school, which included harness repair and leatherwork, communications (line and wireless telegraphy, telephony, and mechanics of electricity), general education for soldiers who had not completed regular gradeschool work, and school for stable sergeants (animal husbandry, anatomy, and diseases of horses taught by a veterinarian). Post schools were taught seven months of the year, late fall to early spring.

While education and training provided one incentive for enlistments, more were needed. The army tried in many ways during 1925 to make service life more attractive to young men. The army needed recruits, and raising pay was out of the question. The one-year enlistment provided one of those attractions. Tried earlier and abolished in 1922 when objected to by influential War Department and army leaders, enlistees could now choose any regiment or branch of service for a one-year committment. This lesser period proved to be much more acceptable for many young men than the earlier three- and five-year periods of committment.

While never popular among recruits or the enlisted men, polo continued to grow in popularity among the officers at Fort D.A. Russell. Polo's popularity, to the exclusion of other sports in fact, caused the announced sale of a pack of "sight hounds" in February 1925. The Thirteenth Cavalry had acquired the pack many years before for hunting coyotes. Sight hounds followed game by sight rather than scent. The pack included three foxhounds, but most were crosses between the Russian wolfhound and the Irish staghound. Rarely used for the past two years, the hounds were quickly bought by local hunters.

A new idea for military/civilian community relations was introduced in early 1925 by the Cheyenne chamber of commerce at the suggestion of Post/Brigade Commander Brigadier General John M. Jenkins. The chamber enthusiastically accepted Jenkins's suggestion and appointed senior members of their group to work with senior officers of the post. The purpose of the combined committee would be to promote common interests. Chamber members named, all prominent in business or ranching, included L.R. Probst as chairman, William G. Haas, Warren Forbes, Allen J. Peterson, and Fred Boice. Military members included the three regimental commanders, Colonel John J. Boniface, Thirteenth Cavalry; Colonel Joseph S. Herron, Seventy-sixth Field Artillery; and newly arrived Colonel Osmun Latrobe, Fourth Cavalry. Also included were senior medical officer Major H.H. Sharpe and Quartermaster Captain Lincoln Martin. This committee, in form and purpose, has functioned now for more than sixty-two years. Social, business, and community relations have long benefited from this ambitious, innovative, and hardworking committee.

The season's social schedule picked up in mid-1925 when the new commander of the Fourth Cavalry and his wife, Colonel and Mrs. Osmun Latrobe, entertained with a dinner dance for about sixty at their quarters on the post. Guests included officers of the Fourth Cavalry and their ladies, and Brigadier General and Mrs. Jenkins. Tables were decorated with unit colors, and the regimental orchestra furnished music for dancing. A confident move for a newly arrived regimental commander, the affair seemed to be a huge success. Normally, quarters were not large enough to accommodate sixty guests at a dinner dance, plus a regimental orchestra and the kitchen help necessary for such an affair. The Latrobes were a popular couple, entertaining frequently during their tour at Fort D.A. Russell.

The approach of spring created a sympathetic attempt by the Thirteenth Cavalry and the chamber of commerce to provide some outdoor entertainment for the principals of the long and involved Teapot Dome trial underway in the federal district court in Cheyenne. Included were the press representatives, witnesses, and counsel, plus many interested spectators. The entertainment started with a Saturday afternoon dress parade and regimental review on the post parade ground. The Black Horse Troop then gave a musical drill, followed by a demonstration of the cavalry charge. The chamber concluded the day's entertainment with a reception at their offices in the old Cheyenne Club building, with Cheyenne residents also invited. The Thirteenth Cavalry took great pride in their performance, and the Teapot Dome trial offered a welcome occasion to parade.

Another parade and inspection occurred the following month for the army chief of staff, Major General John L. Hines. General Hines expressed his satisfaction with the inspection and declared the post and units in "good shape." The following month, Fort D.A. Russell had several more inspections by higher headquarters officers. They included Chief of Cavalry Major General Malin Craig, followed by the newly appointed Ninth Corps Area commander headquartered at the Presidio, San Francisco, Major General Charles T. Menoher. The senior commanders were getting their annual inspections out of the way before the ROTC, CMTC, and National Guard summer camps began.

More than 1,500 men of the civilian components from seven states received training in 1925 from the regular army men of Fort D.A. Russell. The CMTC reported a very successful camp and more applicants than could be accommodated. The Wyoming National Guard, 115th Cavalry, and the Fifty-eighth Machine Gun Squadron reported similar results with their sixth annual summer camp. Army Air Service airplanes, observation types for reconnaissance and adjusting artillery fire, were scheduled to take part in the summer camp maneuvers for the first time. According to Seventy-sixth Field Artillery Commander Colonel Joseph S. Herson, airplanes offered "the application for winning future wars," a view not yet widely held.

The territory of the training area, the Fort D.A. Russell Target and Maneuver Reservation thirty miles west of the post, changed slightly in June. A new 3,000-acre forest reserve had been established on the reservation by presidential order. It would be known as the Pole Mountain District of the Medicine Bow National Forest. The land for the forest reserve would be transferred from the War Department to the Interior Department but would remain available for the War Department's unrestricted use. Some welcome new permanent buildings were erected on the reservation in 1925, including a mess hall, kitchen, and officers' mess. Also, a year-round full-time caretaker was hired, but his tenure proved to be a short one—he was arrested in late June with ninety-one gallons of newly made bootleg whiskey on hand. Apparently the caretaker did not intend for any of the trainees to go thirsty at summer camp.

While training came first, the summer polo schedule followed a close second. The Fort D.A. Russell polo team started the season in June by winning the Ninth Corps Area annual tournament held at Boise, Idaho, and they were ready for the annual two-week post tournament the following month. Each of the three regiments had a strong team entered in the tournament. There were also teams from as far away as Fort Sam Houston at San Antonio, Texas, eager to compete for the "silver." Wyoming Governor Nellie Tayloe Ross, the first female to take office as governor in the United States, opened the tournament by throwing in the first ball. The Thirteenth Cavalry team lost to Fort Sam Houston in the final game of the series, which, all agreed, had been notable for the distinguished level of play.

There were some minor injuries, but nothing serious during the two-week tournament, unusual for the many games played in tough competition. The only serious polo mishap occurred in a game just before the tournament started when Captain George G. Ball of the Fourth Cavalry team received fatal injuries. A popular and highly respected officer, Ball had been president of his 1908 Harvard College graduating class. Funeral services were held in the deceased captain's quarters #57 at Fort D.A. Russell. Following the funeral, his ashes were taken to Weston, Massachusetts, by his widow.

The winter schedule of social activities included a huge Valentine's Day party in February 1926 at post headquarters for 150 guests. Then the annual Fort D.A. Russell Horse Show in the post riding hall helped to brighten the waning days of a cold season. Sponsored by the Fourth Cavalry and featuring their Black Horse Troop F as the star performers, the show received high praise from all attendees. The occasion also celebrated the seventy-first anniversary of the Fourth Cavalry Regiment. A few days later, the Fourth Cavalry hosted a regimental dinner dance at the regimental officers' club in recognition of their Seventy-first anniversary.

Not to be outdone, the Thirteenth Cavalry celebrated their twenty-fifth anniversary in April 1926 with a parade and horse show, plus a dinner dance at the Plains Hotel for officers of that regiment and their ladies. The newly assigned regimental commander, Colonel H.R. Richmond, presided at the festivities.

A new application of weapons appeared in the spring of 1926 when four batteries of Seventy-sixth Field Artillery began antiaircraft machine-gun firing practice on the target range on the west side of the post. The rapid development of airplanes as weapons of war had raised the need for antiaircaft weapons, but some time would pass before the War Department would become concerned. The post's targets for this occasion were makeshift rubber balloons filled with hydrogen, substituting for airplanes. After the balloons were filled with the hydrogen that had been carried to the range in a wagon, they were released by a horseman about a thousand yards in front of the guns. The guns started firing as soon as the horseman got out of the way. Both tracer and regular ammunition were used, and most of the target balloons drifted away from the range of the guns unscathed. The Seventy-sixth Field Artillery commander, Colonel Herron, said that this exercise was the first work of this kind done by line artillery.

The annual summer camps and polo games greatly enhanced the "usual garrison duties" for the summer of 1926. Some rearranging of facilities was also taking place. The *Leader* noted on September 14, 1926, that two bells and a piece of ordnance, all historic war trophies brought back from the Philippines in 1904 by the Eleventh Infantry, had been placed at the base of the flagpole in Trophy Park at Fort D.A. Russell. The bells and cannon had initially been displayed in 1905 at the flagpole when it was located at the original 1867 parade ground on the west side of the post. Since the concerned units, the Ninth and Eleventh Infantry regiments, had long ago departed the post, people had forgotten how historic those trophies really were.

A champion of good public relations, Brigadier General John M. Jenkins had taken great pains to keep the people of Cheyenne informed of activities at Fort D.A. Russell. His association with Cheyenne's leaders had been close since his arrival more than two years before. He had many friends in the town and in the state. But General Jenkins had a point to make when he spoke to the Lions Club meeting in November 1926. He felt that soldiers from Fort D.A. Russell were not being treated well by Cheyenne, and that the city had done nothing in return for the $100,000,000 spent there by soldiers since 1867. About $1,200,000 now went annually into coffers of Cheyenne, according to Jenkins, but in spite of that the city had no welcome for the soldiers. He called on Cheyenne to furnish a clubhouse or some such facility where soldiers and citizens might meet on common ground "instead of the streets and pool halls." Jenkins concluded his talk by telling his Lions Club audience that he liked Cheyenne and was pleased to be serving the last of his forty-three years of service at Fort D.A. Russell. Jenkins's popularity in Cheyenne blunted what would otherwise have been a quick and sharp reaction. No adverse press comment appeared in the days following his diatribe, and his popularity continued at its previously high level.

Some long-awaited good news appeared at the post as 1926 drew to a close: a major modification to an existing building would provide a 450-seat theater, to open in December. Films had previously been shown three nights a week at the Service Club, building #284, but now a dedicated theater would be enjoyed in a remodeled infantry barracks, building #217. These 1884 barracks had originally been built in the form of a large U. Part of one side of the U would now be remodeled to serve as a post chapel. The remainder of the building would be given over to the theater and a generous lobby. The theater would be at the base of the U shape. The recently formed Army Motion Picture Service had provided most of the $4,200 required for the remodeling. The theater included a sloping floor to give a good view of the screen to all patrons of the two shows a night, six nights a week. Admission charge remained at the previous price of fifteen cents.

While neither increases in pay nor promotions came easily to either the members of the military or the civilian employees at Fort D.A. Russell, sometimes outstanding service did get recognized. Mrs. Anne Bresche, superintendent of the post laundry in building #372, received a citation for efficiency and long service. Mrs. Bresche had started work at the post laundry at thirty dollars a month in 1911, the year the post laundry building had been completed. She had become superintendent in 1919, and now her pay amounted to two hundred dollars a month, a very respectable salary indeed.

The services of company laundresses had been discontinued by Congress first in the 1870s and then more positively by the army in the 1880s. It had taken several years to phase the laundresses out of the work force at Fort D.A. Russell because many were married to soldiers and were authorized to accompany their husbands until the end of their enlistment. But in 1883, the army ceased issuing rations to laundresses, thus ending official recognition of the laundresses and their historic institution. After they were gone, most army posts were hard pressed for laundry services. Chinese laborers were hired for a while at Fort D.A. Russell to do the laundry, but that arrangement proved unsatisfactory. The building of a steam laundry in 1911 and the hiring of laundry workers, including Mrs. Bresche, solved the post's laundry problem for many years.

In addition to low cost laundry, the army felt the need for other enticements that would encourage enlistments in 1927. Accordingly, the local army recruiting service offered eligible Cheyenne residents, and men within a hundred-mile radius, a special one-year "hitch" with duty at Fort D.A. Russell, provided they had no prior service. The army didn't want to pay for travel beyond a hundred miles, and the one-year enlistment "at home" again seemed to the Congress like a less expensive way to attract recruits. Despite the low pay, the program enjoyed a measure of success in attracting young men from southeast Wyoming and northern Colorado.

The departure of Brigadier General John Jenkins in June set a new high standard for ceremonial departures that would stand for some time. This despite, or perhaps because of, his very critical comments earlier to the Cheyenne Lions Club. After his farewell appearance at all the civic clubs, the Cheyenne chamber of commerce chose Judge T. Blake Kennedy to give a speech praising Jenkins's good work and fine cooperation with the Cheyenne community. Included in the listing of his many accomplishments were the planting of thousands of trees at the post and the building of a new polo field.

When Brigadier General and Mrs. Jenkins departed the post for the Union Pacific depot in Cheyenne, all available troops of the Thirteenth and Fourth Cavalry, and the Seventy-sixth Field Artillery, were lined along Capital Avenue in Cheyenne all the way to the depot. As the train pulled out of the station for the east, four artillery pieces at Fort D.A. Russell started firing the customary eleven-gun salute, a tribute to a much respected and beloved brigade/post commander. Before his retirement, Jenkins was promoted to major general. A highly decorated veteran of the wars in Cuba, the Philippines, and France, Brigadier General Dwight E. Aultman, soon arrived as Jenkins's replacement.

Soon after General Jenkins's departure, a surprising development threatened to shatter the summer polo schedule and diminish the post's vital support of the Cheyenne Frontier Days activities. Orders were received for both the Thirteenth and Fourth Cavalry to leave Fort D.A. Russell before the July Frontier Days program began. The Thirteenth Cavalry had been ordered to Fort Riley, Kansas, and the Fourth Cavalry to Fort Meade, South Dakota, where it would join the rest of the regiment. Only the Seventy-sixth Field Artillery would remain at Fort D.A. Russell.

In an effort to salvage the city's celebration, Cheyenne Mayor C.W. Riner asked Senator Francis E. Warren to petition the War Department to delay the Thirteenth Cavalry's departure from Fort D.A. Russell until after Frontier Days. The cavalry's participation, particularly the drills of Black Horse Troop F, had always been a special attraction since the arrival of the regiment in 1921. Senator Warren's response appeared in the Cheyenne newspaper. He told the mayor and citizens that the transfers of the Thirteenth and Fourth Cavalry regiments could not be avoided and would take place as scheduled. However, the senator promised that new units would soon arrive at Fort D.A. Russell. These units would increase the post's total strength significantly, to more than 2,000 men. The good news appeared to far outweigh the bad news.

The Thirteenth and Fourth Cavalry regiments bid the post and town a fond farewell on June 16, 1927. Colonel H.R. Richmond led the Thirteenth

The three-quarter-mile-long Argonne Parade ground of Fort D.A. Russell easily accommodated the three regiments of the Fourth Brigade in a 1927 Saturday morning review. The mounted troops, wagons, and gun carriages often passed in review with horses and mules at full gallop.—*WY State AMH Dept.*

Cavalry into Cheyenne and through the business district on the start of a 600-mile overland march to Fort Riley. The Thirteenth Cavalry planned to proceed east from Cheyenne on Lincoln Highway into Nebraska and then south, making twenty-five miles a day initially and increasing that gradually as men and animals became conditioned. The Fourth Cavalry, led by Colonel Osmun Latrobe, chose a more direct route for their march to Fort Meade, South Dakota. They cut across the prairie from the post and intersected Yellowstone Highway north of town.

The departure of the Thirteenth and Fourth Cavalry regiments in 1927 ended a long series of cavalry unit assignments to Fort D.A. Russell. For the next thirteen years, infantry regiments would dominate. The post would be the home of the Fourth Infantry Brigade, the parent unit for two infantry regiments and a battalion, sometimes two, of the Seventy-sixth Field Artillery Regiment. A shift in command also occurred when Fort D.A. Russell moved from the control of the Ninth Corps Area headquartered at the Presidio in San Francisco to the Eighth Corps Area headquartered at Fort Sam Houston in San Antonio, Texas.

True to his promise to Cheyenne, Senator Warren again convinced the War Department to assign more troops to Fort D.A. Russell. The arrival of Colonel J.F. Preston with the First Infantry and Colonel Fred L. Munson commanding the Twentieth Infantry generated a page one banner in the Cheyenne newspaper that read, "GREETINGS AND WELCOME TO

Colonel John F. Preston, commander of the First Infantry, stands at attention on the Argonne Parade in April 1928 with all members of his regiment attired in the regulation lapel blouse with khaki shirt and brown tie. Officers are wearing boots and enlisted men high top shoes with the wool wrap leggins detested by all soldiers. The wool leggins remained a part of the infantryman's uniform until World War II when they were replaced by canvas lace-up leggins and then a combat boot.
—*WY State AMH Dept.*

NEW FORT RUSSELLITES." The edition was devoted to the history of the post and the two newly arrived regiments. The editor carefully pointed out that relations between the post and the city had been good most of the time during the past sixty years, and expected things to be even better during the next sixty years. The good features of the military and civilian communities listed by the newspaper included (a) bus service to town every twenty minutes with a ten-cent fare, (b) a paved road from downtown Cheyenne to the edge of the post, (c) two passenger trains a day going east and west from Cheyenne, (d) four bachelor apartment buildings on post with thirty apartments, each containing two rooms and bath. Each building also contained mess and club facilities at a cost to occupants of about thirty-five dollars per month, (e) officers' quarters included seventeen sets of single quarters for field grade married officers, twenty sets of duplex quarters for captains, and thirteen sets of single quarters for married lieutenants, totaling accommodations for fifty families, (f) a commissary supplying the mess halls stocked with fresh vegetables, butter, eggs, and staple goods, (g) a post exchange with excellent stock, ordering privileges, a good restaurant, and a tailor shop, (h) a post service club where soldiers found wholesome enjoyment and enlightenment. The article concluded with the statement that Fort D.A. Russell meant a lot to the businessmen of Cheyenne, with the quartermaster expending more than half a million dollars yearly in the community, in addition to the pay of the officers and enlisted men.

The newly arrived regiments assumed the task of providing for the 1927 summer camps of the CMTC, ROTC, and National Guard with hardly a pause. They were also able to support the Cheyenne Frontier Days activities at the expected level, but the polo schedule suffered. In fact polo never again attained the level of activity it enjoyed during the mid-1920s with two cavalry regiments assigned. Some concern arose as to whether polo could survive at Fort D.A. Russell without the cavalry. Survive it did, but at a diminished level.

A visit in October 1927 by Army Chief of Staff Major General Charles F. Summeral provided an occasion for military and social activities that much of the community could enjoy. The festivities started with a full-scale review of the Fourth Infantry Brigade, which included the two new infantry regiments, and much of the Cheyenne community attended. A smaller and more select group was invited when Brigadier General Dwight E. Aultman entertained at lunch for the reviewing party. Included among the luncheon guests were Wyoming's Senator Francis E. Warren and Governor Frank C. Emerson.

There was an even more entertaining occasion for the community in the late fall of 1927 when America's march king, John Philip Sousa, and his band arrived in Cheyenne for a performance at the Lincoln Theater. Sousa was officially welcomed by the military staff and regimental bands from Fort D.A. Russell. The three post bands filled the air with Sousa marches as they led the procession of 3,000 citizens from the Union Pacific depot to the theater. On arrival at the theater and before the Sousa band started its performance at 8:30 A.M., the combined Fort D.A. Russell bands occupied the stage and played "Riders of the Flag." This march had been earlier written by Sousa and dedicated to Colonel Osmun Latrobe and the men of the Fourth Cavalry when they were stationed at Fort D.A. Russell.

Although none were so famous or entertaining as John Philip Sousa, the stream of visitors continued as 1927 came to a close. One visitor, unofficial but important, received a great deal of attention. He was General William Heye, chief of staff of the German Republic Army, who was visiting several military installations in this country. Nine years had elapsed since the war with Germany had ended, and much of the bitterness that Americans had earlier felt had diminished. Still, the visit was listed as "unofficial." All the courtesies were extended General Heye, including a parade review of the more than 2,000 officers and men stationed at Fort D.A. Russell. Brigadier General and Mrs. Dwight E. Aultman were also "at home" to the officers and ladies of the post, and their friends in Cheyenne, on the afternoon after the review in honor of General Heye.

1. *Wyoming State Tribune-Cheyenne State Leader*, July 24, 1924, p. 1.

Rancher, merchant and legislator, Senator Francis E. Warren served in successively important capacities starting soon after his 1868 arrival in Cheyenne. On January 1, 1930, Fort D.A. Russell was renamed Fort Francis E. Warren in his honor, and then Francis E. Warren Air Force Base in November 1949. A Civil War veteran, Senator Warren proudly wore the Medal of Honor ribbon in his lapel awarded for "Gallantry on the battlefield at the siege of Port Hudson."—*WY State AMH Dept.*

Chapter Twenty
Senator Warren's Last Visit

The transfer of Fourth Brigade Commander Brigadier General Dwight E. Aultman to Fort Sill, Oklahoma, to head the artillery school, surprised the post and Aultman. He had been less than a year at Fort D.A. Russell. General Aultman had made many improvements and had more in mind, including a plan for naming all streets on the post. He reasoned that unnamed streets caused confusion to visitors looking for a particular place. Streets had been referred to as "the street in front of the officers quarters," or "the street in back of the barracks." Aultman had thousands of trees planted during his short tenure, funds had been obtained to repair many buildings that had fallen into disrepair, old hospital building (building #31) had been made into NCO quarters, road equipment, the first ever obtained, was bought with army funds, and the roads around the post, which were all dirt and gravel, were improved and maintained. General Aultman attributed the success of his post improvement program to the great help he received from two prominent Cheyenne citizens, Fred Warren and George Brimmer.

Post streets were soon named, and the new names were often those of Civil War leaders. There were Warren, Roosevelt, Sherman, and Rosencrans avenues. East-west roads were called avenues and north-south roads were called streets. Circles and parade grounds were also named, with parade grounds taking the names of important World War I battles.

The newly arrived Brigadier General Frank C. Bolles announced that he intended to continue the improvement program started by his predecessors. He also expressed a desire to continue the close community relationship. When the Cheyenne Frontier Days Committee declared that they were receiving the best cooperation from the post ever received since the event started many years before, it was clear that Bolles had established cordial relations.

In continuing the post improvement program, General Bolles hoped to get natural gas to replace the soft coal in use throughout the post, which caused such a "smudge." Also high on Bolles's list was pavement for Randall Avenue from the main gate west through the post, plus some other important streets.

While the post improvement program continued at full speed with most

Brigadier General Charles R. Howland, popular post and Fourth Brigade commander at newly renamed Fort Francis E. Warren, stands with his staff for the brigade to pass in review in the summer of 1930. Howland introduced a post improvement program soon after his arrival in 1929. Included were grass greens for the golf course, a 225-foot-long concrete swimming pool near Crow Creek, and a four-thousand-seat sports stadium named the Warren Bowl used for the next twenty-eight years by the local civilian and military communities.—WY State AMH Dept.

of the labor drawn from the base guardhouse, plus some labor contributed by designated units, the summer camp schedule carried on as usual. ROTC units from the University of Utah and Colorado Agricultural College were among the first to arrive. In August most of the Fourth Infantry Brigade, along with the Wyoming National Guard, was at Pole Mountain participating in maneuvers. Secretary of War Dwight F. Davis arrived in late July to attend the Frontier Days rodeo. He then proceeded to Pole Mountain for several days to inspect and review the camps and maneuvers there, after inspecting Fort D.A. Russell.

More post projects were reported in September and October. An additional chapel was created on the second floor of the brigade/post headquarters building #65. A renewed officers' club also had it's grand opening on the second floor of the building. It included "excellent facilities for dinner dances," a kitchen, dining room, ballroom with maple dance floor, card room, and barber shop, plus other facilities and a civilian steward. The post's nine-hole golf course, which adjoined the nine-hole Cheyenne Country Club, had also seen considerable improvement in the fairways and bunkers. An enlarged post theater now had a stage that could accommodate vaudeville shows as well as motion pictures, and a seating capacity of more than six hundred patrons. The $10,000 cost for modifying the theater had again been borne by the Army Motion Picture Service. The post commander could also boast that for the first time, all married non-commissioned officers entitled to quarters, and deserving such, were housed at Fort D.A. Russell.

The vigorous post improvement program that continued into 1929 included projects of a type that didn't require much money. Today they would be described as "self-help" projects done with available materials and labor. Military appropriations allocated by the Congress in 1929 had reached the niggardly level.

The improvement projects at Fort D.A. Russell did contribute to the well-being of the garrison, but they did not necessarily mean modernization. The increasing popularity in the civilian community of automotive power had not spread to the army. A report appearing in November 1928 revealed that the army still had more than 50,000 horses and mules, about the same number they had possessed ten years before. While the horse population at Fort D.A. Russell had decreased a little in 1927 with the departure of the two cavalry regiments, the two infantry regiments now in place, as well as the field artillery, needed many horses and mules.

Another change of commanders occurred in early 1929, just when incumbent Brigadier General Frank C. Bolles had his improvement program proceeding nicely. The new commander, Brigadier General Charles R. Howland, was an unusual person. He was a highly decorated veteran of the Spanish-American War and World War I, a scholar, and as a bachelor, he still managed to fulfill the social obligations his rank entailed. Howland had graduated from West Point in 1895 and later acquired a law degree. He had also written a comprehensive history of the world war. Personnel at Fort D.A. Russell did not know quite what to expect from their new commander.

While Howland settled into his big quarters #92 and his new command, an unexpected order arrived to immediately deploy the Twentieth Infantry by rail to Bisbee, Arizona. Trouble had erupted on the Mexican side of the border, and army units from several posts had been ordered to respond. More than 800 members, headed by Regimental Commander Colonel W.S. Sinclair, spent a month in Arizona, along with several other army regiments. When the Mexican troubles subsided, the regiment received a warm welcome back home at Fort D.A. Russell, and in Cheyenne.

Social activities on the post picked up after the regiment's return. General Howland's recent arrival also contributed a measure to the social activities, which seemed to increase in pace for the duration of his tour at Fort D.A. Russell. Howland encouraged polo to regain some of its earlier popularity, and each regiment fielded a good team. However, the full summer camp schedule required the polo schedule to be discontinued until after September 1, but then polo play continued until October. Senior officers from higher headquarters visiting the post received "red carpet" treatment that often included a review of troops and then a reception and dinner dance at the officers' club or quarters #92. When General Howland published the fall social calendar, officers' "hops" were shown on the third Friday of each month. For these occasions, he decreed that dinner henceforth would not be served midway through the dance, as had long been done, but served before the dance, as soon became the custom. Anxious to continue good relations with the Cheyenne community and to continue the post improvement program started by his predecessors, Howland worked hard on all fronts.

The last visit of Wyoming's "Grand Old Man," eighty-five-year-old Senator Francis E. Warren, to Fort D.A. Russell provided General Howland an occasion to offer his special brand of hospitality and recognition. Senator Warren was welcomed on July 11, 1929, with a thirteen-gun salute when he arrived with Mrs. Warren at the parade ground to review the Fourth Infantry Brigade. Proudly wearing his Medal of Honor, awarded for bravery during the Civil War, Senator Warren stood at attention for forty-five minutes while the brigade marched by, scorning chairs and invitations to sit down. A grand reception and dinner dance in his honor followed that evening, hosted by General Howland. This event served as the last official occasion for Senator Warren to visit the garrison. But whether he happened to be at the post, in town, or in Washington, he followed events of the military at Fort D.A. Russell with keen interest. He also had been a great supporter of the ROTC and CMTC summer camp programs as well as the National Guard movement.

The annual camps and training maneuvers at Pole Mountain proceeded smoothly during the summer of 1929 until August, when an unfortunate accident killed one soldier and seriously injured ten others. During the exercise of a tactical problem, a team of skittish horses unexpectedly bolted as they were being unhitched from a 75-mm gun carriage. A field artillery battery had been in the process of bringing all its cannon into action when the one team stampeded. All other horses of the battery joined the stampede. Artillerymen were seen being dragged into a "maelstrom" of thudding hoofs and steel wheels. This danger had long existed in field artillery exercises and would not go away until the army replaced the horse with motor vehicles.

The news from Washington, D.C., on November 24, 1929, of the death of Senator Francis Warren saddened all Wyoming. It brought forth memories of his long and dedicated service to the state and the nation. Francis E. Warren had served his interests and grown to be a wealthy man, but as the people of Wyoming saw him, he had first of all served their interests.

State funeral services were held for Warren in the United States Senate Chamber with President Calvin Coolidge, members of his cabinet, and much of Congress there. Warren had set a new record for length of service in the Senate—nearly forty years. The funeral train that brought his body to Cheyenne for burial in Lakeview Cemetery also carried several senators and representatives. Met by a large crowd of citizens at the Cheyenne depot, plus the First Infantry and band, the late senator received full military honors due an army major general. The funeral procession proceeded to the Capitol, where the body lay in state under the rotunda for three hours while thousands of Wyomingites filed by to pay their last respects. The slow movement of the funeral march to the cemetery resumed promptly at 11:45 A.M. while the guns boomed at Fort D.A. Russell. Brigadier General Howland and 2,000 soldiers headed the funeral procession, which stretched for many blocks. At the cemetery, a battery of Seventy-sixth Field Artillery fired three salvos. Then a brief religious ceremony preceded an army bugler sounding taps. Friends said that Warren had died as he wished, active and in harness.

A week after Senator Warren's burial in Cheyenne, a local newspaper carried this headline: "POST RE-NAMED FRANCIS E. WARREN." The name had been changed by presidential direction to Fort Francis E. Warren to honor the late senator, effective January 1, 1930. The name Fort D.A. Russell would be given to Camp Marfa at Marfa, Texas. It seemed fitting and proper, after carrying the name Fort D.A. Russell for more than sixty-two years, that "the post near Cheyenne" should now be named Fort Francis E. Warren for one of Cheyenne's own, a man who richly deserved such an honor.

A smartly formed gun crew of the Seventy-sixth Field Artillery, which served at Fort Francis E. Warren during the 1930s, is shown in 1932 on a mixed team of mules and horses attached to a caisson.—*WY State AMH Dept.*

EPILOGUE

The brigade enjoyed an unusually high measure of stability during the decade of the 1930s at Fort Francis E. Warren, with two infantry regiments assigned, the First and Twentieth, plus a part of the Seventy-sixth Field Artillery. The units participated annually at Pole Mountain in summer maneuvers with National Guard and Reserve units, and otherwise attended to garrison duties. When field artillery batteries were scheduled to fire on the range near the Iron Mountain road, which ran through the post to Cheyenne, local newspapers warned all ranchers to use another road. Brigadier General Charles R. Howland continued his energetic post improvement program, which included building a sports complex in 1930 near the main gate south of Randall Avenue with a $5,300 donation from the citizens of Cheyenne. The stadium consisted of "a dirt berm and poured concrete." Volunteer soldiers and civilian employees of the garrison did the work. Named the Warren Bowl, the stadium seated 4,157. It served the post and Cheyenne football and track teams for the next thirty years.

An outdoor swimming pool was constructed near Crow Creek and the base golf course, first opened in August 1914, came in for significant improvements, including the first grass greens in the state. Polo remained a popular sport, and a local February 1930 newspaper article reported that mules were coming into their own as polo mounts. A number of mules were being trained by enlisted men of each regiment, and both the First and Twentieth Infantry had two polo teams mounted on mules.

Brigade commanders were reassigned about every two years, and December 1931 witnessed the arrival of Brigadier General Frank Cocheu to replace Howland, Cocheu was replaced in February 1933 by Brigadier General Casper H. Conrad. An additional brigadier general, Hamilton M. Hawkins, arrived in June 1933 to establish a regional headquarters for the Civilian Conservation Corps at Fort F.E. Warren. Brigadier General Conrad's efforts to continue the earlier post improvement program were largely frustrated by the lack of military appropriations. However, Conrad identified a number of priority projects, including a theater, chapel, indoor swimming pool, and a coal unloading ramp. When Brigadier General Charles Humphrey, Jr., replaced Conrad as brigade/post commander in October 1935, the prospects for military appropriations had greatly improved. The growing threat in Europe and Asia to the United States and world peace became a primary concern of the Roosevelt administration, (1933-1945). Restructuring and modernizing the United States Army gained a high priority.

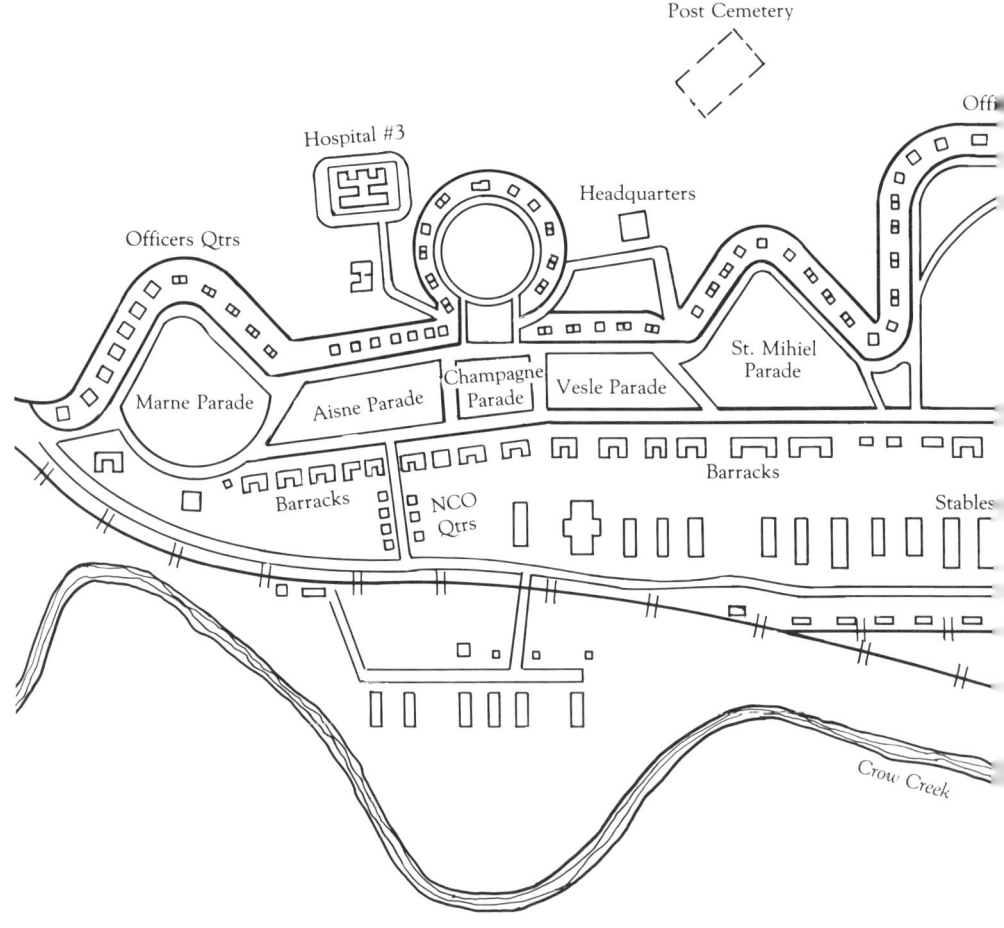

While Fort D.A. Russell built to the east from the original 1867 post, Cheyenne expanded to the west and by 1930 when the name changed to Fort Francis E. Warren their boundaries had come together. The physical arrangement of the military installation of 1930 remains much the same in 1989.

Warren

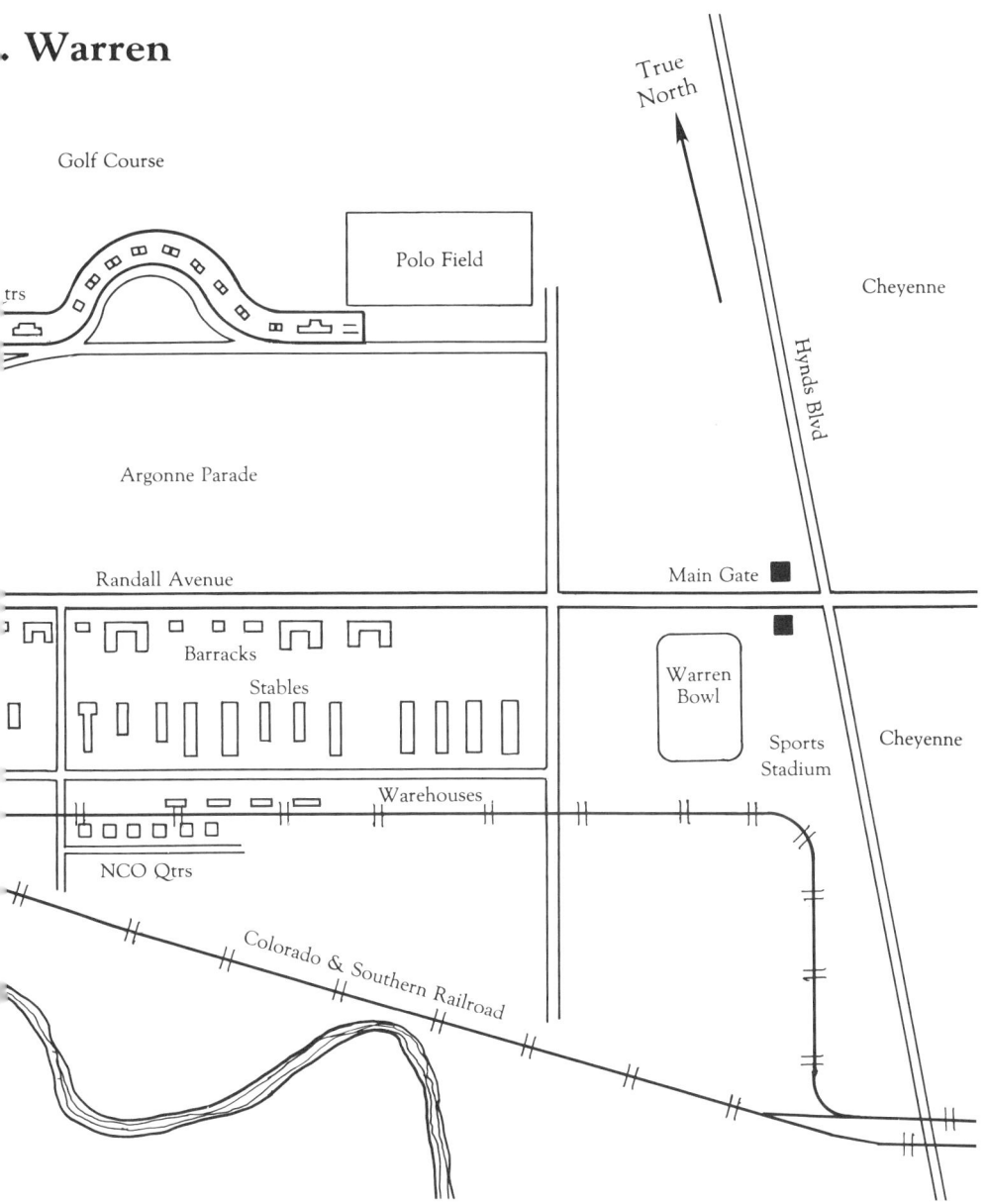

The largest peacetime national defense appropriation in the nation's history was approved by the Congress in June 1936, enlarging the armed forces and providing for needed construction and repairs. The post's military population numbered about 2,500 in mid-1936, but soon grew to more than 4,000—3,900 enlisted men and 150 officers. Additional enlistments authorized by the army filled up the vacancies in the regiments. With the arrival of Brigadier General E.D. Peek to replace Humphrey in July 1937, appropriations for new construction became available. In January 1938, a local news report named Major John R. Hermann as the first army man ever named to the Cheyenne Frontier Days Committee. The committee had finally recognized the prominent part played by Fort Francis E. Warren in each Frontier Days event, starting from the first one held in 1897.

A new post theater and gymnasium were completed in 1939, and both are still in use fifty years later. More post chapels would come later—five in 1941-1942. The modernizing and motorizing of regiments, started in 1936, had been almost completed by mid-1939. Both infantry regiments had also been equipped with the new Garand semiautomatic rifle, replacing the 1903 Springfield rifle. Only two mules remained at Fort F.E. Warren on May 31, 1939. There were some riding horses, but the draft animals, mules

Machine Gun Company D, Twentieth Infantry, had not been motorized in 1933, but relied on mule power for moving weapons and supplies. The barracks in the background, built in 1885, were occupied by the Twentieth Infantry in the 1930s and now house the base library, education offices, classrooms and other base support facilities. First used in World War I, the .30 caliber Browning machine gun was considered a formidable weapon.—*WY State AMH Dept.*

and horses, had been replaced by trucks to haul the men and supplies, and pull the big guns. Late 1939 witnessed the transfer of the Fourth Infantry Brigade headquarters from Fort F.E. Warren and the move of the two infantry regiments to Camp Jackson, South Carolina, for winter maneuvers. The regiments returned in mid-1940, but were permanently transferred in March 1941, and the remaining units of the Seventy-sixth Field Artillery departed a few months later. After seventy-three years, the last combat arms units of the regular army to be assigned to the post had gone. However, two National Guard Artillery regiments, the 183rd Field Artillery from Idaho and the 188th Field Artillery from North Dakota, soon arrived for a few months to occupy the barracks vacated by the First and Twentieth Infantry regiments.

A startling Cheyenne newspaper headline on June 21, 1939, declared that Greeley, Colorado, forth miles south, might be made a "No Man's Land For Soldiers From Ft. Warren." It served as an example of actions some other communities had taken or were considering. The vast majority of the army's enlistees were conscientious, hardworking, and law-abiding soldiers. However, some were not, and those few miscreants throughout the army were responsible for the low level of esteem in which all soldiers of the United States Army were held during the latter part of the 1930s. There were many reasons for this condition, including lack of command attention and social conditions of the times. Several soldiers from the post were in jail in Greeley for robbing parked cars, and some were in the Cheyenne jail for other reasons. Relations between the city council and the post command section remained good, but the soldiers of the post did not share in those good relations. Their frequent involvement in auto accidents, robberies, breaking and entering, and other infractions of the law reported in the Cheyenne newspapers combined to give the average citizen a reduced respect for the army enlisted man. Not until the Selective Service Act became law and United States entered World War II would the former good image of the soldier be restored in Cheyenne.

The 1940s saw more change at the post than any other decade in its history. In mid-1940 the Congress approved several acts that enabled the army to embark on a large expansion program that included induction of the National Guard into federal service, calling up of the Organized Reserves, and the first peacetime draft of civilians, the Selective Service and Training Act of September 14, 1940. The post was designated one of several "kindergarten" camps, or "replacement centers," located throughout the United States where selectees would be given thirteen weeks of basic military training before assignment to a unit. Brigadier General F.E. Uhl replaced Peek as brigade/post commander and a building program started in November 1940, south of Crow Creek away from the main post, to accommodate the thousands of trainees expected. The post received its first group of selectees for training, 583, in mid-January 1941. In early 1941, the First and Twentieth Infantry regiments, and later the Seventy-sixth Field Artillery, were transferred to several posts in the Midwest and West to provide the nucleus for new regiments. By March

1941, some 4,500 Quartermaster Corps draftees had arrived for thirteen-week training courses. The post newspaper, the *Sentinel*, served as the primary vehicle for circulating local news.

The construction program progressed well in early 1941, and 121 two-story wooden temporary barracks were completed by March. Also soon

By mid-1941, a new area of temporary barracks and other buildings had been constructed south of Crow Creek to accommodate the thousands of arriving, newly inducted quartermaster corps trainees. The permanent post can be seen above Crow Creek relatively undisturbed while the new construction appears in the lighter area below Crow Creek where the ground has been graded.—U.S. *Dept. of Agriculture*

available for the new trainees were thirty new mess halls, a post office, five recreation hall/theaters, a post exchange, guest houses, warehouses, a firehouse, five administrative buildings, three guardhouses, officers' quarters, and an infirmary. Despite several attempts by Congress to raise military pay, the basic pay of a soldier did not increase from thirty dollars a month to fifty dollars until the next year, after the war had started.

In March 1941, the Fort Francis E. Warren Replacement Training Center was taken over by the Quartermaster Corps and redesignated the Quartermaster Replacement Training Center (QRTC). Brigadier General John A. Warden arrived in May 1941 to assume command of the QRTC while Uhl moved to command the Seventh Corps Area with headquarters at Omaha. Colonel George Blair served as post commander, and the post/QRTC commands continued as separate commands for the time. By June 1941, 9,500 draftees had arrived and 282 temporary wooden frame buildings had been constructed on the south side of Crow Creek with all utilities and streets completed. There were five Quartermaster Corps training regiments in January 1942, four white and one black regiment. Four of those regiments occupied the recently constructed facilities south of Crow Creek, and the fifth regiment occupied the permanent barracks vacated by the First and Thirteenth Infantry regiments on the main post. A Quartermaster Corps officers' candidate school and officers' training course also became a part of the center.

Additional construction was authorized the day after Pearl Harbor, and a total of 387 buildings were ultimately constructed, sufficient for a garrison of 20,000 men. The QRTC and post were combined in November 1942, with General Warden serving as both post and QRTC commander. As recruits continued to arrive in ever increasing numbers, the post population passed the 20,000-man capacity level and for a short time exceeded 26,000. Attempts to accommodate this many men were made by increasing the number in each barracks and putting up 360 pyramidal tents, six men to a tent, on the prairie inside the main gate of the post. The Cheyenne U.S.O. facility in Cathedral Hall at Twenty-first Street and Capitol offered the primary off-post social, entertainment, and communications center for officers and enlisted men.

Soon after Brigadier General H.L. Whittaker assumed command of the QRTC from Warden in February 1943, the large number of Quartermaster Corps trainees arriving every thirteen weeks stopped. The unhappy three-month experiment of consolidated QRTC and post staffs also came to an end for the time being. The acceptable number of trainees on the post had been exceeded, and the Quartermaster Corps had enough to satisfy its forseeable needs. In the meantime, a new and permanent addition to the army arrived—female soldiers. The first contingent of the Fifty-sixth Womens' Army Auxiliary Corps (WAAC) Headquarters Company reported in March 1943, 150 strong to assume duties in the service clubs, theaters, hospital, and the headquarters. The WAAC later changed to WAC, Women's Army Corps.

Another change soon followed with the deactivation of the QRTC in

Newly arrived commander of the Quartermaster Replacement Training Center at Fort Francis E. Warren, Brigadier General John A. Warden, stands in Frontier Park sixth from the left with his staff and Indians for the July 1941 Frontier Days celebration in Cheyenne.—*WY State AMH Dept.*

The cooks and stewards of Company D, First Regiment, Quartermaster Replacement Training Center, stand ready to serve Thanksgiving Dinner in their newly constructed mess hall south of Crow Creek in November 1941.—*WY State AMH Dept.*

October 1943 and the arrival of a Quartermaster Unit Training Center (QUTC) from Vancouver, Washington. Supposedly in keeping with the mission change from individual training to unit training, this change found the enlisted strength of the center reduced to less than 3,000 men. The rapid and drastic reduction in the number of troops caused the Seventh Service Command headquarters at Omaha to announce in July 1943 that Fort Francis E. Warren was not being abandoned.

The total post population increased when a prisoner of war camp was established in late 1943 on Crow Creek to house German prisoners. Even though the army considered the presence of German prisoners at Fort Francis E. Warren a classified matter, a Cheyenne newspaper report on December 1, 1943, carried the caption, "American Soldier Finds Cousin In Nazi War Prisoners' Camp at Post." Private T.M. Mitsch, a German-born American citizen in the United States Army, recognized his cousin, Karl Gartner, who had been captured by the American forces in North Africa. The newspaper reported that an army guard had chased Mitsch away from the camp, and he did not get to talk to his cousin before leaving for California. The camp at one time housed 894 German prisoners. Initially located in temporary quarters, the camp moved to a brick horse barn complex near Crow Creek that had previously been used as a laundry school. Accommodations were remodeled to comply with all Geneva Convention requirements. Eight German and one Italian prisoner who died while in confinement were buried next to the post cemetery. The last contingent of 203 German prisoners left the post in late April 1946 to return to Germany. Italian soldiers were also retained at Fort Francis E. Warren, but Italy had already surrendered when those Italians arrived in Wyoming. The Italians were not held in the same prisoner of war status as the German POWs. In May 1944, some former Italian prisoners of war were receiving noncombat-type training at the post.

Training special quartermaster units became the primary mission after 1943, but other units were also trained. Railroad battalions of the Transportation Corps began training in 1944 using facilities of the Union Pacific Railroad. In May 1944 the center's name changed again; it became the Army Service Forces Training Center (ASFTC). This change did not signify a mission realignment but more of a recognition of the much reduced requirement for Quartermaster Corps training. A consolidation of command occurred again in February 1945 when Whittaker took charge of the full post.

The training program continued at Fort Francis E. Warren after V-E Day, May 8, 1945, but at an even more reduced level and slower pace. After President Harry S. Truman announced the capitulation of the Japanese on August 14, 1945, a discharge center was established at the post, and by October more than 200 soldiers were being released to civilian life each day.

In November a curious memorial to the heroes of World War II received a grand dedication. Located in the park in front of the post theater on Randall Avenue, the memorial had a thirty-five-foot concrete base with a six-foot medallion featuring a bare bucking horse. It was dedicated on

November 20, during the annual Western Governors' Conference held that year in Cheyenne. The governors spent the day at Fort Francis E. Warren touring the post, attending briefings, dedicating the memorial, and attending a hosted lunch at the officers' club. Wyoming Governor Lester E. Hunt chaired the four-day conference, and Brigadier General H.L. Whittaker presided at the war memorial dedication ceremony with the western governors attending. Probably one of the first in the country to be dedicated after the end of World War II, and faithfully maintained since, the war memorial's bucking bronco serves as its focus, with no mention of battles, heroes, or even World War II.

When Whittaker received his reassignment orders in March 1946, training activities of the ASFTC had almost ended. Post strength had been reduced to a caretaker force. The future appeared uncertain indeed. The War Department's announcement in April 1946 that the cavalry had been terminated as a separate branch of the army gave no joy to the horse cavalry aficionados in Cheyenne hoping for a return to the post of the good old days. Colonel Paul H. Hallowell became post commander for a few months, to be succeeded in October 1946 by a former cavalry officer who had served at Fort D.A. Russell with the Fourth Cavalry in 1924-1925, Colonel Percy S. Hayden. A long line of officers (eighteen) had served as post commander for varying periods between 1940 and 1946. The QRTC had four commanders of the center, two who acted as combined post/center commanders.

The uncertain future of Fort Francis E. Warren continued through 1946 and well into 1947. The army was being reduced to a fraction of its wartime size, and some of the oldest and most established posts were being deactivated. In April 1947, good news for the community arrived in the form of a Cheyenne newspaper headline that announced, "AIR CORPS TO USE FORT WARREN." An aviation engineering school arrived from Geiger Field, Washington, on June 1, 1946. Commanded by Colonel John C.B. Elliott, the school taught individuals in airfield engineering, construction, and allied subjects. The Aviation Engineers belonged to the Army Corps of Engineers and did not work for the Army Air Forces. The post newspaper soon had a new name, *Sky Dozer*. Then the National Security Act of 1947 established a new defense organization that included a separate Department of the Air Force. The United States Air Force began functioning as the nation's primary airpower agency on September 18, 1947, when W. Stuart Symington took the oath of office as the first secretary. However, the new air force did not know if it wanted an old army post on Crow Creek near Cheyenne that no longer had the faintest semblance of a flying field.

To further cloud the scene, an article in the October 1947 Cheyenne *Eagle* reported that an agreement between Generals Eisenhower and Spaatz, chiefs of staff of the army and air force, had placed Fort Francis E. Warren back under the jurisdiction of the army; it was no longer a part of the new air force. The fear of closure surfaced again in March 1948, when the *Eagle* reported that the post had been declared surplus and would be abandoned soon. While Wyoming Senators Joseph C. O'Mahoney and E.V. Robertson denied that the post would be closed, the senators admitted that they were conferring with Army Secretary Kenneth C. Royall and Air Force Secretary Stuart Symington as to "the future utility of Fort Warren." Robertson thought that "the post would revert back to the army ground forces when the present technical schooling of aviation engineers here is completed."

Closure seemed so certain that the Cheyenne chamber of commerce decided to appoint a seven-man delegation to go to Washington and "fight for the fort." It became known at this time that the army surgeon general had recommended basic training not be held at Fort Francis E. Warren, or at any other Rocky Mountain post that had a high incidence of rheumatic fever and certain other streptococcal infections. The chamber of commerce maintained with good evidence that the high incidence of rheumatic fever at the post was caused by congested living conditions. Further, they showed that the post and Cheyenne fell far below the general average for cases of that disease and all other diseases. A laboratory for the study of rheumatic fever was installed at the base hospital in 1948, and more than 800 patients were examined by the X-ray technicians during January 1949. While this debate continued in Washington, the post population stood at 4,800 officers and men.

Several things happened in 1948 that caused the Truman administration to reexamine the dwindling strength of the nation's armed forces, and halt that trend. For instance, a decision to keep United States Army units in Germany did not meet with any significant opposition from the American people. Our former ally, the Soviet Union, had begun a concerted campaign to blockade and isolate Berlin, and had commenced other hostile actions in various forums and parts of the world. A proposed 20,000-plane air force served as a discussion point to counter this new threat, and in May 1948 a seventy-group air force was approved by the Congress. This meant that more men had to be enlisted, and more planes and airfields built immediately.

Soon after President Harry Truman visited Cheyenne and Fort Francis E. Warren on June 6, 1948, a United Press dispatch from Washington announced that the post would be "reactivated." The efforts of the Cheyenne chamber of commerce to "fight for the fort" had paid off, along with the concerted efforts of the Wyoming congressional delegation. While the status of the Aviation Engineers "remained unsettled," automotive, supply, and administrative training units began arriving from Lowry Field in Denver to set up training courses in those fields for air force recruits. The USAF Technical School designated in June 1948 became the 3450th Technical Training Wing in August 1948, under the auspices of the newly organized Air Training Command headquartered at Barksdale Field, Louisiana.

A joint Army and Air Force Adjustment Regulation 1-1-1 dated November 30, 1947, tried to help all Army personnel, other than Army Air Forces, to select the service they preferred, army or air force. The post and school commander, Colonel John C.B. Elliott, quickly transferred his regular army commission of twenty years in the Corps of Engineers to the air force. In mid-1948, many of the non rated personnel at the post (295 officers and 4,870 enlisted men) were still in the process of deciding whether to go army or air force. There were also 619 civilian employees at the post who didn't have to make that decision.

The record blizzard that struck the northern High Plains in January 1949 suspended training activities for a while, until the storm subsided and both military and civilian personnel could return to their jobs. Fort Francis E. Warren provided assistance in manpower and equipment for the next three months to the southeast Wyoming and northern Colorado areas in a project named "Operation Snowbound." Military crews were opening snowbound roads and highways as far away as Rawlins and Casper, and conducting rescue operations of travelers and ranchers isolated by the severe storm.

The USAF announced in February 1949 the termination of eighteen Aviation Engineer specialist courses. Henceforth these specialists would be trained by the Department of the Army for both services. Colonel Charles B. Backes, a command pilot with considerable flying experience, became commander in July 1949, when Elliott received an assignment to the National War College. Backes would serve as commander until 1953. Technical training held a high priority in the air force, and by October 1949, the 3450th Technical Training Wing offered courses in administration, auto and utilities maintenance, engineering, and the maintenance of engineering equipment. A fixed-wire communications school was added in late 1949. Despite the earlier apparent willingness to make the post an air force training base, the air force did not change the name of Fort Francis E. Warren to Francis E. Warren Air Force Base until October 1949. It took awhile longer for the local newspapers to refer to the post as the base, but by the end of 1949, the name Francis E. Warren Air Force Base seemed to come easier. The base newspaper also received a new name about this time; it changed from the *Sky Dozer*, given to it by the Aviation Engineers, to the *Mustang*.

While the base population grew, available family housing did not increase on base or in the Cheyenne area. Most officers and noncommissioned officers who desired to live on base were accommodated, but the lower grades had to hunt for a place for their families. Many more enlisted men, now called airmen, married at a younger age, made possible in part by better pay and benefits. The services recognized the need to provide more family housing. The authorization for the construction on-base of 722 family units in November 1949 provided the occasion for Wyoming's newly elected Senator Lester Hunt to explain his role on the Senate Armed Services Committee. Hunt declared that the "base is made permanent by the new housing unit. There is no cause to believe that Fort Warren will ever close." While construction was expected to commence soon, it took two years to get started, and 500 units were built, not 722. Still, 500 units would alleviate the severe housing shortage affecting air force personnel.

The air force also adopted in 1949 a new blue uniform for winter wear, staying for many more years with the cotton khaki uniform for summer months or topic climates.

The 3450th Training Wing continued to grow as additional technical training courses were added, and by the end of 1949, more than 9,000 military personnel were assigned, 377 officers and 8,684 airmen, of which 5,290 were students. Most students were young airmen, new to the air force and transferred here from Lackland Air Force Base, Texas, where they underwent three months of basic military training. The civilian employee force numbered 671.

A January 23, 1950, local newspaper headline announced that "FRANCIS E. WARREN AIR FORCE BASE IS NOW CHEYENNE'S LEADING INDUSTRY." The air force had released to the Cheyenne chamber of commerce the information that more than 8,000 airmen plus their families were living on base and in Cheyenne. Further, the monthly military payroll exceeded $1,130,000. Additionally, some 900 civil service (civilian) employees received a monthly payroll of $237,000 that combined annually with the military for over $16 million, much of it spent locally.

In 1951, a year after the Korean War broke out, the base military population had grown to better than 12,000 more than two-thirds of whom were students. Four major training departments that would remain intact throughout the 1950s were fixed-wire communications, administrative and supply, automotive, and utilities. There were also some special training courses established at various times for special purposes. Three new brick academic buildings were completed south of Crow Creek in 1952 to accommodate the growing student body. The 3450th Training Wing was also responsible for more than 10,000 air force students in twenty-seven civilian contract schools located around the country. Instructors from Francis E. Warren Air Force Base were on the road constantly visiting these contract schools and monitoring the progress of the students. Francis E. Warren Air Force Base would remain for most of the 1950s as a very large technical training facility of the Air Training Command.

The completion and occupation in 1952 of 500 Wherry Housing units on-base, started in late 1950, vastly improved the military family housing situation in the Cheyenne area. The $4 million government-subsidized housing project built and managed by a consortium of Cheyenne builders and named after the legislative sponsor Senator Kenneth Wherry, also provided a significant boost to the building industry of Cheyenne. Base Commander Colonel Charles Backes presided at the dedication ceremony on June 31, 1951, at which Wyoming Governor Frank Barrett, and Senators J.C. O'Mahoney and Lester C. Hunt also spoke.

Colonel Backes also dedicated the new base golf course that month; the course boasted again of being the only one with grass greens and grass fairways in Wyoming. The holes and fairways had been rearranged and refurbished but located on the same site. A new club house, lounge, and pro

A mid-1950s aerial photo of Francis E. Warren Air Force Base looking west shows the 500 Wherry Housing units completed in 1952 on the land where the Fort D.A. Russell flying field had existed in 1919-1920. Some of the temporary World War II wooden buildings south of Crow Creek later torn down or removed can be seen in the upper left of the photo.—*F.E. Warren AFB Base Museum Collection.*

shop had also been dedicated, structured from a reclaimed Civilian Conservation Corps building. The post's golf course had remained a first class course through the 1930s, but the lack of maintenance during World War II and the years after had led to its deterioration. Being an avid golfer, Colonel Backes made restoration of the course a high priority project when he assumed command in 1949. The course achieved a first-class rating in the early-1950s and for the next twenty years entertained many regional and national air force golf tournaments.

The recently organized air force 3600th Air Demonstration Team of four F-84G jet aircraft from Luke Air Force Base, Arizona, performed over Frontier Park on July 18, 1953, during the annual Cheyenne Frontier Days celebration. Later renamed the Thunderbirds, the team has received tremendous acclaim and invitations to return to Cheyenne every year since. The Thunderbirds proved to be every bit as popular as the black horse cavalry troops from Fort D.A. Russell had been in the earlier years.

An expected Korean War armistice in mid-1953 did not diminish the national determination to build up the military forces, nor did it diminish the student load at Francis E. Warren Air Force Base. Some students were believed by some to be the brave bandits who successfully robbed the post exchange of $7,100 late on the evening of October 1, 1953, leaving three airmen and the post exchange manager tied up. Colonel William A.R. Robertson relieved Backes of command in late 1953 and served for two years, to be relieved in 1955 by Brigadier General Orin L. Grover. School problems reported in the last half of 1955 included instructor instability plus a large number of substandard students being assigned. Also, difficulty had been reported with the two chaplain service courses added in 1955. Chaplains assigned for training had no formal military indoctrination prior to arrival, and the military regime took a little getting used to for these gentlemen of the cloth. The assigned base officer complement included fifty rated officers who were expected to get their required monthly flying time in order to receive their monthly flying pay. There were twenty-five permanent party pilots, seven attached pilots from other agencies in the area, eight student pilots, and ten observers. Fourteen military administrative aircraft were hangared at the Cheyenne Airport; three C-47s, one L-20, seven T-6s, one B-25, and two C-45s.

Colonel Hilbert F. Muenter arrived as commander in 1956 to replace Brigadier General Orin L. Grover and soon reorganized the command into a wing-base concept with four functional training departments. They were (1) officer training, (2) supply and administration, (3) fixed-wire training, and (4) automotive and utilities. Some 14,336 students graduated during the last six months of 1956, an increase of 3,600 over the previous reporting period. Three new four-story brick airmen dormatories and a dining hall were dedicated in May 1957 south of Crow Creek to accommodate the increasing student population. A few months later a new brick $850,000 service club named the Satellite was dedicated across the street for airmen and their guests. It seemed that the base planners were locating all new buildings in the open spaces south of Crow Creek and starting the nucleus of a new base. Such a move could encourage the early demolition of the still-used stately but deteriorating 1884 and 1904 brick barracks and houses of the earlier Fort D.A. Russell garrison.

The unveiling of a Russian ICBM in Moscow's Red Square in November 1957 caused the base's training mission to be rapidly reduced and subsequently transferred. President Dwight Eisenhower announced the next day that a crash program for ICBM missile development would be started immediately in order to catch up with the Soviet Union's perceived lead in missile technology. Then on November 22, 1957, the *Wyoming State Tribune* reported that Francis E. Warren Air Force Base would become an Atlas ICBM missile headquarters under the Strategic Air Command with missile launch sites to be constructed in the surrounding countryside.

When the Air Training Command turned the base over to the Strategic Air Command (SAC) on February 1, 1958, students and training courses had partly been moved to Chanute Air Force Base, Illinois, Sheppard Air Force Base, Texas, and Amarillo Air Force Base, Texas. The transfers were completed in 1959 and the base military population reduced to less than 5,000, quite a reduction from the 26,000 of World War II and even Air Training Command's 12,000 of just a few years earlier. The 4,000 to 5,000 military population also proved to be more acceptable to the Cheyenne community, which then numbered a little more than 39,000. Wyoming and Cheyenne were delighted with the prospective economic input of the missile construction project—$100 million. Cheyenne's Mayor Worth Story said, "Cheyenne is proud to have the first missile base in the country and proud to be the nation's No. 1 target for enemy missiles."

The 4320th Strategic Wing (Missile) came into being at Francis E. Warren Air Force Base on February 1, 1958, but was redesignated three weeks later by SAC as the 706th Strategic Missile Wing. Colonel Hilbert F. Muenter was in command of each of these. Brigadier General William L. Large, Jr., took command in January 1959. An experienced missile officer, General Large's assignment indicated the importance and priority of the first Atlas missile base. Colonel Muenter and the remaining vestiges of the former training mission were transferred to Air Training Command facilities soon after. The base settled back to an even more comfortable 3,500 military population, with most activities located in the permanent red brick building part of the base north of Crow Creek. The World War II vintage temporary wooden buildings south of Crow Creek were rapidly sold and moved or torn down starting in October 1959.

Work had started in April 1958, under the supervision of the Army Corps of Engineers, on the first of twenty-four Atlas missile sites to be located in southeast Wyoming, western Nebraska, and northern Colorado. Colonel William S. Rader succeeded General Large as commander of the 706th Strategic Missile Wing in June 1959. The next month saw the Thirteenth Air Division headquarters activated at Francis E. Warren Air Force Base and located in building #65, Colonel Rader designated commander. The Thirteenth Air Division was soon renamed the Thirteenth Strategic Missile Division in keeping with SAC's plan to assign missile wings to it. The commander of such a division was normally a brigadier general, but it took almost two years (March 1, 1961) before Rader pinned on a general's star. Colonel George T. Chadwell arrived in August 1959 and assumed command of the wing, replacing Colonel Rader. The 706th (Atlas) and 703rd (Titan) Strategic Missile wings were assigned to the Thirteenth Strategic Missile Division, the latter wing located at Lowry Air Force Base, Colorado. The first Atlas site, designated Site A, was located twenty-one miles northwest of Francis E. Warren Air Force Base. Sites B, C, and D were located northeast, southeast, and southwest of the base. The first Atlas "D" missiles started arriving in October 1959, and in the next two years the full complement of twenty-four Model D and E Atlas missiles had been installed.

The Strategic Air Command (SAC) made many changes at their newly acquired base near Cheyenne. Funds became available that had long been lacking for maintenance and repair of the old buildings. Family houses got a good overhaul, as did the airmen's barracks and most of the administrative buildings. At long last, an indoor swimming pool was authorized. Installed in building #217, an 1884 barracks that had been used for a theater since the mid-1920s, the pool immediately became one of the most popular recreational facilities on the base. The 500-unit on-base Wherry Housing Project, built in 1951-1952, was purchased by the air force in 1958 from the Cheyenne owners so that it could be operated as military housing. Authorization in 1961 for a new Capehart Housing Project of one hundred family units on the northwest corner of the base promised to further alleviate the local military housing shortage.

SAC also discarded some facilities considered no longer essential. The Pole Mountain preserve thirty miles west of the base was declared excess in 1959 and turned over to the Departments of Interior and Agriculture to be administered by the Forest Service and Bureau of Land Management for recreational and grazing uses. The Wyoming National Guard had stopped "going to Pole Mountain" after they acquired a large maneuver area on the North Platte River near Guernsey, Wyoming, in 1937. For many years after 1940, Pole Mountain served mainly as a military hunting and fishing preserve. An editorial in the *Wyoming State Tribune* on July 7, 1960, rejoiced that fishing was now for all at the Pole Mountain Reserve, when previously it had just been for the military at Warren AFB.

As the Atlas missiles arrived and became operational, the base had periodic practice alerts with the gates closed to most traffic. Mainly a communications exercise, base alerts also required the units to practice their assigned wartime tasks. SAC had installed chain link fence and guards on all the gates; only authorized personnel were permitted to enter on a routine basis. The previous ninety years had seen Cheyenneites driving out in their buggies or automobiles just to look around or attend the band concerts. Now a base band no longer existed to give concerts even if the citizens of Cheyenne could get on the base to hear it. Base bands were no longer authorized. The Warren Bowl, a sports complex built in 1930 with the help of the citizens of Cheyenne and a lot of volunteer garrison labor, also came down. Rarely used by the military after 1940 or the Cheyenne schools after 1959 (the year Cheyenne's Memorial Stadium was dedicated), the Warren Bowl had deteriorated. Interstate 25 needed space, the main gate had to be moved, and SAC had the wherewithall to solve these and other problems by demolishing this earlier much beloved stadium.

While base facilities were being overhauled and restructured, so were the organizations. The 706th Strategic Missile Wing was redesignated the 389th Strategic Missile Wing on July 1, 1961, with Colonel George T. Chadwell remaining in command. News of the successful testing of the new solid-fueled Minuteman missile inspired Mayor Worth Story and a delegation of the Cheyenne chamber of commerce to journey to Washington, D.C., and make it known that Cheyenne would like to have that new weapons system deployed in southeast Wyoming. An editorial in the December 14, 1961, edition of the *Wyoming State Tribune* also invited the Department of Defense to build a Minuteman missle base at Cheyenne. The newspaper said that the community would welcome it.

The announcement on March 27, 1962, that Francis E. Warren Air Force Base had been selected as the support base for an undisclosed number of dispersed Minuteman missile sites came as good news to Cheyenne, since Atlas site construction had recently ended. The press reported that Cheyenne's new mayor, Bill Nation, was elated with the $158 million project. Construction would start in a few months and employ more than 2,000 men. Later announcements designated the activation date as July 1, 1963, for the new Ninetieth Strategic Missile Wing. The air force had finally chosen a proud and historic predecessor unit number to designate the new Minuteman wing. The Ninetieth had first been a distinguished bombardment group in World War II, and then an equally distinguished strategic reconnaissance wing until the late 1950s. It would also be recognized an outstanding missile wing. The new missile wing would have an old flying unit designation and 200 Minutemen missiles deployed individually in hardened underground silos within a hundred miles in southeast Wyoming, western Nebraska, and northeast Colorado.

About the time construction started on the Minuteman silos, the Cuban Missile Crisis arose. The 389th Strategic Missile Wing was placed on increased alert on October 21, 1962, with all Atlas missile sorties in launch configuration. The wing's posture did not return to normal until November 27, 1962, when the situation with Cuba and the Soviet Union had significantly improved.

As the first commander of the Ninetieth Strategic Missile Wing, Colonel Floyd Wikstrum would see his unit grow in the next two years from a handful of people and no missiles to an operationally ready 200 Minuteman missile wing. The Minuteman missile proved to be far superior to the Atlas missile in accuracy, reaction time, in-flight performance, and reliability. Consequently, an early decision was made by the Department of Defense to retire the Atlas missiles as the Minuteman could be produced and made operational. When the last of the Atlas missiles had been deactivated in 1965, the 389th Strategic Missile Wing also became extinct.

A Geodetic Survey Squadron arrived from Orlando, Florida, in late 1964 to help the Ninetieth Strategic Missile Wing, and all other Minuteman wings in SAC, fix the exact location of Minuteman missiles and their targets. Existing geodetic information did not permit the high level of accuracy that the Minuteman guidance system could produce. The exact position on the face of the earth had to be determined for each missile, as well as its position in relation to the location of the potential targets. Aerial photographs, ground surveys, and satellite reconnaissance provided the main sources of information for the Geodetic Survey Squadron.

More support for the wing of a different kind arrived in November 1965. The assignment of a squadron of sixteen UH-1F helicopters would provide faster and more secure transportation for maintenance and security personnel, and missile crews, to the outlying sites. The helicopters would also be helpful to the Geodetic Survey Squadron's crews in reaching some very isolated and hard to reach areas.

Brigadier General Lewis E. Lyle replaced Brigadier General William S. Rader as commander of the Thirteenth Strategic Missile Division in January 1965. Rader served as division commander for more than five and a half years, an unprecedented tour for a general officer and a division commander. Lyle was promoted to major general three months later, the first two-star general to serve at this post/base. A year later, July 1, 1966, the Thirteenth Strategic Missile Division was deactivated. Most of the Atlas and Titan wings had been deactivated, several new Minuteman missile and B-52 bomb wings had been activated, and SAC had reassigned units to different divisions and numbered air forces. They had also moved or deactivated several division headquarters. Francis E. Warren Air Force Base had enjoyed the prestige that went with having a higher headquarters headed by a general officer on base for seven years. Now both the general and the division headquarters would be gone for the next five years.

The original 200 Minuteman single-warhead missiles deployed in the Ninetieth Strategic Missile Wing missile field were modified in the late-1960s with a nose cone that contained three warheads per missile. Each of the three reentry vehicle warheads were independently targetable, a tremendous improvement in the effectiveness of the Minuteman force. An economic resource impact statement released in 1968 gave the base population as 3,358 military, 650 civilian employees, and 6,722 dependents of the military. The economic outlay for the base had been influenced by the missile modification program and grew to $62,330,300 for 1967, with about half of that amount estimated to be remaining in the local area. The military population had remained about the same since SAC acquired the base ten years before, and would not vary much except for the periods when major missile modifications were underway. A major modification to the Minuteman missile system, now nearly ten years old, tremendously.

On July 1, 1971, in another realignment of units, the Fourth Strategic Missile Division commanded by Brigadier General Robert R. Scott arrived at Francis E. Warren Air Force Base to serve as the higher headquarters for the entire 1,000 Minuteman missile force assigned to several wings and bases in several states. Cheyenne and the wing were both pleased to have a division headquarters and a general officer back on the base. Two years later, there was another reassignment by SAC of wings to divisions, and the Fourth Strategic Missile Division's name changed to the original name given in 1951, the Fourth Air Division, with both missile and bomber wings and bases assigned. The headquarters remained in building #65 with much the same supervisory mission and number of personnel, about fifteen military, until 1988, when it was deactivated in yet another SAC realignment of units.

Designated a National Historic Landmark in 1975, Francis E. Warren Air Force Base had been earlier entered on the National Register of Historic Places. These measures provided some assurance of maintaining the historic integrity of the early installation and its beautiful historic buildings. Civil engineering personnel of the base have long been aware of the significance to military and western history that is represented there, and have done a great job of preserving the old buildings. Federal recognition enables base civil engineering personnel and the State Historic Preservation Officer (SHPO) to jointly comment on programs affecting properties within the designated historic district, and stop those considered incompatible with it.

The next significant change to the Ninetieth Strategic Missile Wing's missile force came in September 1986, when the air force began replacing fifty of the 200 Minuteman missiles with the latest in missile technology, the ten-warhead Peacekeeper. The fifty Peacekeeper missiles moved into the existing Minuteman silos with some modification to the silos. Much-needed maintenance and repair funds, and some new buildings, also came with the Peacekeeper. Open bay barracks built in 1910 were modified to meet modern-day airmen dormitory standards. New and attractive red brick buildings were built south of Crow Creek for the commissary and exchange, allowing those two stores to move from the riding hall built in 1910 and a barracks of 1884 vintage. The new buildings were designed in keeping with the architectural style and setting of the old post.

A military family housing project also opened in 1987, with 265 new units located south of Crow Creek not far from the commissary and exchange. To maintain a similar number of on-base family housing units, 265 Wherry Housing units were demolished in 1988, leaving only 235 of the original 500 units completed in 1952. Considered substandard from the start, the military had accepted Wherry Housing as being better than nothing at a time when military family housing was in short supply throughout all the services. A greenbelt recreational area is planned for the land where the 265 units were demolished, the same area where the Fort D.A. Russell landing field had been located in 1919. A proper monument marking that early landing field was dedicated near the main gate in 1981 by the Fort Warren Flight #54, Order of Daedalians.

A rail-garrison basing mode for the future missile force is being considered by the Congress, with Francis E. Warren Air Force Base one of several candidate bases. Under this system, several trains would be retained at the rail-garrison base with missiles on board, ready to move from the base in case of increasing international tension or warning of an impending attack. These missiles could be fired from the trains at any location in the nation. The rail-garrison basing mode is one of several systems being considered for employing ICBMs in the future.

While Cheyenne had grown to more than 57,000 people, the military population of Francis E. Warren Air Force Base has remained about the same for the past thirty years, a number compatible with the facilities of the base and the Cheyenne community's ability to cope with the transient military. A Base FY 88 Economic Resource Impact Statement lists 4,022 military personnel (634 officers and 3,388 enlisted), 807 civilian employees and 8,821 military dependents. These totals include the parent Ninetieth Strategic Missile Wing plus several tenant organizations that support the wing, such as the helicopter, geodetic survey, and communications squadrons. The economic impact generated by the base has grown significantly; it amounted to $184,526,324 in 1987, not including the pay of retired military members in the area. There are some 1,565 military retirees of all services with about 1,200 being former members of the air force. Payments to the local military retirees totaled $17,775,504 in 1987.

The relationship between Francis E. Warren Air Force Base and Cheyenne continues to develop and improve even after 121 years. Both the military and civilian communities have worked hard to insure that such a relationship continues. It has been more than forty years since the Cheyenne community worried seriously about the base closing, the longest period yet enjoyed. From 1867 to 1950, the westward moving frontier and then changing national and international conditions created a base closure crisis about every ten years. Wyoming and Cheyenne delegations usually have been quick to scream bloody murder to Washington when a local force reduction occurred or a threat arose to the future of the military installation next door.

But the deactivation of the Fourth Air Division headquarters on August 23, 1988, did not arouse a murmur of protest, or anything loud enough to be reported in the press. Perhaps the elected representatives believed there would be no injury to Cheyenne or Wyoming. In his deactivation ceremony speech in front of the headquarters building #65 on August 23, 1988, Brigadier General Arlen D. Jameson made these remarks: "In the ever changing posture of strategic forces, the inactive Fourth Air Division might not be inactive for long. In any case, the beautiful headquarters facilities that the brigades and air divisions have so long occupied at Francis E. Warren Air Force Base will not be left empty, and who knows . . ."

SAC DIVISIONS, WINGS, AND COMMANDERS, 1958-1988

THIRTEENTH STRATEGIC MISSILE DIVISION, 1959-1966, Deact.

Col. William S. Rader	July 1, 1959-March 1, 1961
Brig. Gen. William S. Rader	March 1, 1961-January 15, 1965
Brig. Gen. Lewis E. Lyle	January 15, 1965-July 1, 1966

FOURTH STRATEGIC MISSILE DIVISION, 1971–1973, Redesignated
- Brig. Gen. Robert R. Scott   July 1, 1971–June 7, 1972
- Brig. Gen. Gerald G. Fall   June 7, 1972–February 28, 1973

FOURTH AIR DIVISION, 1973–1988, Deactivated
- Brig. Gen. Gerald G. Fall   March 1, 1973–July 31, 1974
- Maj. Gen. Melvin G. Bowling   August 1, 1974–August 7, 1975
- Brig. Gen. Harold E. Gross   August 8, 1975–May 22, 1978
- Brig. Gen. John R. Lasater   May 23, 1978–June 15, 1979
- Brig. Gen. David L. Patton   July 16, 1979–August 24, 1981
- Maj. Gen. Ellie G. Shuler   September 7, 1981–July 4, 1984
- Brig. Gen. Robert L. Kirtley   July 7, 1984–June 6, 1985
- Brig. Gen. Denis L. Walsh   June 13, 1985–June 11, 1987
- Brig. Gen. Arlen D. Jameson   June 11, 1987–August 23, 1988

4320TH STRATEGIC WING (MISSILE), 1958, Redesignated
- Col. Hilbert F. Muenter   February 1, 1958–February 12, 1958

706TH STRATEGIC MISSILE WING (ATLAS), 1958–1961, Redesig.
- Col. Hilbert F. Muenter   February 24, 1958–January 1, 1959
- Brig. Gen. William L. Large   January 1, 1959–June 1, 1959
- Col. William S. Rader   June 1, 1959–August 24, 1959
- Col. George T. Chadwell   August 24, 1959–July 1, 1961

389TH STRATEGIC MISSILE WING (ATLAS), 1961–1965, Deact.
- Col. George T. Chadwell   July 1, 1961–December 12, 1963
- Col. Julian R. Summers   December 12, 1963–March 25, 1965

NINETIETH STRATEGIC MISSILE WING, 1963–1988, Active
- Col. Floyd E. Wikstrum   July 1, 1963–August 26, 1965
- Col. Donald W. Johnson   August 26, 1965–August 16, 1966
- Col. Robert J. Hill   August 16, 1966–August 2, 1968
- Col. Robert R. Scott   August 2, 1968–August 18, 1969
- Brig. Gen. Harold A. Strack   August 18, 1969–January 3, 1972
- Col. Paul E. Bell   January 3, 1972–July 2, 1973
- Col. Bobbie G. Guthrie   July 2, 1973–June 13, 1974
- Col. Christopher S. Adams   June 13, 1974–December 3, 1975
- Col. Ray E. Miller   December 3, 1975–September 29, 1976
- Col. James E. Cowan   September 29, 1976–March 23, 1979
- Col. Charles H. Greenley   March 26, 1979–June 11, 1981
- Col. Martin M. Burdick   June 11, 1981–December 14, 1982
- Col. James P. Henry   December 14, 1982–January 24, 1984
- Col. Arlen D. Jameson   January 24, 1984–June 17, 1986
- Col. Gary L. Curtin   June 17, 1986–June 8, 1988
- Col. John A. Gordon   June 8, 1988–Present

Members of the Cheyenne Military Affairs Committee are shown gathered with senior air force officers at the Site Activation Task Force (SATAF) command post in June 1965 when the last flight of ten Minuteman missiles were turned over to the Ninetieth Strategic Missile Wing by the Air Force Systems Command. Standing left to right: Tom Searle, Clem Deaver, Clyde Gaymon, Abe Nuss, Brigadier General William Rader, Bob Smith, Major General Austin Davis, Mayor Bill Nation, Brigadier General H.J. Sands, Boeing rep Bob Randall, Charles Carey, Percy Hilde, Don Stanfield, Leo Herman, George Kaufman, Haskell Cohen, George Guy, Pete Cook, and Val Christenson. Seated: Colonels William Todd, Floyd Wikstrum and William Brier.—*Ninetieth SM Wing History Office*

The headstone of First Sergeant John Limeburner, Company D of the Fifth Cavalry who died April 13, 1871, age twenty-eight, remains one of the handsomest in the base cemetery. Limeburner was shot by one of his buddies in a "house of loose architecture" located between the post and Cheyenne, according to a local newspaper report. Paid for by his soldier friends who earned only a few dollars a month, the headstone includes this: "A Tribute of Respect By His Comrades." Retired Air Force Senior Master Sergeant Edward A. Tarbell, seen above, remains active in volunteer community work that includes serving as vice-president of the base historical society and doing research of base cemetery burials, some of which have proven to be very interesting. Tarbell arrived at Francis E. Warren AFB as a communications NCO during the Atlas-Minuteman missile transition and retired in 1965.—*1988, Author's Photo*

The three headstones seen nearest Retired Air Force Senior Master Sergeant Edward A. Tarbell are early officer burials in the base cemetery. They are Lieutenant William W. Bell (left), shot by Private Brown on June 13, 1868, near present-day Laramie while the Eighteenth Infantry marched from Fort Fetterman to take station at Fort D.A. Russell. Summarily executed, Brown was buried in the wagon ruts on the Laramie Plain and Bell received a Christian burial two days later in this plot. The center headstone marks the grave of Lieutenant George F. Mason, Fifth Cavalry, killed in a shoot-out with civilian employee A.J. Botsford in March 1870. The headstone right in-line is that of Captain James Cahill, Company K of the Second Cavalry, who died of delerium tremens on February 5, 1868 while under post arrest.—*1988, Author's Photo*

Third generation Cheyenneite William A. Corson, Jr., recalls being inducted into the army in 1943 at Fort Francis E. Warren and, earlier, the wonderful stories his grandfather, Samuel Corson, told him about the early social affairs and other activities at Fort D.A. Russell and Cheyenne Depot that usually included the Cheyenne community. Samuel Corson arrived in 1882 from Scotland and successfully entered the business arena with some encouragement from early Wyoming cattleman Alexander Swan of the Swan Land and Cattle Company. The Daughters of the American Revolution dedicated this marker in 1927 on the former site of the Cheyenne Depot flagpole. Wyoming Governor Frank C. Emerson gave the dedication address. The D.A.R. members, like many others, preferred to use the name "Camp Carlin," taken from the name of the first commander of the Cheyenne Depot, Quartermaster Captain Elias Brown Carling.—1988, *Author's Photo.*

The Order of Daedalians dedicated a memorial marker in 1981 near the main gate on the site of the 1919 Fort D.A. Russell flying field. Active for about eighteen months, the flying field served as the first military/civilian airfield in southeast Wyoming. Retired Air Force Colonel William W. Brier (left) presided at the 1981 dedication as flight captain of Fort Warren Flight #54, Order of Daedalians, which is a society of active and retired military pilots. Another Daedalian and former flight captain, retired Air Force Colonel Merle "Hap" Johnson (right), arrived at Francis E. Warren AFB in 1963 during the Atlas to Minuteman missile transition from a SAC bomb wing in Arizona, quite a change of pace as Johnson recalls.—*1988, Author's Photo*

Built in 1903 as a regimental guard house, building #218 served that purpose as long as cavalry and infantry regiments garrisoned the post. In 1974 the F.E. Warren AFB Federal Credit Union moved into building #218 and has made good use of it since. A member-owned-federally-charted financial institution organized in 1951, the Credit Union provides a convenient and accommodating facility for members of the military, civilian employees, and the families. In addition to the main office in building #218, there is a branch facility in Cheyenne. Pictured on Randall Avenue in front of the Credit Union are the chief officers: Mrs. Shirley Howard, a Wyoming native started to work for the Credit Union twenty-nine years ago. She has been president of the F.E. Warren AFB Federal Credit Union since 1974. Senior Master Sergeant H.A. Stephens joined the Credit Union eighteen years ago when he retired from the Air Force. He now serves as vice president and manager of the base facility.—*1988, Author's Photo*

Mr. Jack B. Knudson, deputy base civil engineer, has focused for the past twelve years on the maintenance, repair, operation and preservation of buildings and facilities at this historic military base. A native of North Dakota, Knudson received a bachelor of science degree in electrical engineering from the University of North Dakota in 1961. The riding hall in background (building #314), built in 1907, served the cavalry, infantry and artillery units for mounted indoor training when the winter Wyoming weather made outdoor activity impractical. Many former "army brats" can recall their riding lessons in this hall more than fifty years ago. The riding hall also accommodated indoor polo games. During World War II, when the horses and mules were gone, the riding hall served as a motor pool for the Quartermaster Corps, and in 1947 it became a commissary where military families could finally purchase groceries on the post. The commissary moved to newly constructed quarters south of Crow Creek in 1987 and the riding hall served temporarily as headquarters for the Civil Engineering Squadron. It will soon become a recreation arena with running track, tennis courts, basketball courts and other athletic facilities.—*1988, Author's Photo*

When Major Tom Burgess arrived at F.E. Warren AFB from a tour of duty in Alaska to take over the positions of base supply officer and commander of the Ninetieth Supply Squadron, he also became president of the base historical society and prime manager of the base museum. Built in 1893 as a regimental headquarters at a time when Fort D.A. Russell accommodated only an eight-company regiment, building #210 now accommodates three floors full of interesting and pertinent historical artifacts and memorabilia. The base museum is staffed and operated by volunteers, members of the base historical society.—*Author's Photo.*

Retired Air Force Colonels William W. Brier (right) and Conley B. Stroud served successively as commanders of the 809th Combat Support Group (Base Command 1964 through 1967) during the transition from Atlas to Minuteman missiles at Francis E. Warren Air Force Base. The 389th Strategic Missile Wing (Atlas) phased out when the Ninetieth Strategic Missile Wing had received all 200 Minuteman missiles and become operationally ready. The 809th Combat Support Group, which supported both the Atlas and Minuteman wings during the transition, was then designated the Ninetieth Combat Support Group. Missiles statically displayed near the main gate are Peacekeeper (left), Minuteman III, and the early Minuteman I. The Atlas, not displayed, was even larger than the Peacekeeper.) 1988, *Author's Photo*

Lieutenant Colonel G.L. "Bud" Heaton, USAF (Ret), joined the First Infantry Regiment in 1940 as a former star football player from the University of Wyoming and a brand new second lieutenant from the university's ROTC detachment. A native of Cheyenne, Bud served at Fort Francis E. Warren with the First Infantry. Regimental headquarters was located in building #242 just behind Bud Heaton. Built in 1909 as a standard regimental band quarters, the band building is now occupied by the Base Operations & Training Division.

Mrs. Claudia Wiggins and Mr. William M. Metz head the Real Property Records Office and the Historic Preservation Office respectively of the Ninetieth Civil Engineering Squadron. Their temporary offices in the former regimental headquarters building seen in back provides a commanding view of the central part of the base and Randall Avenue. Built in 1911 as a regimental headquarters, building #233 has served since 1940, when the last infantry regiment departed, as home for various agencies. As a teenager in the late 1950s, Mrs. Wiggins lived on-base with her parents, Chief Master Sergeant and Mrs. Hugh H. Himes, and retains many fond memories of growing up on an air force base.—1988, *Author's Photo*

Colonel Howard W. Brimmer, USA (Ret) first saw Fort D.A. Russell, now Francis E. Warren Air Force Base, after graduating from West Point on November 1, 1918, in the third graduating class that year and just ten days before World War I ended. It immediately became one of his favorite posts because there were lots of horses. Brimmer served three tours at "the post near Cheyenne" (1932-1936, 1946-1949, and 1952-1953) retiring in 1953 near his favorite post where he had family and many friends. In the early 1930s, then Captain Brimmer commanded Battery C, Seventy-sixth Field Artillery, which occupied barracks #250, now headquarters of the Ninetieth Strategic Missile Wing. The corner room behind the sign served as Captain Brimmer's office and orderly room. It is now occupied by the Wing Deputy Commander for Operations.—1988, *Author's Photo*

The dedication of this war memorial in November 1945 remains vivid in Mr. Fred A. Garvalia's memory now at the age of seventy-three because of all the dignitaries attending and the location of his office as first sergeant of the Military Police Company just across the street on Randall Avenue. The Western Governors' Conference attendees, hosted in Cheyenne by Wyoming Governor Lester Hunt, spent the day at Fort Francis E. Warren. Although not readily discernible as a war memorial, it might have been one of the first in the nation to be dedicated following World War II.—1988, *Author's Photo*

Harriett Elizabeth (Liz) Rhone and James W. Byrd first met in building #284 (background) when Sergeant Byrd returned from Europe after WWII. They married in 1947. Built in 1906 as a rec center and gym, a PX, library, social center and snack bar were included during the war. Administration offices, barber and beauty shops, a branch bank, laundry/dry cleaning, and a liquor store were added later. Now empty, it will soon become the Base Legal Center. Retired from teaching in 1986, Liz Byrd now serves in the Wyoming State Senate. Jim's career has included eight years as chief of police and four years as U.S. marshal.—*Author's Photo*

Brigadier General Robert R. Scott, USAF (Ret) served at Francis E. Warren Air Force Base as a wing (1968) and division (1971-1972) commander before retiring to work for a Cheyenne bank. Scott also served as head of the "Save the Cannon Committee" when it appeared in 1981 that the rare sixteenth century English Falcon cannon would be sent to the Smithsonian or London Tower. The cannon and two bells from Balangiga had been brought from the Philippines in 1904 by the Eleventh Infantry as war trophies. Scott is shown presiding at the well-attended dedication ceremony for the restored Falcon cannon and its new shelter in September 1985 in Trophy Park.—*USAF Photo*

Air Force Technical Sergeant Wesley P. Prill works in the Ninetieth Headquarters Squadron most of the time but also serves as commandant of the U.S. Fifth Cavalry (Reorganized), a thirty-member volunteer group of military and civilian troopers who are much in demand for parades and ceremonial occasions. This unit has represented the base and Wyoming in the last three presidential inaugural parades in Washington, D.C. Uniforms and equipment are furnished by members and are similar to that used by the Fifth Cavalry in the Indian Wars. A very distinguished cavalry regiment, the Fifth was stationed at Fort D.A. Russell from 1876 to 1880. The McClellan saddle on Prill's registered quarter horse, Little Bit, and Prill's uniform are authentic and very proper for an Indian Wars Fifth Cavalry trooper. The U.S. Fifth Cavalry (Reorganized) is now headquartered in the veterinary stable #329.—1988, *Author's Photo*

Retired Wyoming Supreme Court Justice Rodney M. Guthrie had an uncle, William E. Guthrie, held for several months at Fort D.A. Russell in 1892 along with some forty-two other "rancher regulators" for involvement in what became known as the Johnson County War. Eight days after the so-called regulators had set out on April 5 from Cheyenne looking to the north for rustlers, the army was called in to rescue them when they were surrounded by irate citizens at the TA Ranch near Buffalo, Wyoming. Forty-three regulators were escorted back to Fort D.A. Russell by the army for a trial that never occurred. In the background are the bells taken from the village of Balangiga as war trophies by the Eleventh Infantry and brought from the Philippines to Fort D.A. Russell in 1904.—1988, *Author's Photo*

The stone horse head over the entrance of building #329 designated veterinary stables throughout the United States Army in the early part of the twentieth century. Wing Historian Technical Sergeant Danny Sprong writes the quarterly history that records the pertinent activities at Francis E. Warren Air Force Base for posterity and higher headquarters. He also serves as the in-house authority on the historic military installation. Built in 1907, this veterinary stable could accommodate thirty horses in separate, or isolation, stalls and included an operating room and living quarters for the stable sergeant. It now accommodates the U.S. Fifth Cavalry (Reorganized).—1988, *Author's Photo*

Colonel Paul Chenchar, USAF (Ret), arrived at Francis E. Warren Air Force Base in 1964 as the Minuteman missiles were becoming operational. Wyoming native and graduate of the University of Wyoming, in 1946, Chenchar was an aircrew member on the B-29, Dave's Dream, that dropped the first peacetime atomic weapon at the Bikini Atoll. He was also a good friend of the late Colonel George T. Chadwell, commander of the 389th Strategic Missile Wing (Atlas) in the early 1960s and for whom the airmens' dining hall in back of Chenchar is named. During World War II and during the 1950s, more than thirty mess halls were in daily operation on the post/base serving three meals a day. Now, many airmen are authorized separate rations that enables them to dine wherever they please. The single remaining on-base airmens' dining hall, Chadwell Dining Hall located in a former horse barn, is a delightfully furnished and well-equipped facility that bears no resemblance to the mess halls of forty years ago. The exterior of the former stable that houses Chadwell Dining Hall has retained its historic integrity as have most of the other twenty-three former horse stables on the base. The stanchion used to hoist hay into the haymow of the stable, now Chadwell Dining Hall, can be seen above Colonel Chenchar's ten gallon hat.—1988, *Author's Photo*

Deactivating the Fourth Air Division headquarters in August 1988 brought members of the Civilian Advisory Council (CAC) of Cheyenne to the ceremony held in front of the headquarters building #65, with Brigadier General Arlen Jameson presiding. The CAC is a joint body of leading Cheyenne businessmen and senior air force officers who meet for lunch monthly and discuss subjects of mutual interest. The Council has been instrumental for the past sixty years in maintaining good relations in the military/civilian community. Shown left to right are the author, General Jameson, long-time CAC chairmen and Cheyenne attorney Mr. Dean W. Borthwick, Ninetieth Strategic Missile Wing Commander Colonel John Gordon, and CAC member Mr. Gred A. Garvalia.—*USAF*

Arriving from an extended assignment in the Panama Canal Zone in 1930, Mrs. Elsie Christman, moved into senior NCO quarters #276, then into quarters #275 next door seen in the background. The Christmans lived in quarters #275 until 1949 when they bought a house in Cheyenne. Mrs. Christman fondly recalls her friends and neighbors of fifty years ago with delightful stories and she still hears from some of them occasionally. Sergeant Fred Christman had transferred from the army to the air force in 1948 and retired in 1959 after fifty-five years of active service, a near record at the time. Three sets of family NCO quarters were built in 1884, and two sets survive in classic condition. They are now used as guest quarters for visiting service families.) 1988, *Author's Photo*

Colonel and Mrs. Gilmore M. (Janice) Dahl both hail from Kansas and Kansas State University. They moved into quarters #8 in June 1987 from a two-year assignment with the United States Joint Advisory Group in Bangkok, Thailand. A twenty-eight year veteran, Colonel Dahl had earlier served a tour of duty in Thailand during the Vietnam War and flew some 206 combat missions with the Thirteenth Tactical Fighter Squadron in an F-4 Phantom fighter. Built in 1908, quarters #8 is distinguished from other senior officers quarters by a slightly different exterior profile and interior arrangement. Colonel Dahl serves as commander of the Ninetieth Combat Support Group.—1988, *Author's Photo*

Captain and Mrs. Alan L. Dobson (Rae Lyn) have occupied quarters #27 for two years with their two daughters, Tiffany aged ten and Amber five, and loved every minute of it. The Dobsons are from Brookville, Pennsylvania where they attended school as childhood sweethearts. Quarters #27 is one of the seven surviving "captains" quarters built in 1885 soon after the post was declared permanent. Spacious by most standards, the two-story houses boast fourteen-foot ceilings and 3,300 square feet of living space that includes three bedrooms and a maid's quarters, four baths, a formal dining room, formal living room, large kitchen and a family room. These hundred-year-old houses have been preserved in the original architectural style outside and inside. Captain Dobson serves as adjutant of the 319th Strategic Missile Squadron.—1988, *Author's Photo*

Colonel and Mrs. John (Marilyn) Gordon, with daughter Jennifer, occupy quarters #92, probably the handsomest house on any United States' military installation. Colonel and Mrs. Gordon are both Missourians and products of the University of Missouri. Colonel Gordon is commander of the Ninetieth Strategic Missile Wing and the senior officer at Francis E. Warren Air Force Base. Quarters #92 was built as a general officers quarters in 1910 when the post grew to brigade size with a general commanding. The army built two other houses of the same design and style at Fort Totten, New York and Fort Monroe, Virginia. Today the other two houses suffer sadly from neglect and modification while quarters #92 sits as originally seen and just as majestically as it did in 1910.—*1988, Author's Photo*

In the mid-1880s, the post commander at Fort D.A. Russell installed a fence and gate to remind horse-drawn vehicles from Cheyenne to slow down and proceed on post at not more than a gentle trot. Everyone was welcome to visit the post and no passes or authorization for admittance was required. Lieut. Col. Robert M. Middleton of the Ninetieth Security Police Group believes that vehicular traffic has not changed much in the last one hundred years—drivers still want to charge through the main gate at full speed. However, the security police guarding the main gate, the base, and the two hundred outlying missile sites consider speeders a minor concern these days.—*Author's Photo*.

Wyoming Governor Mike Sullivan did the honors at the F.E. Warren AFB Airman of the Quarter Banquet held at the NCO Club in October 1988. Staff Sergeant Ken Lorimer (L) of the Ninetieth Security Police Group received the NCO of the Quarter award and Airman First Class Orlando Vilches, Ninetieth Civil Engineering Squadron, received the Airman of the Quarter recognition. Military guests are often seen at functions held at the governor's mansion in Cheyenne and Governor and Mrs. Sullivan are frequent visitors to, and strong supporters of activities at the missile base.—*USAF Photo by SSGT Ron Rush.*

SOURCES

PART I. AN ARMY POST BEYOND THE FRONTIER, 1867-1869
CHAPTER ONE. FINDING THE RIGHT SPOT
ON CROW CREEK

T.A. Larson's *History of Wyoming* (Lincoln: University of Nebraska Press, 1978), is the definitive history of the state and the best source for basic historical information. Volume 2 of General W.T. Sherman's *Personal Memoirs of Gen's W.T. Sherman* (New York: Charles L. Webster and Co., 1891), gives an excellent account of Sherman's activities after the war, including some of his important letters and speeches. For Sherman's letters to Augur and Augur's letters to Sherman and Stevenson, see the National Archives file on U.S. Continental Commands, Department of the Platte Records 1858-1895, Letters Received A-Y 1867-1869, Record Group 533, Rolls 6 and 7. These records were viewed on film at the Coe Library, University of Wyoming. The monthly Post Returns of Fort D.A. Russell start in September 1867 and continue up to the 1920s. They list the units on station, number of officers and enlisted men, commanding officer, and any unusual events that occurred that month. National Archives microfilm records of Fort D.A. Russell Post Returns made available by courtesy of F.E. Warren Air Force Base Librarian Mrs. Ellen Tarbell.

For more information on the siting and early days of Fort D.A. Russell and Cheyenne, see Gilbert A. Stelter, "The Birth of a Frontier Boomtown: Cheyenne in 1867," *Annals of Wyoming*, Vol. 39 (April 1867), pp. 5-64. *Annals of Wyoming* is a biannual historical publication of the State Historical and Publications Division. Another good source is Henry C. Parry, "Letters from the Frontier, 1867," *Annals of Wyoming*, Vol. 30 (October 1958), pp. 127-148. Major General Grenville M. Dodge, *How We Built the Union Pacific* (Denver: Sage Books, 1965) gives Dodge's account of the July 4, 1867, meeting at Crow Creek Crossing and other excellent information on early Cheyenne. The best account of the North brothers and the Pawnee Scouts is contained in George Bird Grinnell's *Two Great Scouts and Their Pawnee Battalion* (Cleveland: The Arthur H. Clark Company, 1928). General Order 33, dated July 31, 1867, establishing Fort D.A. Russell can be found in National Archives Records of the Adjutant General's Office 1780-1917, Orders and Circulars 1866-67, Vol. 932, G.O. No. 33, Headquarters Department of the Platte, Omaha, Nebraska, Record Group 94. National Archives film at Coe Library, University of Wyoming.

CHAPTER TWO. BUILDING BARRACKS AND CHASING INDIANS

The *Cheyenne Daily Leader* started publication on September 19, 1867, and provides one of the best sources of information. The Wyoming State

Historical and Publications Division in Cheyenne maintains a microfilm library of Cheyenne newspapers.

The Post Return for September shows Special Order No. 26, dated September 7, 1867, Department of the Platte, establishing the post on September 8, 1867, not entirely in keeping with the earlier General Order 33 shown in chapter 1. A good account of the first summer and fall at Fort D.A. Russell is seen in William H. Bisbee, *Through Four American Wars* (Boston: Meador Publishing Company, 1931), p. 183. Also Frenchman Louis L. Simonin, *The Rocky Mountain West in 1867* (Lincoln: University of Nebraska Press, 1966), p. 63. Other excellent observations were recorded by the Reverend Joseph W. Cook, *Diary and Letters* (Laramie: The Laramie Republican Co., 1919).

CHAPTER THREE. FIRST SPRING CAMPAIGN
AND THE TREATY OF 1868

The *Cheyenne Daily Leader* reported trends in desertions from the post as well as unit movements and the troop strength as a matter of general interest to the community. Excellent reports of Indian movement into or through the area appeared promptly. The paper also supplied a good account of the Peace Commission's activities in 1868 and their progress at Fort Laramie with the Indian chiefs, which resulted in the important Treaty of 1868. Mrs. Elizabeth Burt, wife of Major Andrew Burt, kept a journal all her adult life and left a detailed record of the Burts' thirty years at various western posts, including three tours of duty at Fort D.A. Russell. Mrs. Burt's journal is seen in the excellent book produced by Merrill J. Mattes, *Indians, Infants and Infantry: Andrew and Elizabeth Burt on the Frontier* (Denver: The Old West Publishing Company, 1960), p. 25. Andrew Burt retired from the army in 1902 as a general officer after forty years of service.

The temporary order curtailing army unit activity against Indians away from their reservations is found in records of the War Department, U.S. Command, Department of the Platte, Letters Sent April 2, 1866-October 30, 1877, (RG 98, Roll 7), National Archives film on file at Coe Library, University of Wyoming. Pressure from the public caused Sherman to change that policy, as seen in Robert G. Athern, *William Tecumseh Sherman and the Settlement of the West* (Norman: University of Oklahoma Press, 1956), p. 217. Reports of patrols sent out from Fort D.A. Russell appear in the records of U.S. Army Continental Commands, Department of the Platte Records 1858-1895, (RG 533, Roll 7), National Archives film on file at Coe Library. Sherman's pointed response to Colorado Governor Hunt's request for more protection from the army or a federalized state militia appeared in the *Leader* on September 10, 1868. The Reverend Joseph W. Cook's record of the vigilantes' activities in October 1868 is the best as shown in his *Diary and Letters*, p. 104.

CHAPTER FOUR. THE ARMY AND INDIAN POLICY

A good report of Captain E.R. Arms's scouting expedition into western Nebraska appeared in the *Cheyenne Daily Leader*, December 28, 1868, while other scouting reports of that period are included in the U.S. Army

Continental Commands, Department of the Platte Records 1858-1895, (RG 533, Roll 7). Post trader J.D. Woolley's store is described briefly in U.S. War Department, Inspector General's Office, *Outline Description of the Posts and Stations of Troops* (Washington: Government Printing Office, 1872), p. 91. General Augur's telegram asking the laundresses of the Thirtieth Infantry to be patient is in the Records of the War Department, Department of the Platte, Letters Sent April 2, 1866-October 30, 1867, (RG 98, Roll 7). The *Leader* reported on the Dick Douglas affair on February 12 and 16, 1869, and offered the first of many critical comments to follow on Grant's Indian policy on March 21, 1869. Don Rickey, Jr., also provides excellent information on Grant's peace policy in his *Forty Miles a Day On Beans and Hay* (Norman: University of Oklahoma Press, 1963), p. 8.

The *Cheyenne Daily Leader* kept in close touch with the permanent and temporary movement of units in and out of Fort D.A. Russell and the arrival of the paymaster in September 1869, in this case, both items being of great interest and economic importance to Cheyenne. An early report on the Fort D.A. Russell cemetery is included in "National Cemeteries in Wyoming Territory, 1869," *Annals of Wyoming*, Vol. 17, No. 1 (January 1945), p. 75.

PART II. INDIAN WAR ON THE HIGH PLAINS, 1870-1879.

CHAPTER FIVE. PATROLLING AND ESCORTING

The Post Return for April 1870 cites the Department of the Platte letter requiring that all scouting parties be accompanied by an officer. It also shows a near-complete deployment of units from Fort D.A. Russell for the season to various outposts and areas. Lieutenant Colonel C.H. Alden served as the first post surgeon and played an important role in designing the plan for the garrison in 1867. His annual reports extend far beyond the post hospital to include morale and welfare activities and the post garden. Alden's reports are in the publication *War Department Surgeon General's Office*, Circular Number 4, "Report on Barracks and Hospitals with Description of Military Posts," (Washington, D.C.: Government Printing Office, December 1870), p. 322.

The expedition of the Big Horn Mining Association received close attention from the *Cheyenne Daily Leader* in the spring and summer of 1870. General Christopher Augur's letter to Washington giving details of the association's final disarray is included in Records of the War Department, U.S. Army Command, Department of the Platte, Letters Sent April 2, 1866-October 30, 1877, (RG 98), National Archives film at the Coe Library, University of Wyoming.

The subject of drunken paydays appeared for many years in the *Leader* almost every time the paymaster arrived at Fort D.A. Russell, which was every three to five months. General Augur's statement on the need for the army paymaster to appear more frequently and on a regular schedule can be found in Records of the War Department, U.S. Army Continental

Commands, Department of the Platte, Records 1858-1895, Letters Sent 1866-1877, (RG 533), National Archives film at the Coe Library, University of Wyoming.

CHAPTER SIX. THE PEACE POLICY
AND GOLD IN THE BLACK HILLS

The *Cheyenne Daily Leader* provided excellent reports in April 1873 of the roving troublesome bands of Oglala Sioux in western Nebraska and eastern Wyoming. Also see Robert M. Utley's very informative *Frontier Regulars: The United States Army and The Indians* (Bloomington: Indiana University Press, 1977), pp. 198-207. Reports of 1873 scouting parties are included in Records of the War Department, United States Army Continental Commands, Department of the Platte, Records 1858-1895, "Quarterly Report of Scouts Made From Fort D.A. Russell," National Archives. The story of the 1874 Sioux Expedition and establishment of Camp Robinson is well told by Roger T. Grange, Jr., "Fort Robinson: Outpost on the Plains," *Nebraska History*, Vol. 3, No. 3 (September 1958), p. 197. Family life in the 1870s at Fort D.A. Russell has been recorded by Martha Summerhayes in *Vanquished Arizona: Recollections of My Army Life* (Philadelphia: J.B. Lippincott Company, 1908), p. 197.

CHAPTER SEVEN. CAMPAIGNS OF 1876

The *Cheyenne Daily Leader* gave a good account of the early activities of the Cheyenne and Black Hills Stage Line in the February 3, 1876, edition. Also see Agnes Wright Spring, *The Cheyenne and Black Hills Stage and Express Routes* (Glendale: The Arthur H. Clark Co., 1949).

The *Leader* announced the launching of the winter campaign from Fort D.A. Russell on February 22, 1876, and at least three excellent published accounts are available. They are J.W. Vaughn, *The Reynold's Campaign on Powder River* (Norman: University of Oklahoma Press, 1961); Anson Mills, *My Story* (Washington, D.C.: Press of Byron S. Adams, 1918, published by the author); and *General George Crook: His Autobiography*, edited by Martin F. Schmitt (Norman: University of Oklahoma Press, 1946).

A report of the departure of Crook's summer campaign from Fort D.A. Russell appeared in the *Leader* on May 19 and 24, 1876. An excellent account of that campaign is also presented in Jesse Wendell Vaughn, *With Crook at the Rosebud* (Norman: University of Oklahoma Press, 1956). Also see John G. Bourke, *On the Border With Crook* (New York: Charles Scribner's Sons, 1891). The winter campaign is reported by the *Leader* on November 4 and 19, 1876, along with some of the exploits of the Pawnee Scouts. The story of Frank and Luther North and the Pawnee Scouts is best told by George Bird Grinnell in *Two Great Scouts and their Pawnee Battalion*, and by Robert Bruce, *The Fighting Norths and Pawnee Scouts* (Lincoln: Nebraska State Historical Society, 1932).

CHAPTER EIGHT. INDIAN WARS ENDED, ALMOST

On May 30, 1877, the *Cheyenne Daily Leader* again reported the departure of a Fort D.A. Russell unit on temporary duty and in very picturesque language. Captain Charles King served as Adjutant, Fifth Cavalry, at Fort D.A. Russell for two years, 1876–1878. An Apache bullet he received earlier in Arizona caused his retirement in 1879. King had started writing while at Fort D.A. Russell, and his literary career blossomed soon after his retirement. In a letter dated June 16, 1983, Agnes Wright Spring tells of corresponding with Charles King about 1919. He admitted to writing one of his early and most popular books while stationed at Fort D.A. Russell, the title, *Laramie or the Queen of Bedlam*. He recreated life in the barracks at Fort Laramie in this novel and told a romantic tale of the bachelor officers' quarters there known as "Bedlam." He wrote dozens of historical novels, wonderful to read even today, which reinforced the army's late–eighteenth–century image.

George F. Price tells of Fort D.A. Russell and the Fifth Cavalry Indian scouts in the summer of 1877–1878 as well as the railway strike riot duty in his *Across the Continent With the Fifth Cavalry* (New York: Antiquarian Press, 1959). Frequent articles on Fort D.A. Russell and Cheyenne Depot were contributed to the Cheyenne newspapers by Mrs. Theresa Jenkins, wife of John D. Jenkins, who worked at Cheyenne Depot from 1876 until 1890. Mrs. Jenkins contributed the 1877 article titled "Fort Russell Scene of the Gayest of Social Functions" to the *Kemmerer Kamera*, August 27, 1919. An excellent account of the company laundresses and military dependents is told by Patricia Stallard in *Glittering Misery: Lives of Army Dependants in the Trans–Mississippi West, 1865–1898* (Fort Collins: The Old Army Press, 1978). Also see George A. Forsyth, *The Story of the Soldier* (New York: D. Appleton and Company, 1900). The *Leader* provided excellent coverage of the two Cheyenne bands in northwestern Nebraska evading the Fifth Cavalry in January–March 1879 in an attempt to reach their traditional hunting territory in Montana.

The *Leader* reported on February 7, 1878, that the Senate had confirmed Nathan C. Meeker, editor of the *Greeley Tribune*, as agent for the Utes at the White River Agency in Colorado. The September, October, and November 1879 editions of the *Leader* provide detailed information on the "Thornburgh Massacre" and movement of troops to the White River Agency area. Also see the Post Returns for those months and George F. Price, *Across the Continent With the Fifth Cavalry*, p. 173.

PART III. REFURBISHING FORT D.A. RUSSELL, 1880–1889

CHAPTER NINE. SURVIVING THE CUT OF POSTS

The *Cheyenne Daily Leader* continued in the 1880s as the main source of Fort D.A. Russell information, with particularly good coverage of the visit of President Rutherford B. Hayes and General W.T. Sherman in September 1880. Sherman's report to the secretary of war was also reported in the November 16, 1880, edition. The prohibition edict is included in the Post Return for March 1881, and cites G.O. 24, Headquarters of the Army, Adjutant General's Office, Washington, dated February 22, 1881. The joint resolution of Congress pertaining to the post traders is contained in the Army Continental Commands, Department of the Platte Records

1858-1895, (RG 533, Roll 6), National Archives film at the Coe Library, University of Wyoming.

An excellent account of a later effort to find the remains of the Sir John Franklin Expedition that Lieutenant Schwatka searched for can be found in Bil Gilbert, "A Frozen Sailor Summons Up Tale of Heroism," *Smithsonian* (June 1985). The best source of information on old posts is Herbert M. Hart, *Old Forts of the Northwest* (New York: Superior Publishing Company, 1963).

CHAPTER TEN. MAKING THE POST PERMANENT, FINALLY

The Post Return for April 1883 included G.O. #8 dated April 1, Department of the Platte, subject "Issue of Rations to Laundresses to Cease After June 18, 1883." The *Cheyenne Daily Leader* provided the usual good coverage of the arrival of a new regimental commander, Colonel John T. Mason, in June along with the post social activities and President Chester Arthur's visit in August 1883. In January 1884, the *Cheyenne Daily Leader* was sold to a group of Cheyenne Democrats, and the name changed for the next three years to the *Cheyenne Democratic Leader*. The new *Leader* reported the demise of the post trader system at Fort D.A. Russell in the February 10, May 27, and July 6, 1885, editions. Also see Records of the Quartermaster General Consolidated Correspondence, (RG 92), National Archives records on file at the Ninetieth Civil Engineering Squadron, Francis E. Warren AFB. A great deal of political pressure was brought to bear on the army, and some post traders survived longer at other western posts. A note submitted to the quartermaster general said that the post trader at Fort D.A. Russell was being discontinued due to the proximity of Cheyenne. Fort Laramie retained John Hunton as post trader up to the time of its closing in 1890.

T.A. Larson provides an excellent account of the so-called "Chinese Massacre" at Rock Springs in September 1885 in his *History of Wyoming*, p. 141. The need of owning a cow is discussed in Merrill J. Mattes's recording of Mrs. Elizabeth Burt's journals, *Indians, Infants and Infantry*, p. 175. The *Leader* told on February 11, 1886, about the problem Fort D.A. Russell was having with pet goats allowed to run loose.

CHAPTER ELEVEN. SCALING DOWN TO SIZE:
A SINGLE-REGIMENT POST

On March 20, 1887, *Cheyenne Daily Leader* published reports that the president intended to eliminate fences around government land and expressed some concern on June 3 about the unexpected arrival of the troop of black cavalry from Fort Robinson. The *Leader* also provided the news of the post gaining its own post office and postmistress on January 22 and June 30, 1888. The progress of the building program and the new canteen appeared on April 22 and 26 and May 24, 1888. The story of the paymaster losing his payroll bag appeared in the local newspaper, the *Army and Navy Journal* (March 26, 1887), and Oliver Knight, *Life and Manners in the Frontier Army* (Norman: University of Oklahoma Press, 1978), p. 25.

PART IV. CHEYENNE DEPOT, QUARTERMASTER SUPPLY, 1867-1889

CHAPTER TWELVE. ALSO KNOWN AS CAMP CARLING OR OR CARLIN

Local contractors and suppliers are shown in the U.S. Army Continental Commands, Department of the Platte Records; 1858-1859 Contract Register, Quartermaster Department 1868-1878, (RG 533), National Archives film at Coe Library, University of Wyoming. The Jenkins family provided an excellent source of information on Cheyenne Depot during the early part of the century. See J.F. Jenkins, "Camp Carlin or Cheyenne Depot," *Annals of Wyoming*, Vol. 5, No. 1 (July 1927). John F. Jenkins, his wife Theresa, and John's brother, James, all came to Cheyenne about the same year, 1876. John and James worked at the Cheyenne Depot until it closed in 1889. John served as a justice of the peace in Cheyenne in the 1920s. Theresa wrote many fine articles about the "old days" for the Cheyenne newspapers.

Many of the activities of Cheyenne Depot are shown in Richard Guentzel, "The Department of the Platte and Western Settlement, 1866-1877," *Nebraska History* (Fall 1975). Also Agnes Wright Spring, "Site of Pioneer Military Depot Seethes with Activity," *Wyoming Stockman Farmer*, Vol. 7, No. 2 (February 1941). A description of the depot is given in War Department Quartermaster General's Office, "Outline Description of Military Posts and Reservations in the United States and Alaska," (Washington: Government Printing Office, 1904). The April 1, 1890, edition of the *Leader* reviewed the fate of Cheyenne Depot and that of five other army installations in Wyoming recently closed.

For a full account of Thomas Moore's funeral and biography see the *Wyoming Tribune*, May 15, 19, and 22, 1896. A letter from Russell L. Tracy of Salt Lake City dated October 5, 1936, to Mr. Mark Chapman of Cheyenne gives Tracy's recollections of Cheyenne Depot during the 1880s, including Thomas Moore and the white mule, Steamboat. Copy of letter on file at the Wyoming State Historical and Publications Department.

PART V. CLOSING OUT THE NINETEENTH CENTURY, 1890-1899

CHAPTER THIRTEEN. WOUNDED KNEE, THE JOHNSON COUNTY WAR, AND WAR WITH SPAIN

General Schofield's important 1890 report to the secretary of war appeared in the *Cheyenne Daily Leader*, November 7, 1890. The Senate bill providing for the disposal of abandoned military lands is included in the Post Return for March 1890 and the *Leader* on April 1 and July 1, 1890. The movement of Fort D.A. Russell troops and supplies to the area of the Pine Ridge Reservation during the "Ghost Dance" movement is related in the *Leader*, November 21-22, 1890, and the Post Return for December 1890. The battle at Wounded Knee Creek is well told by Rex Alan Smith, *Moon of Popping Trees* (Lincoln: University of Nebraska Press, 1981).

Colonel Henry R. Mizner's eloquent memorial service tribute to General W.T. Sherman was carried in the *Cheyenne Daily Leader*, February 21, 1891. The *Leader* also printed on March 8 the announcement of 2,000 Indians to be enlisted in the army soon and Colonel Mizner's charges against post surgeon Captain A.H. Appel on May 14, 1891.

Fort D.A. Russell's accepting prisoners from the Johnson County War is contained in the Post Return for April 1892. A full account of that event can be found in T.A. Larson, *History of Wyoming*, and Helena Huntington Smith, *The War On Powder River* (Lincoln: University of Nebraska Press, 1966). A good description of the life and times of a soldier, including those at Fort D.A. Russell, in the late nineteenth century is told by George A. Forsyth, *The Story of the Soldier* (New York: D. Appelton and Company, 1900).

Fort D.A. Russell troops employed against the Commonwealers at Green River and at the railroad workers' strike in Wyoming and Colorado are shown in the Post Returns for May through August 1894. Colonel Poland's report is filed under Annual Report of 17th Infantry Regimental Commander Colonel John S. Poland, April 17, 1894, at the Wyoming State Historical Publications Division. When Fort D.A. Russell troops were sent to Jackson Hole to cope with 300 Bannock Indians supposedly full of fight, the *Leader* reported the event on July 23, 24, 25, 27, 30, and September 4, 1895. Also see "The Indian Troubles," *Harpers Weekly* (August 17, 1895).

Improvements in the post canteen system and a name change to "post exchange" appears in the *Wyoming Tribune*, May 8, 1895. Also the Post Return for August 1896 shows AGO General Order 6, July 26, 1895, "Post Exchange Regulations." The *Cheyenne Daily Sun-Leader* wrote of the two expeditions to Alaska on September 18 and December 23, 1897. Also see Post Returns for September and December 1897.

The assembling of the Wyoming National Guard at Fort D.A. Russell prior to their departure for the Philippine Islands is related by T.A. Larson in the *History of Wyoming*. Also see *American Military History*, Maurice Matloff, editor (Washington: Office of the Chief of Military History, United States Army, 1969), p. 287. Matloff shows the National Guard moving from local loosely knit militia units in the 1870s to organized militia units in the late 1890s, when they were called the National Guard. When the United States declared war on Spain, the National Guard provided the principal reserve force standing behind the regular army. The *Cheyenne Daily Sun-Leader* reported Colonel Jay L. Torrey's call for volunteers to join the Second United States Volunteer Cavalry Regiment on April 17, 1899, and the progress and later movement of that unit. An account of the three U.S. volunteer cavalry regiments, including the Second, and their contribution to the Spanish-American War is provided in C.P. Westermeier, *Who Rush to Glory* (Caldwell, Idaho: The Caxton Printers, Ltd., 1950).

PART VI. THE "NEW" FORT D.A. RUSSELL, 1900-1909
CHAPTER FOURTEEN. THE POST EXPANDS TO BRIGADE SIZE

The Cheyenne newspapers and the monthly Post Returns continue to provide the majority of information on Fort D.A. Russell. Although commonly used after 1900, the term National Guard became the official title of the American Militia after passage of the National Defense Act of 1916. See "350 Years Young, National Guard Commemorates Birthday," *Heliogram Of the Council on America's Military Past*, No. 181 (November 1986), Fort Myer, Virginia.

The post's water dispute with Cheyenne and the progress of the building program, including a crematorium for burning horse manure, were reported in the *Cheyenne Daily Leader*, December 2 and 22, 1902, and April 3, May 1, and 19, 1903. President Theodore Roosevelt's visit to Fort D.A. Russell is told by Fenimore Chatterton, *Yesterday's Wyoming: The Intimate Memoirs of Fenimore Chatterton* (Sheridan, WY: Powder River Publishers & Booksellers, 1957), p. 71.

CHAPTER FIFTEEN: LARGE-SCALE SUMMER MANEUVERS
AT POLE MOUNTAIN

The arrival of the bells and cannon were reported by the *Cheyenne Daily Leader* on May 16, 1905. Recognition of the cannon as a rare item came in a letter from H.L. Blackmore, deputy master of the armouries, H.M. Tower of London, dated July 1, 1979, copy in the files of the Wyoming State Historical and Publications Department. For more information on the cannon and bells see Gerald M. Adams, "The F.E. Warren AFB War Trophies from Balangiga, P.I.," *Annals of Wyoming* (Spring 1987). Brigadier General T.J. Windt's ill-chosen words on soldiers marrying were reported in the *Leader*, August 29, 1905. The Eleventh Infantry's role in the San Francisco disaster appeared in the *Leader* on April 27, 1906, and the Post Returns for April through July 1906. The story of the replacement of the Krag with the Springfield 1903 rifle is told in *American Military History: United States Army* (Washington, D.C.: Government Printing Office, 1969).

The item on dogs at Fort D.A. Russell bothering mounted officers appeared in the *Cheyenne State Leader* on September 2, 1909. General Smith's remarks to the Industrial Club were printed on November 24, 1909.

PART VII. MEXICAN TROUBLES
AND A WAR IN EUROPE, 1910-1919

CHAPTER SIXTEEN. THE BRIGADE SEEKS GOOD RELATIONS
WITH CHEYENNE— MOST OF THE TIME

An add-on to the building program mainly completed was reported in the *Cheyenne State Leader* on March 16 and April 5, 1910. The heated disagreement between the Medical Corps and brigade commander on the use of building #65 appeared in the *Leader* on April 15 and May 28, 1910.

Lieutenant Bloom's tour of duty at Fort D.A. Russell did not pass without incident, as reported in the *Leader* on October 12, 1911, and February 17, 1912. A fistfight with a noncommissioned officer occurred when Lieutenant Bloom did not receive what he judged to be a proper hand salute. Captain Mitchell's activities at Fort D.A. Russell appeared in the Post Returns for January and September 1912, and the *Leader*, July 2, August 20-21, and September 7, 1912. Also see John L. Frisbee, "Mitchell of the Signal Corps," *The Retired Officer* (March 1986). Charges of wrongdoing against Senator Francis E. Warren were reported in the *Leader* on August 30, September 3, and 15, October 3, 1912, and January 28, 1913. The partial mobilization of the Wyoming National Guard in 1916 was reported in the *Leader* on May 14, June 2, July 2, and November 8, 1916.

CHAPTER SEVENTEEN. WAR, DEMOBILIZATION, AND THE AVIATION ERA

The restructuring of the army in 1917 is given in *American Military History*, Maurice Matloff, editor, p. 374. Conversion of eight cavalry outfits in training at Fort D.A. Russell to field artillery is reported in Post Returns for May through September 1917. Also see the *Leader* for May 16 and July 26, 1917. The discussion on the objection to the use of the word "sammies" appeared in the *Leader* on June 15, 1918. Major E.W. Stone's charges against Cheyenne appeared in the *Leader*, April 22, 1919. The visit of the Far West Flying Circus to Cheyenne is reported in the *Leader* on May 1, 1919. For other aviation activity at Fort D.A. Russell in the 1919-1920 period see Gerald M. Adams, "Cheyenne's Colorful Aviation History: No Airfield Now—But We Did Have a Dandy," *Cheyenne Sunday Tribune-Eagle* (December 7, 1980). The *Leader* reported on the flight of planes from the Transcontinental Reliability Test landing at the post on October 4, 7, 9, 10, 13, 14, 16, 17, and 18, 1919.

PART VIII. THE POSTWAR ARMY AT FORT D.A. RUSSELL, 1920-1929

CHAPTER EIGHTEEN. THE FLYING FIELD MOVES TO CHEYENNE

Secretary of War Baker's telegram preventing a joint military/civilian airfield was printed by the *Wyoming State Tribune*, July 23, 1920. The survey visit of Rickenbacker and Acosta appeared on August 4, 1920, and Rickenbacker's unfortunate landing the next year was reported in the *Wyoming State Tribune* and *Cheyenne State Leader*, May 27, 1921. The two Cheyenne daily newspapers combined in March 1921 and were known as the *Tribune-Leader*. Also see Gerald M. Adams, "The Air Age Comes to Wyoming," *Annals of Wyoming*, Vol. 52, No. 2 (Fall 1980).

The visit of the chief of chaplains, Colonel John T. Acton, and his plea for a dedicated post chapel was reported in the *Tribune-Leader* on January 27, 1922. The account of the untimely death of Lieutenant Colonel James Longstreet and the impressive procession to the funeral train appeared, fully and beautifully written, in the *Tribune-Leader* on July 15 and 17, 1922.

CHAPTER NINETEEN. A COMMUNITY RELATIONS COMMITTEE IS BORN

The Fort D.A. Russell cavalry and field artillery participation in the Frontier Days parade is described in the *Tribune-Leader*, July 24, 1924. A review of the units, buildings, land, and other assets at Fort D.A. Russell in December 1924 is given in the December 11 edition of the *Tribune-Leader*. The military committee described in the *Tribune-Leader* on February 27, 1925, has continued to serve a very useful purpose but in an expanded form. A civilian Advisory Council composed of senior chamber of commerce members and senior military members meets monthly or at the call of the president. There is also a Military Affairs Committee with chamber members and military members. The chamber members are appointed for two year terms.

The summer maneuvers of 1925, including Army Air Service airplanes, are reported on June 3, August 1-2 and 12, 1925, in the *Tribune-Leader*. Fort D.A. Russell's first attempt at antiaircraft artillery firing practice is described on April 8, 1926, in the *Tribune-Leader*. The restoration of the Falcon cannon is described in Gerald M. Adams, "The F.E. Warren Air Force Base War Trophies from Balangiga, P.I.," *Annals of Wyoming* Vol. 59, No. 1 (Spring 1987). Brigadier General John M. Jenkins's scolding but well accepted presentation to the Cheyenne Lions Club appeared in the *Tribune-Leader*, November 10, 1926.

The departure of the two cavalry regiments from Fort D.A. Russell is well described in the June 16, 1927, edition of the *Tribune-Leader*. Colonel Osmun Latrobe, Fourth Cavalry commander, became military aide to President Calvin Coolidge in February 1928. Almost the entire July 1, 1927, edition of the *Tribune-Leader* was devoted to the good features of Fort D.A. Russell, the new units assigned, and the good relations existing between the post and town. An excellent account of John Philip Sousa's visit to Cheyenne and appearance with his very popular band at the Lincoln Theater appeared on October 20, 1927, in the *Tribune-Leader*.

CHAPTER TWENTY. SENATOR WARREN'S LAST VISIT

General Aultman's ambitious post improvement program is included in the March 3, 29, and June 15, 1928, editions of the *Tribune-Leader*. General Bolles's continuation of the post improvement program and efforts to maintain good community relations are related in the April 18 and 19, May 18 and 19, and August 10, 1928, editions of the *Tribune-Leader*. General Howland's special brand of hospitality and entertainment received the attention of the *Tribune-Leader* on June 13, July 9 and 11, and October 1, 1929. Senator Warren's last visit to the post on July 11 is particularly well described. Senator Warren's death and the ceremonies in Washington and Cheyenne are well reported in the *Tribune-Leader*, November 29, 1929. The announcement of the presidential decree renaming Fort D.A. Russell Fort Francis E. Warren effective January 1, 1930, appeared on December 6, 1929, in the *Tribune-Leader*.

EPILOGUE

The most fruitful source of information from the 1930s to the present continues to be the Cheyenne newspapers, available at the microfilm library of the Wyoming State Archives, Museums and Historical Department in the Barrett Building at Cheyenne. Property records of the Ninetieth Civil Engineering Squadron, F.E. Warren AFB, are also helpful. The Wing History Office kindly made the unclassified quarterly historical reports from 1949 to 1966, and other useful unclassified material, available. The unclassified *Economic Resource Impact Statement* prepared annually by the Cost Branch of the Resource Management Deputate, Ninetieth Stragegic Missile Wing, and widely distributed contains a wealth of data.

Very useful information has also been gained from many conversations with the following retired air force friends who served at the base during the early missile days and are now living in Cheyenne. They are Brigadier General Robert R. Scott, Lieutenant Colonel G.L. "Bud" Heaton, Colonel Merle "Hap" Johnson, Colonel Conley B. Stroud, and Chief Master Sergeant Edward A. Tarbell. Also Colonel Howard W. Brimmer, USA-Ret., who first saw Fort D.A. Russell soon after finishing at West Point on November 1, 1918, the third graduating class that year. He served three tours at post/base near Cheyenne before retiring in 1953. Another valuable source of information of the 1930s and 1940s, Mrs. Elsie Christman, arrived at the post in 1930 with her husband, Master Sergeant Fred Christman, moved into family quarters [#275], and stayed there until 1949. Other Cheyenneites, excellent sources of information on the city/state and the post/base and most generous in sharing, were Mrs. Katherine Halverson, Mr. William Corson, Mr. Fred Garvalia, retired Judge Rodney M. Guthrie, and Mr. Ralph Robinson. Ranch friends Mr. Merrill Farthing and Mr. and Mrs. Wayne Bonham (Wayne & Biddy) kindly provided information about the Pole Mountain area and other historic sites in the Laramie Mountains, plus remembrances of military activities in earlier years.

BIBLIOGRAPHY

BOOKS

The American Military On The Frontier. Proceedings of the Seventh Military History Symposium, USAF Academy, 1976. Washington: Office of Air Force History, 1978.

Athearn, Robert G. *Union Pacific Country*. Lincoln: University of Nebraska Press, 1971.

Athearn, Robert G. *William Tecumseh Sherman and the Settlement of The West*. Norman: University of Oklahoma Press, 1956.

Biddle, Ellen McGowan. *Reminiscenses of a Soldiers Wife*. Philadelphia: J.B. Lippincott Company, 1907.

Billington, Ray Allen. *America's Frontier Heritage*. New York: Holt, Rinehart and Winston, 1966.

Bisbee, William H. *Through Four American Wars*. Boston: Meador Publishing Company, 1931.

Bourke, John G. *On The Border With Crook*. New York: Charles Scribner's Sons, 1891.

Bratt, John. *Trails of Yesterday*. Lincoln: University of Nebraska Publishing Company, 1921.

Brown, Dee. *The Gentle Tamers: Women of the Old West*. New York: G.P. Putnam's Sons, 1962.

Bruce, Robert. *The Fighting Norths and Pawnee Scouts*. Lincoln: Nebraska State Historical Society, 1932.

Burroughs, John R. *Guardian of the Grasslands: The First Hundred Years of the Wyoming Stock Growers Association*. Cheyenne: Pioneer Printing and Stationery Co., 1971.

Byrne, Bernard J. *A Frontier Army Surgeon*. Crawford, N.J.: Exposition Press, 1935.

Chatterton, Fenimore. *Yesterday's Wyoming: The Intimate Memoirs of Fenimore Chatterton*. Sheridan, WY: Powder River Publishers & Booksellers, 1957.

Cook, Joseph W. *Diary and Letters*. (Arranged by the Rt. Reverend N.S. Thomas) Laramie: The Laramie Republican Company, 1919.

Crook, General George, edited by Martin F. Schmitt. *General George Crook: His Autobiography*. Norman: University of Oklahoma Press, 1946.

Dodge, Maj. Gen. Grenville M. *How We Built the Union Pacific Railway*. Denver: Sage Books, 1911.

Eggenhofer, Nick. *Wagons, Mules and Men: How the Frontier Moved West*. New York: Hastings House Publishers, 1961.

Finerty, John F. *War-Path and Bivouac*. Chicago: M.A. Donahue & Co., 1890.

Forsyth, George A. *The Story of the Soldier*. New York: D. Appleton and Company, 1900.

Ganoe, William A. *The History of the United States Army*. New York: D. Appleton and Company, 1924.

Gould, Lewis L. *Wyoming: A Political History, 1868-1896*. New Haven: Yale University Press, 1968.

Grange, Roger T., Jr., *Fort Robinson: Outpost On The Plains*. Nebraska State Historical Society, 1958.

Greely, Adolphus W. Major General U.S.A., Retired. *Reminiscences of Adventure and Service: A Record of Sixty-five Years*. New York: Charles Scribner's Sons, 1927.

Grinnell, George Bird. *Two Great Scouts and Their Pawnee Battalion*. Cleveland: The Arthur H. Clark Company, 1928.

Griswald, Wesley S. *A Work of Grants*. New York: McGraw Hill Book Company, 1962.

Hafen, LeRoy R. and Francis Marion Young. *Fort Laramie and the Pageant of the West, 1834-1890*. Glendale: The Arthur H. Clark Company, 1938.

Hart, Herbert M. *Old Forts of the Northwest*. Seattle: Superior Publishing Company, 1963.

Heitman, Francis B., comp. *Historical Register and Dictionary of the United States Army*. 2 vols. Washington, D.C.: Government Printing Office, 1903.

Hyde, George E. *Spotted Tail's Folk*. Norman: University of Oklahoma Press, 1961.

Jackson, W. Turrentine. *Wagon Roads West*. New Haven: Yale University Press, 1952.

Leckie, William H. *The Buffalo Soldiers*. Norman: University of Oklahoma Press, 1967.

Johnson, Jerrell G. *The Sutler's Store*. Tempe: Beaumares Books, 1973.

King, Captain Charles, U.S.A. *Campaigning With Crook*. Norman: University of Oklahoma Press, 1964.

King, James T. *War Eagle: A Life of General Eugene A. Carr*. Lincoln: University of Nebraska Press, 1963.

Knight, Oliver. *Following the Indian Wars*. Norman: University of Oklahoma Press, 1953.

Larson, T.A. *History of Wyoming*. Second Edition, Revised. Lincoln: University of Nebraska Press, 1978.

Lewis, Loyd. *Sherman: Fighting Prophet*. New York: Brace and Company, 1932.

Mattes, Merrill J. *Indians, Infants and Infantry*. Denver: The Old West Publishing Company, 1960.

Majors, Alexander. *Seventy Years on the Frontier*. Chicago: Rand, McNally & Company, 1893.

McKay, R.H. *Little Pills: An Army Story*. Pittsburg, Kansas: Pittsburg Headlight, 1918.

Mills, Anson. *My Story*. Washington, D.C.: Press of Byron S. Adams, 1918. (Published by the author.)

Muller, William G. *The Twenty-Fourth Infantry: Past and Present*. Fort Collins: The Old Army Press, 1972.

Nadeau, Remi. *Fort Laramie and the Sioux*. Lincoln: University of Nebraska Press, 1967.

North, Luther. *Man of the Plains: Recollections of Luther North*. Edited by Donald F. Danker. Lincoln: University of Nebraska Press, 1961.

Office of the Chief of Military History. *American Military History*. United States Army, Washington, D.C., 1969.

Parker, James. *The Old Army: Memories 1872-1918*. Philadelphia: Dorance & Company, 1929.

Price, George F. *Across the Continent with the Fifth Cavalry*. New York: Antiquarian Press, 1959.

Prucha, Francis Paul. *Indian Policy in the United States*. Lincoln: University of Nebraska Press, 1981.

Rickey, Don. *Forty Miles A Day on Beans and Hay*. Norman: University of Oklahoma Press, 1963.

Russell, Don. *Buffalo Bill, The Lives and Legends of*. Norman University of Oklahoma Press, 1960.

Sheridan, Philip H. *Personal Memoirs of P.H. Sheridan*, vol. 2. New York: Charles L. Webster & Company, 1885.

Simonin, Louis L. *The Rocky Mountain West In 1867*. Translated and annotated by Wilson O. Clough. Lincoln: University of Nebraska Press, 1978.

Smith, Helena Huntington. *The War on Powder River*. Lincoln: University of Nebraska Press, 1966.

Smith, Rex Alan. *Moon of the Popping Trees*. Lincoln: University of Nebraska Press, 1981.

Stover, Earl F. *Up From Handyman: The United States Army Chaplains, 1865-1920*. Washington, D.C.: Office of Chaplains, GPO, 1977.

Summerhayes, Martha. *Vanished Arizona: Recollections of My Army Life*. Philadelphia: J.B. Lippincott Company, 1908.

Trenholm, Virginia Cole. *Footprints on the Frontier*. Douglas, Wyoming: Douglas Enterprise Co., 1945.

Tuttle, Edmund B. *Six Months on the Plains: Or the Travelers Guide to Cheyenne and the Rocky Mountains*. Chicago: Horton & Leonard, 1868.

Utley, Robert M. *Frontier Regulars: The United States Army and the Indians, 1866-1891*. Bloomington: Indiana University Press, 1977.

Vaughn, J.W. *The Reynolds Campaign On The Powder River*. Norman: University of Oklahoma Press, 1961.

Vaughn, Jesse Wendell. *With Crook at the Rosebud*. Norman: University of Oklahoma Press, 1956.

Wellman, Paul I. *The Indian Wars of the West*. Garden City, N.Y.: Doubleday and Co., 1947.

Westermeier, C.P. *Who Rush To Glory*. Caldwell, Idaho: The Caxton Printers, Ltd., 1958.

Whitman, S.E. *The Troopers: An Informal History of the Plains Cavalry, 1865-1890*. New York: Hastings House Publishers, 1962.

Young, Otis E. *The West of Philip St. George Cooke, 1809-1895*. Glendale: The Arthur H. Clarke Company, 1955.

ARTICLES AND LETTERS

Adams, Gerald M. "The Air Age Comes to Wyoming." *Annals of Wyoming* vol. 52, no. 2, (Fall 1980).

Adams, Gerald M. "The F.E. Warren Air Force Base War Trophies From Balangiga, P.I.." *Annals of Wyoming* vol. 59, no. 1 (Spring 1987).

Brinkerhoff, Sidney B. and Pierce Chamberlain. "The Army's Search for a Repeating Rifle, 1873-1903." *Military Affairs* 32 (1968).

Brown, Jesse. "The Freighter in Early Days." *Annals of Wyoming* 17 (July 1947).

Bryan, Lieutenant F.T. "Report of, Concerning His Operations in Locating a Practical Road Between Fort Riley to Bridgers Pass, 1856." *Annals of Wyoming* vol. 17, no. 1 (January 1945).

Cabannis, A.A. "Troop and Company Pack Trains." *Journal of the U.S. Cavalry Association* 3 (1890).

Capron, Cynthia J. "The Indian Border War of 1876, from letters of Lieut. Thaddeus H. Capron." *Journal of the Illinois State Historical Society* vol. 13, no. 4 (January 1921).

Capron, Cynthia and Thaddeus H. Letters and Papers. Western History Research Center, University of Wyoming, Laramie.

Clough, Wilson. "Fort Russell and Fort Laramie Peace Conference in 1867." *Sources of Northwest History* no. 14, reprinted from *The Frontier* vol. 11, no. 2 (January 1931).

Coffman, Edward M. "Army Life on the Frontier, 1865-1898." *Military Affairs* 20 (1956).

Crane, Paul and T.A. Larson. "The Chinese Massacre." *Annals of Wyoming* 12 (1940).

Danker, Donald F. "The Violent Deaths of Yellow Bear and John Richard, Jr." *Nebraska History* (Summer 1982).

Farnham, Wallace. "Grenville Dodge and the Union Pacific: A Study of Historical Legends." *Journal of American History* 51 (March 1965).

Gilbert, Bill. "The Last Voyage of Sir John Franklin." *Smithsonian* vol. 16, no. 3 (June 1985).

Guentzel, Richard. "The Department of the Platte and Western Settlement." *Nebraska History* 56 (Fall 1975).

Henry, Bvt. Brig. Gen. Guy V. "Wounded In An Indian Fight." Collections of the Wyoming Historical Society (1897).

"The Indian Troubles." *Harpers Weekly* 39 (August 17, 1895).

Jenkins, J.F. "Camp Carlin or Cheyenne Depot." *Annals of Wyoming* vol. 5, no. 1 (July 1927).

Jenkins, Theresa P. "Fort Russell, Scene of the Gayest of Social Functions." *Kemmerer Kamera* (August 27, 1919).

Mattison, Ray H. "The Army Post On the Northern Plains, 1865-1885." *Nebraska History* 35 (March 1954).

"National Cemeteries in Wyoming Territory, 1869." *Annals of Wyoming* vol. 17, no. 1 (January 1945).

Parry, Henry C. "Letters from the Frontier." *Annals of Wyoming* 30 (1958).

Rankin, M. Wilson. "The Meeker Massacre." *Annals of Wyoming* vol. 16, no. 2 (July 1944).

Ryan, Garry David. "Camp Walbach, Nebraska Territory: The Military Post at Cheyenne Pass." *Annals of Wyoming* vol. 35, no. 1 (April 1963).

Spring, Agnes Wright. "Old Letter Book." *Annals of Wyoming* vol. 13, no. 4 (October 1941).

Spring, Agnes Wright. "Site of Pioneer Military Depot Seethes With Activity." *Wyoming Stockman Farmer* vol. 47, no. 2 (February 1941).

Spring, Agnes Wright. Letter to the author, 16 June 1983.

Stelter, Gilbert A. "The Birth of a Frontier Boom Town: Cheyenne in 1867." *Annals of Wyoming* vol. 39, no. 1 (April 1967).

Steward, Miller J. "To Plow, To Sow, To Reap, To Mow: The U.S. Army Agriculture Program." *Nebraska History* (Summer 1982).

Tapson, Alfred J. "The Sutler and the Soldier." *Military Affairs* 21 (Winter 1957).

Tracy, Russel L. Letter to Mr. Mark Chapman of Cheyenne, 5 October 1936.

Welty, Raymond. "The Protection of Overland Trails." and "Supplying the Army on the Frontier." Welty Papers in the Nebraska State Historical Society.

Welty, Raymond. "The Army Fort on the Frontier." *North Dakota Historical Quarterly* 2 (April 1928).

Whitaker, Robert J. "The Early Exploration of Cheyenne Pass." *Annals of Wyoming* (Fall 1975).

NEWSPAPERS

Cheyenne Daily Leader, September 19, 1867–May 23, 1884.
Cheyenne Democratic Leader, May 23, 1884–June 14, 1887.
Cheyenne Daily Leader, June 14, 1887–June 24, 1895.
Cheyenne Daily Sun–Leader, June 24, 1895–May 11, 1900.
Cheyenne Daily Leader, June 1900–May 11, 1909.
Cheyenne State Leader, May 11, 1909–March 15, 1921.
Wyoming State Tribune–Cheyenne State Leader, March 15, 1921–January 1930.
Cheyenne Daily Sun, March 3, 1876–June 24, 1895.
Cheyenne Daily Tribune, December 1884–1893.
Wyoming Tribune, 1894–March 15, 1921.

DOCUMENTS

Fort Francis E. Warren, 1930. Published through courtesy of Cheyenne Chamber of Commerce. An excellent seventy-page document portraying the post's units, commanders, facilities, and activities of 1930. Available at the Laramie County Library, Cheyenne.

U.S. Army. Continental Commands. National Archives Record Group 533 on film.

—Roll 1. Department of the Platte, June 3, 1869. General Order #34 gives the dimensions of Fort D.A. Russell at 4512 acres, plus a description of several scouts sent out.

—Roll 2. Department of the Platte, August 1874. Describes a scout sent to Republican Valley.

—Roll 3. Department of the Platte. Register of contracts 1866–1867 in effect at Fort D.A. Russell.

—Roll 4. Department of the Platte Records: 1858–1895, Contract Register, Quartermaster Department 1868–1878.

—Roll 5. Sioux Expedition, 1874, Selected Documents, Register of Letters Received, Department of the Platte, 1866–1868, Letters Received A–Y.

—Roll 6. Department of the Platte Records: 1858–1895, Letters Received A–Y 1866, 1867–1869.

—Roll 7. Department of the Platte. Letters Sent, 1866–1877. Telegrams Sent, 1867–1868. Telegrams Received, 1866–1874.

U.S. Army. Department of the Platte, *Annual Reports of the Commanding General*, 1892–1897. On file at the U.S. Army Military History Institute, Carlisle Barracks, Pennsylvania. Reports give an excellent account of the treatment afforded the Johnson County Invaders and deployment of troops to the "Ghost Dance" movement.

U.S. Army. Military Division of the Missouri. *Outline Description of the Posts in the Military Division of the Missouri*. Chicago: Headquarters, Military Division of Missouri, 1872.

U.S. Army. *Monthly Post Returns from Fort D.A. Russell, 1867-1929*. National Archives microfilm rolls #1050-1055.

U.S. War Department. Inspector General's Office. *Outline Descriptions of the Posts and Stations of Troops*. Washington, D.C.: GPO, 1872.

U.S. War Department. Judge Advocate General's Office. *United States Military Reservations, National Cemeteries and Military Parks*. Washington, D.C.: GPO, 1910.

U.S. War Department. Quartermaster General's Office. *Posts and Stations, 1871*. Washington, D.C.: GPO, 1872.

U.S. War Department. Quartermaster General's Office. *Military Posts in the United States and Alaska*. Washington, D.C.: QMGO, 1905. (p. 41 has a detailed map of Fort D.A. Russell.)

U.S. War Department. Surgeon General's Office. *A Report on Barracks and Hospitals*. Washington, D.C.: GPO, 1870. (Includes a map of Fort D.A. Russell, a blueprint of the hospital, and Lieutenant Colonel C.H. Alden's excellent description of the post in 1870.)

Index

Acosta, Bert, 174
Acton, Chaplain Col. John T., 177
Air Mail Service, 174, 182
Alden, Lt. Col. C.H., 9, 43, 91
Alkali Station, 27
Antelope Station, 31, 98
Appel, Capt. A.H., 115, 116
Arapaho Indians, 5, 7, 11, 13, 21, 26, 51, 57
Armes, Capt. E.R., 31
Army Service Forces Training Center (ASFTC), 211
Arthur, Pres. Chester A., 85
Atlas, 219, 220, 221, 222, 232
Augur, Brig. Gen. Christopher C., 3, 5, 7, 11, 23, 33, 44, 45, 47
Aultman, Brig. Gen. Dwight E., 192, 195, 197

Backes, Col. Charles B., 214, 215, 218
Bailey, Major Harry L., 131
Baker, N.A., 10
Baldwin, Lt. John A., 83
Baldwin, Brig. Gen. William H., 133
Ball, Capt. George G., 189
Barkley, Lt. D., 123
Barrett, Governor Frank A., 215
Bash, Maj. Daniel N., 98
Battle of the Little Big Horn, 50, 59
Baxter, George W., 95, 96
Bells of Balangiga, 136, 236
Bell, Lt. William W., 228
Bennett, Capt. Clarence E., 114
Big Horn Mining Association, 43, 44
Bisbee, Lt. William H., 9, 121
Blair, Col. George, 209
Bloom, Lt. Frank, 156
Boice, Fred, 188
Bolles, Brig. Gen Frank C., 197, 199
Bomford, Col. James V., 49, 51
Boniface, Col. John J., 186, 188
Borthwick, Dean W., 239
Botsford, A.J., 42, 228
Bozeman Trail, 13, 22, 23, 25, 59
Brackett, Col. Albert G., 74, 76, 77, 78
Bradley, Lt. Col. Luther P., 34
Bresche, Mrs. Anne, 191
Bresnahan, L.R., 129
Brewster, Col. Alden F., 186
Brier, Col. William H., 226, 229, 232
Brimmer, Col. Howard W., 234

Bresnahan, L.R., 129
Brier, Col. William H., 226, 229, 232
Brimmer, George, 197
Brisbin, Major James F., 25, 26
Brooke, Brig. Gen. John R., 97, 114, 120
Burt, Capt. Andrew and Elizabeth, 22, 25, 91

Cahill, Capt. James, 228
Campbell, Terr. Governor John A., 35, 43
Camp Brown, 42, 65
Camp Collins, 4, 23
Camp Kendrick, 159
Camp Marfa, renamed Ft. D.A. Russell in 1930, 201
Camp Pilot Butte, 87, 121, 122, 123
Camp Walbach, 6
Canby, Brig. Gen. Edward R.S., 50
Capehart Housing, 220
Carey, Senator & Governor J.M., 129, 145
Carey, Governor & Senator Robert D., 165, 172, 179
Carling, Capt. Elias B., 17, 103, 108, 109
Carr, Major Eugene A., 35
Carr, T. Jeff, 118, 119
Carrol, Pvt. Frank, 154
Cattlemen, Johnson County War, 110, 111
Chaffee, Lt. Gen. Adna R., 133
Chamber of Commerce or Industrial Club, 142, 144, 145, 153, 154, 169, 188, 213, 221
Chambers, Col. Alexander, 95, 96, 98
Chatterton, Governor Fenimore, 131
Cavalry:
  1st Regt., 123, 129, 161
  2nd Regt., 10, 13, 22, 25, 26, 27, 31, 33, 34, 35, 57, 59, 60, 67, 132
  3rd Regt., 47, 48, 51, 53, 54, 58, 59, 60, 69, 75, 76, 77, 78, 81, 96, 107
  4th Regt., 186, 189, 190, 192, 193, 195
  5th Regt., 35, 37, 42, 46, 47, 60, 63, 64, 65, 66, 67, 68, 69, 75, 76
  8th Regt., 141

263

9th Regt., 123, 148, 152, 154, 156, 157
10th Regt., 130, 132
12th Regt., 158
13th Regt., 176, 177, 182, 185, 186, 187, 189, 190, 192, 193
15th Regt., 165, 166, 167, 169, 173, 176
24th Regt., 161, 162
25th Regt., 161, 162
312th Regt., 163
315th Regt., 163
2nd U.S. Volunteer Regt., 112, 122, 124
Chadwell, Col. George T., 221, 238
Chenchar, Col. Paul, 238
Cheyenne & Black Hills Stage Line, 57
Cheyenne Depot also called Camp Carling or Carlin, 4, 9, 10, 13, 14, 17, 27, 33, 42, 53, 60, 67, 81, 85, 96, 99, 100, 103, 106, 107, 108, 109, 229
Cheyenne Electric Streetcar Company, 142, 155
Cheyenne Frontier Days Celebration, 154, 163, 166, 174, 176, 185, 186, 192, 195, 197, 206
Cheyenne Indians, 5, 7, 13, 21, 31, 35, 51, 57, 59, 61, 66, 67, 85, 86
Cheyenne Literary Club, 162
Cheyenne Motor Bus Company, 186
Cheyenne & Northern Railway, 90, 99, 100, 114
Cheyenne Pass, 4, 5
Chinese Massacre, 87
Chrisman, Mrs. Elsie, 240
Christensen, Val, 226
Civilian Conservation Corps (CCC), 203
Civilian/Military Advisory Council, 188, 226, 239
Clark, Major R.D., 67
Cleveland, Pres. Grover, 95, 96
Cocheu, Brig. Gen. Frank, 203
Cody, William F., 63, 68
Cohen, Haskell C., 226
Colliers, 156, 157
Commonwealers, 119
Conrad, Brig. Gen. Casper H., 203
Cooke, Brig. Gen. Phillip St. George, 3
Cook, Rev. Joseph, 16, 18, 27
Cook, Mauor P.S., 142, 172
Cook, Pete, 226
Coppinger, Brig. Gen. Joseph J., 121
Corson, William A., 229
Craig, Maj. Gen. Malin, 188
Crook, Brig. Gen. George, 48, 53, 58, 60, 63, 65, 91
Crow Creek Crossing, 4, 5, 7, 9, 23
Custer, Lt. Col. George A., 52

Dahl, Col. & Mrs. Gilmore M. (Janice), 241
Davison, Brig. Gen. P.W. 164, 174
Davis, Maj. Gen. Austin, 226
Deaver, Clem, 226
Denver Pacific Railroad, 26, 44
Department of the Platte, 3, 11, 23, 25, 50, 51, 83, 91, 98
DeRussy, Maj. Isaac D., 81
Dervees, Capt. Thomas B., 31, 32
Dineen, W.E., 186
Dobson, Capt. & Mrs. Alan L. (Rae Lynn), 241
Dodge, Grenville M., 4, 5, 7
Dodge House, 12
Donaldson, Col. T.Q., 186
Douglas, Wy., 116
Dugan, Sam, 27
Dugan, Col. T.B., 173, 174, 175, 176
Dull Knife, 61, 67
Duncan, Lt. Col. Thomas, 35

Economic Resource Impact Statement (ERIS), 224
Egan, Capt. James, 33
Eisenhower, Gen. & Pres. Dwight D., 212, 219
Elliott, Col. John C.B., 212, 214
Emerson, Gov. Franc C., 195, 229
Evans, Sgt. Felix, 139

Falcon cannon, 136, 137, 236
Far West Flying Circus, 165
Flying Field at Fort D.A. Russell, 165, 167, 168, 169, 229
Field Artillery:
   2nd Regt., 139, 141
   4th Regt., 150, 152, 154, 155, 157
   76th Regt., 178, 179, 185, 186, 190, 192, 203, 207
   8th Batt., 135, 137
   12th Batt., 139
   13th Batt., 130, 132, 137
   19th Batt., 139
Forbes, Warren, 188
Ford House, 24
Fort Bridger, 22, 25, 42, 81, 91, 114
Fort C.F. Smith, 22, 25, 91
Fort Douglas, 87
Fort Fetterman, 4, 23, 46, 57, 58, 59, 63, 64, 81, 107, 114
Fort Fred Steele, 23, 69, 114
Fort Francis E. Warren Target and

Maneuver Reserve, originally the Wood & Timber Reserve (1880), then the Crow Creek Forest Reserve (1900), Fort D.A. Russell Target and Maneuver Range (1904), and the Pole Mountain District of the Medicine Bow National Forest, 130, 132, 133, 137, 138, 139, 141, 146, 154, 156, 157, 186, 189, 198, 200, 220
Fort Kearny, 4, 23, 33
Fort Laramie, 11, 12, 13, 21, 22, 44, 46, 52, 57, 60, 65, 85, 91, 96, 107, 114
Fort Laramie Treaty of 1868, 22, 23, 25, 43
Fort Logan, 98, 129, 132, 179
Fort Omaha or Omaha Barracks, 49, 58, 81, 95, 132
Fort McKenzie, 157
Fort McPherson, 4, 35, 50, 60, 65, 129
Fort Morgan, 4, 23
Fort McKinney, 65, 66, 110, 116, 120
Fort Meade, 115, 186
Fort Niobrara, 121, 135
Fort Phil Kearny, 13, 22
Fort Reno, 13, 22
Fort Riley, 130, 192
Fort Robinson, 60, 67, 85, 91, 96, 114, 121, 158
Fort Sanders, 4, 81, 109
Fort Sedgwick, 4
Fort Sidney or Sidney Barracks, 65, 85, 115
Fort Washakie, 135
Forsyth, Lt. Col. George A., 118
Fourth Brigade, 178, 193, 195, 198
Frazer, Major H., C., 165
Freund rifle, 68

Galbreath, Capt. Jacob G., 123
Ganno, Col. James M.J., 129
Garand rifle M1, 206
Garrison, Chaplain Joseph G., 179, 182
Garvalia, Fred A., 234, 239
Gartner, Karl (POW), 211
Gaymon, Clyde, 226
Geodetic Survey Squadron, 222, 224
Gerhardt, Lt. Charles, 122
German Prisoners of War, 211
Ghost Dance or Messiah Craze, 114, 115
Gibbon, Col. John, 59
Gordon, Col. John A., 239, 242
Grant, Gen. and Pres. Ulysses S., 24, 26, 31, 33, 34, 43, 49, 54
Grant's Peace Policy, 34, 50
Greybull, 44
Goose Creek, 59, 60
Grover, Brig. Gen. Orrin L., 218
Guthrie, Judge Rodney M., 237
Guthrie, W.E., 111, 237
Guy, George, 226

Haas, William G., 188
Hallowell, Col. Paul H., 212
Hammond, Chief Musician Wade H., 152
Harding, Pres. Warren G., 182, 183
Harney, Brig. Gen. W.S., 11, 21
Harper, Col. Ray B., 176, 178
Harrison, Pres. Benjamin, 98, 116
Hart, Maj. Verling K., 66, 156
Hawkins, Brig. Gen. Hamilton M., 203
Hayden, Col. Percy S., 212
Hayes, Pres. Rutherford B., 75, 76, 77, 78, 115
Heaton, Lt. Col. G.L. "Bud," 233
Helicopter Squadron, 222, 224
Heine, Col. Wilhelm, 12
Henry, Capt. Guy V., 47, 49, 59, 60
Herman, Maj. John R., 206
Herman, Leo, 226
Herron, Col. Joseph S., 188, 190
Heye, German General William, 195
Hilde, Percy, 226
Hillsdale Station, 42
Hines, Maj. Gen. John L., 188
Holbrook, Maj. Gen. W.A., 178
Hook, Mayor H.M., 9
Horn, Col. James J., 108, 116
Howard, Brig. Gen. Oliver O., 85, 96
Howland, Brig. Gen. Charles R., 198, 199, 200, 201, 203
Howard, Mrs. Shirley, 230
Hoyt, Governor John W., 78
Humphrey, Brig. Gen. Charles F. Jr., 203
Hunt, Colorado Governor, 26
Hunt, Wyoming Governor and Senator Lester E., 212, 214, 215, 234

Infantry:
 1st Reg., 193, 194, 203, 207
 2nd Regt., 131, 132
 4th Regt., 37, 45, 58, 59, 60, 67, 81
 7th Regt., 83
 8th Regt., 49, 116, 120, 121, 122
 9th Regt., 35, 37, 45, 47, 49, 59, 60,

265

81, 83, 84, 85, 86, 90, 93
11th Regt., 132, 135-139, 142, 152, 154, 157, 236
14th Regt., 45, 60
17th Regt., 95, 96, 98, 113, 115, 116, 119-121
18th Regt., 22, 23, 27, 33, 34, 129-131
20th Regt., 193, 199, 203, 207
23rd Regt., 53, 129
24th Regt., 123, 158
27th Regt., 25, 34
30th Regt., 7, 9, 10, 12, 13, 18, 23, 33
53rd Regt., 176, 178, 179, 182
InterOcean Hotel, 57
Irvine, W.C., 111

Jackson Hole, 121
Jameson, Brig. Gen. Arlen D., 224, 239
Jenkins, Brig. Gen. John M., 183, 185, 186, 188, 190-192
Jenkins, Mrs. Theresa, 64
Johnson, Pres. Andrew, 3, 11
Johnson County War, 110, 116, 237
Johnson, Col. Merle "Hap," 229
Johnston, Col. Albert S., 6

Kaufman, George, 226
Keefe, Mayor M.P., 131
Kelly, A.D., 172
Kendrick, Governor and Senator John B., 159, 162, 163
Kennedy, Judge T. Blake, 192
King, Charles, 63
King, Col. John H., 35, 37, 43, 47, 49
Knudson, Jack B., 230
Krag-Jorgensen rifle M1893, 119, 139

LaFollette, Senator Robert M., 157
Lakeview Cemetery, 108, 158, 172, 173, 201
Langtry, Lillie, 85, 88
Large, Brig. Gen. William L., Jr., 219
Latrobe, Col. Osmun, 188, 193, 195
Laundresses, 32, 33, 66, 83, 84, 191
Lawrence Fork also called Laurens Fork, 7
Lester, Mrs. Lucinda, 97
Limeburner, 1st Sgt. John M., 46, 227
Lodgepole Creek Trail, 3, 4
Lovell, Lt. Robert A., 83
Longstreet, Lt. Col. James Jr., 178, 179
Lyle, Maj. Gen. Lewis E., 222

Mackenzie, Col. Ranald S., 61
Marsh, Professor O.C., 44
Mason, Lt. George F., 42, 228
Mason, Col. John T., 84
Martin, Capt. Lincoln, 188
Maynard, Lt. Melvin, 169
McCoy, Timothy J., State Adj. Gen., 175
Meeker, Nathan C., 69
Menoher, Maj. Gen. Charles T., 188
Merritt, Col. Wesley, 56, 66, 69, 75
Metz, William M., 233
Miles, Maj. Gen. Nelson A., 65, 120
Mills, Capt. Anson, 58
Minuteman, 221-223, 226, 232
Mitchell, Capt. William, 156
Mitsch, Pvt. T.M., 211
Mizner, Col. Henry R., 96, 97, 115, 116
Mizner, Lt. John K., 5
Modoc Indians, 50
Moonlight, Thomas, Terr. Governor, 96
Moore, Capt. Alexander, 58
Moore, Thomas, Honorary Col., 108, 114
Muenter, Col. Hilbert F., 218, 219
Munson, Col. Fred L., 193
Mustang, 214
Myers, Col. A.L., 137

National Historic Act, 223
Nation, Mayor Bill, 226, 231
Nez Perce Indians, 65
North, Maj. Frank, 5, 60, 61, 63, 115
Noyes, Capt. Henry C., 58
Nuss, Abe, 226
Nutt, Lt. Clifford M., 167

Oelrichs, Harry, 85, 88
Ogallala Station, 25, 43
O'Mahoney, Senator Joseph C., 213, 215
O'Neil, Brig. Gen. J.P., 167
Operation Snowbound, 214
Ord, Brig. Gen. E.O.C., 47, 50, 53
Order of Daedalians, 223, 229
Oregon Trail, 3, 4

Pardee, Lt. Julius H., 53
Pawnee Indian Scouts, 5, 31, 35, 51, 60, 61, 63
Payne, Capt. John S., 68
Peace Commission, 11, 13, 21, 22, 49, 55
Peacekeeper, 223, 232
Pearson, Capt. Samuel B., 158

Peek, Brig. Gen. Edward D., 206
Pershing, Gen. John J., 138, 157, 158, 161, 163, 172, 173, 175, 183, 186
Peterson, Allen J., 188
Petrikin, Engineer Lt. Reuben W., 9
Pine Bluffs, 7, 42, 86
Plains Hotel, 158, 183, 190
Plum Creek, 35
Poland, Col. John S., 116, 119, 120
Pole Mountain, See Fort D.A. Russell Target & Maneuver Reserve.
Poore, Brig. Gen. Benjamin, 167, 169
Pope, Brig. Gen. John, 58
Post Exchange, 121
Powder River, 58
Preston, Col. J.F., 193, 194
Prill, TSgt. Wesley P., 237
Probst, L.R., 188
Promontory Point, 35

Quakers or Society of Friends, 34
Quartermaster Replacement Training Center (QRTC), 209, 210, 212
Quartermaster Unit Training Center (QUTC), 211

Rader, Brig. Gen. William S., 219, 222, 226
Randall, Boeing Rep. Bob, 226
Randall, Lt. Col. George M., 122
Rawlins, Maj. Gen. John A., 5
Rawlins, 23, 68, 69
Reno, Major Marcus A., 67
Reynolds, Col. Joseph J., 48, 51, 57, 107
Richmond, Col. H.R., 190, 192
Rickenbacker, Capt. Eddie, 174, 175
Riner, Mayor C.W., 192
Riner, Mayor C.W., 192
Riner, Judge John A., 172
Robertson, Senator E.V., 213
Robertson, Col. William A.R., 218
Robinson, Lt. Levi H., 52
Rock Springs, 87
Roosevelt, Pres., Franklin D., 203
Roosevelt, Pres. Theodore R., 129, 131, 132, 138
Rosebud Creek, 59
Ross, Governor Nellie T., 189
Ross, Governor William B., 186
Royal, Lt. Col. WIlliam B., 58
Russell, Brig. Gen. David A., 7

Sage, Brig. Gen. W.G., 176, 177
Sammies, 162, 163
Sands, Brig. Gen. H.J., 226
Sanford, J.B., 11

Schofield, Lt. Gen. John M., 113, 120
Schurz, Secy of Interior Carl, 68
Schwatka, Lt. Frederick G., 78
Scott, Brig. Gen. Robert R., 222, 236
Searle, Tom, 226
Selective Service Acts of 1917 and 1940, 161, 207
Sharpe, Major H.H., 188
Sherman, General William T., 2, 3, 4, 11, 21, 24, 26, 31, 34, 41, 55, 76, 77, 103, 115
Sherman Station, 31, 32
Sheridan, General Philip H., 21, 24, 26, 34, 50, 51, 53, 58, 64, 97, 98
Short, Col. Walter C., 163
Shoshoni Indians, 121
Simonin, Louis L., 12
Sinclair, Col. W.S., 199
Sioux Indians, 5, 7, 13, 28, 51, 54, 55, 57–59, 61, 114; Brule, 7, 21, 46, 65, 66, Spotted Tail Agency, 44, 52, 53, 55, 65, 66, Rosebud Agency, 81; Oglala , 7, 11, 21, 46, 50, 59, 66, 98, 114, Red Cloud Agency, 44, 47, 49, 50, 52, 53, 55, 59, 65, 66, 81, Pine Ridge Agency, 81, 98, 114; Hunkpapa, 63, 66, 114
Sky Dozer, 214
Slim Buttes, 60
Smith, Bob, 226
Smith, Brig. Gen. Frederick A., 142, 143, 145, 151, 153
Smith, Lt. Louis, 123
Smoke, Capt. Samuel A., 159
Sousa, John Phillip, 195
Spaatz, Major Carl A., 165, 212
Spencer, Sgt. Park B., 119
Springfield Rifle M1873, 78, 91, 119
Springfield Rifle M1903, 139, 206
Sprong, TSgt. Danny, 238
Stanfield, Don, 226
Steamboat the mule, 108
Stelter, Gilbert A., 7
Stevenson, Col. John D., 7–9, 12, 13, 17, 18, 23
Stevens, SMSgt. H.A., "Steve," 230
Stimson, Sec. of War Henry, 156
Stone, Major E.W., 165
Stroud, Col. Conley B., 232
Story, Mayor Worth, 219, 221
Strategic Air Command (SAC), 219, 220, 223
Strategic missile units activated at F.E. Warren AFB, 1958–1989
    4320th Wing, 219
    706th Wing, 219–221

267

389th Wing, 221, 232
90th Wing, 221–225, 232
13th Air Division, 219
13th Strategic Missile Division, 219, 220, 222, 224
4th Strategic Missile Division, 222, 223, 225
4th Air Division, 223–225, 239
Summerall, Maj. Gen. Charles F., 195
Summerhayes, Lt. John W. and Martha, 52
Summit Springs, 35
Symington, Sec. of Air Force W. Stuart, 212

Taft Pres. William H., 138, 146, 155, 156
Tarbell, SMSgt. Edward A., 227, 228,
Taylor, N.G., 11
Taylor, Col. Sydney W., 141
Technical Training Wing, 3450th, 213, 215
Terry, Brig. Gen., Alfred H., 11, 59
Thornburgh, Major Thomas T., 69
Tisdale, John, 111
Todd, Col. William, 226
Torrey, Col. Jay L., 112, 122, 125
Tracy, Russell L., 108
Transcontinental Reliability Test of 1919, 167–169
Trophy Park, 136, 137, 190
Truman, Pres. Harry S., 211, 213
Tuttle, Chaplain E.B., 16

Uhl, Brig. Gen. F.E., 207, 209
Union Pacific, 3–5, 13, 23, 24, 26, 27, 31, 44, 53, 76, 77, 87, 103, 123, 165, 183, 211
Ute Indians, 66, 69, 75, 78, 95
Camp on White River, 71, 75, 78, 95

Van Horn, Col. James J., 114, 120
Van Voast, Major James, 27

Vigilantes, 27

Wales, Lt. Edward, 169
Warden, Brig. Gen. John A., 209, 210
Warren Bowl, 198, 220, 221
Warren, Governor and Senator Francis E., 87, 95, 98, 130, 132, 135, 138, 141, 142, 145, 146, 155–157, 162, 163, 175, 176, 183, 186, 195, 196, 200, 201
Warren, Fred, 197
Wells Fargo, 24, 25
Wessels, Lt. Col. Henry W., 23, 27
Western Governors' Conference of 1945, 212
Wherry Housing, 215, 216, 220, 223
Whitcomb, E.W., 111
White, A.S., 11
Whittaker, Brig. Gen. H.L., 211, 212
Wiedman, Post Trader Charles A., 77, 78, 85
Wiggins, Mrs. Claudia, 233
Wikstrum, Col. Floyd E., 221, 226
Wilson, Pres. Woodrow, 157, 159, 162, 167
Windt, Brig. Gen. T.J., 137, 138
Wittenmeyer, Brig. Gen. Edmund, 177, 182
Wolcott, Frank, 111
Wolf, Pvt. Frank M., 142
Wood, Maj. Gen. Leonard, 157
Womens' Army Auxiliary Corps (WAAC), later Womens' Army Corps (WAC), 209
Woolley, Post Trader J.D., 17, 32, 77, 78
Wounded Knee Creek, 115
Wovoka, 114
Wyoming Stock Growers Assn. (WSGA), 116

Yeatman, Col. Richard T., 142
Yellowstone Park, 51, 65, 85

About the Author

During his thirty-seven-year career in the Air Force, Gerald M. Adams flew high altitude reconnaissance missions for the Eighth Air Force in Europe during World War II. Later, he served in SAC; the Air Staff in the Pentagon; SHAPE in Paris; the U.S. Mission to the UN; Vietnam and the JCS at Offutt AFB, before concluding his career at F.E. Warren AFB.

A native of Nebraska, the author holds a B.A. degree from the University of Maryland and an M.A. from C.W. Post College at Brookville, New York and a second M.A. from the University of Wyoming, Laramie. Now retired, Col. Adams and his wife Kathleen live in Cheyenne where he pursues his interests in historical research and writing, being a regular contributor to several historical publications. **The Post Near Cheyenne** is his first book.